Job Insecurity and Work Intensification

Based on the findings of the recently published Joseph Rowntree Report,
this book provides an up-to-the-minute review of current research on flexibility, job insecurity and work intensification. It examines the impact of
these developments on individuals, their families, the workplace and the
long-term health of the British economy, as well as providing an analysis
of the impact across a wide range of other countries including the United
States, France, Germany, Sweden and Japan. Key questions addressed
include:

- How are jobs more insecure?
- Does 'just-in-time' labour mean more flexible contracts or more flexible
  workers?
- How does workplace stress affect individual health and family relationships?
- What are the business costs of stress and insecurity?

Timely and thought-provoking, *Job Insecurity and Work Intensification* is essential reading for all those involved in the fields of employment relations,
human resource management (HRM) and the sociology of work.

Brendan Burchell is Senior Lecturer in the Faculty of Social and Political
Sciences, University of Cambridge. **David Ladipo** is Lecturer in Sociology
and Social Policy, University of Nottingham. **Frank Wilkinson** is Reader in
Applied Economics, University of Cambridge.

Routledge Studies in Employment Relations
Series editors: Rick Delbridge and Edmund Heery
Cardiff Business School

Aspects of the employment relationship are central to numerous courses at both undergraduate and postgraduate level.

Drawing from insights from industrial relations, human resource management and industrial sociology, this series provides an alternative source of research-based materials and texts, reviewing key developments in employment research.

Books published in this series are works of high academic merit, drawn from a wide range of academic studies in the social sciences.

Job Insecurity
and Work Intensification

Edited by Brendan Burchell,
David Ladipo and
Frank Wilkinson

London and New York

First published 2002 by Routledge
11 New Fetter Lane, London EC4P 4EE

Simultaneously published in the USA and Canada
by Routledge
29 West 35th Street, New York, NY 10001

Routledge is an imprint of the Taylor and Francis Group

Typeset in 10/12pt Baskerville by Graphicraft Limited, Hong Kong
Printed and bound in Great Britain by Biddles Ltd,
Guildford and King's Lynn

British Library Cataloguing in Publication Data
A catalogue record for this book is available from the British Library

Library of Congress Cataloging in Publication Data
Job insecurity and work intensification / edited by Brendan
Burchell, David Ladipo and Frank Wilkinson.
     p.   cm. — (Routledge studies in employment relations)
   Includes bibliographical references and index.
   1. Job security—Great Britain.   2. Job stress—Great Britain.
3. Unemployment—Great Britain—Psychological aspects.
4. Labor market—Great Britain.   5. Industrial relations—Great
Britain.   I. Burchell, Brendan.   II. Ladipo, David.
III. Wilkinson, Frank.   IV. Series.

HD5708.45.G7 J63 2001
331.25'96—dc21   2001019751

ISBN 0-415-23652-5 (hbk)
ISBN 0-415-23653-3 (pbk)

Contents

Illustrations

Figures

Tables

Boxes

Contributors

Brendan Burchell is a Senior Lecturer in the Faculty of Social and Political Sciences at the University of Cambridge, and a Fellow of Magdalene College. His first degree was in psychology, but now his research interests consist mainly of the interdisciplinary study of the labour market, and the impact of the labour market on the individual's health and well-being.

Maria Hudson is an ESRC-funded PhD student in the Faculty of Economics and Politics, University of Cambridge and was previously a Research Fellow at the ESRC Centre for Business Research (CBR), University of Cambridge. She is also a member of Newnham College and a Research Associate at the CBR.

David Ladipo worked as a Research Fellow at the ESRC Centre for Business Research at the University of Cambridge between September 1997 and June 1999, since when he has been employed as a Lecturer in the School of Sociology and Social Policy at the University of Nottingham.

Roy Mankelow, a retired Senior Manager of Grindlays Bank, is a Research Associate at the ESRC Centre for Business Research, University of Cambridge.

Jane Nolan is an ESRC-funded PhD student in the Faculty of Social and Political Sciences at the University of Cambridge and a member of Newnham College.

Ines Wichert is an ESRC-funded PhD student in the Faculty of Social and Political Sciences at the University of Cambridge and a member of Hughes Hall.

Dr Frank Wilkinson is Reader in the Department of Applied Economics, University of Cambridge, and Fellow of Girton College. His research is concerned mainly with the effects of industrial and labour institutions and organisations on economic performance.

Acknowledgements

Our thanks go, first and foremost, to the Joseph Rowntree Foundation for their generous funding of the Job Insecurity and Work Intensification Survey, upon which so much of this book is based. We are particularly grateful to Derek Williams and the members of the Advisory Committee who helped steer the survey through from inception to completion. We also acknowledge the special contribution made by the Royal College of Midwives which provided us with an additional grant to extend the scope of our research.

Throughout the course of our research we have relied upon the advice and assistance of Hannah Reed and Diana Day. They deserve an equal share of any praise (or blame!) this book may attract.

Special thanks also to Stephanie Auge, Mel Bartley, David Biggs, Tom Bramble, Linda Brosnan, Kathrin Buhr, Janine Clemence, Simon Deakin, Lord Eatwell, Chris Gilson, Joan Haddock, Amanda Harding, Jean Hartley, Alan Hughes, Will Hutton, Oliver James, Sue Konzelmann, Joy Labern, Sue Moore, Kate Purcell, Richard Sennett, Rachel Simpson and Paul Teesdale.

Finally, we owe a particular debt of gratitude to all the employees and employers who took time out of their very busy schedules to subject themselves to our interviews.

Introduction

The research upon which this book is based was initiated at a time of unprecedented interest in job insecurity. By 1997, it was widely assumed that job insecurity had increased rapidly over the past decade.[1] There was also an emerging understanding that job insecurity was not only unpleasant for individuals (in terms of their psychological well-being), but that it raised serious problems for family stability and for organisational efficiency by lowering the commitment and motivation of employees. But while the popular press began to pay more attention to the negative consequences of job insecurity, the need for a flexible workforce that could compete in global markets was becoming the top priority for managers and policy makers alike.

In light of this contradiction between the fear of insecurity and the demand for flexibility, we embarked on a year-long survey of the British workforce. Brendan Burchell and Frank Wilkinson raised the funds for the project and steered it through the initial planning stages. Maria Hudson, David Ladipo and Hannah Reed were appointed as research fellows on the project. Roy Mankelow, a Research Associate of the Centre for Business Research, joined the project for its duration. And Jane Nolan and Ines Wichert took up PhD places, funded by the Economic and Social Research Council, to work alongside the project as full members of the research team. The addition of so many members of the team, many of them unplanned, gave the project a far wider remit than initially planned. Between us we brought expertise from Economics, Economic History, Labour Law, Social and Organisational Psychology and Sociology.

As this book demonstrates, our research interests were not limited to one specific labour market phenomenon. On the contrary, we sought to examine the complex set of relationships through which macroeconomic pressures, such as the globalisation of product and capital markets, are passed via the workplace onto individuals and their families. To do this, we needed a methodology that would reflect the 'big picture' and still enable us to conduct detailed analyses of the microeconomic effects of job insecurity and work intensification. This simultaneous requirement for depth and breadth was achieved by a combination of qualitative and quantitative data collection and analysis.

During the course of our survey, we interviewed dozens of managers and hundreds of employees. As the fieldwork progressed, our ideas and prior assumptions were constantly challenged and, in some areas, our final conclusions differ quite markedly from the ideas we held at the beginning of the project. And perhaps the most significant change in our conception of the phenomena we observed was that we needed to broaden our notions of job insecurity. To start with, we had to recognise the distinction between job *stability* (as measured by the length of time individuals spend with their employer) and job *insecurity* (as measured by the fear of job loss). But the results of our work quickly indicated to us that feelings of insecurity are not restricted to the fear of job loss. Debilitating anxieties can also be triggered by workplace changes which threaten to deprive workers of their control over the pace and flow of work, and the enjoyment of reasonable working hours.

Our findings also suggested that the *intensification* of work could prove an even greater problem – in terms of stress, psychological health and family tension – than the prevalence of job insecurity. Hence the range of topics addressed within this volume. Over the following chapters, we will describe the pressures on organisations and show how they have responded to these pressures by reorganising their workforce. We will analyse the implications of these changes for workforce insecurity and indicate the extent to which the working lives of employees have been changed for the better or worse. We will also consider the ways in which these changes have affected their trust in management and the related need for effective representation. And, towards the end of the book, we examine the extent to which job insecurity and work intensification are affected by the laws and institutions which regulate the market economy.

The JIWIS sample

The twenty workplaces included in the Job Insecurity and Work Intensification Survey (JIWIS) were not a random sample of UK workplaces, but were chosen to reflect a diverse set of industries, sectors and sizes. The majority were, for convenience, based in East Anglia, but in order to obtain some of the specific cases we were after, we also went as far afield as Wales and Scotland. Two were chosen because they had been widely reported in the media as having zero-compulsory-redundancy policies. We often sampled organisations in pairs, to look at different reactions to similar external pressures: we interviewed in two financial services organisations, two Further Education colleges, two privatised utilities and two employment agencies. Some of the organisations were very profitable, others were declining. Because of our special interests in midwifery, we included six birthing units in our sample. The public and private sectors were both represented.

In some cases we were unable to access certain types of employers. For instance, dozens of security and cleaning sectors (renowned for their poor employment conditions) were approached, but none of them would agree to take part in the research. But overall we were confident that we saw a very heterogeneous range of employment practices. A full list of these organisations is given in Appendix A.

The fieldwork

In order to collect data from the organisations, we interviewed at three levels in all of the organisations: senior managers, line managers and employees.

In each organisation a senior manager was interviewed, usually by two members of the research team. In some cases, in order to get an authoritative response to the complete range of questions, more than one senior manager was interviewed – typically one in the personnel or human resources department, and one with more general responsibilities. These interviews typically lasted about two hours, and covered a wide range of topics from employment practices and policies to product markets and profits. Both qualitative and quantitative data were collected, and a detailed case study for each of the organisations was written soon after the interviews.

Employees were also interviewed in the workplace (with the exception of some of the agency workers, who were interviewed in their own homes). A total of 340 employee interviews were conducted, each lasting an average of just over an hour. Employees were also asked to fill in a self-completion questionnaire, usually before they met the researcher: this took an average of about thirty minutes. (The more straightforward closed questions were typically included in the self-completion questionnaire, and the more complex sections with multiple skips and open-ended questions were administered face-to-face.) Occasionally the self-completion questionnaire was also administered face-to-face, for instance in cases where the respondent had poor literacy skills.

The number of employees interviewed in each establishment was roughly proportional to the size of their organisation. These interviews were conducted over a period of approximately twelve months, from late 1997 to late 1998. Eighty-four of the 340 employees were midwives; the rest of them formed a fairly representative cross-section of the population (where the results are substantially different with and without the sub-sample of midwives, this is made clear in the presentation of results). Where possible, line managers were also asked to comment (in a self-completion questionnaire) on the security of the jobs performed by the employee respondents and the relative scarcity of their skills.

The quality of the employee data differs from that of more conventional cross-sectional surveys. For instance, although the employees in our sample did seem to be fairly representative of the UK workforce (when we compared some of the important demographic and attitudinal data to the results of other surveys) this was perhaps more by luck than design. On the other hand, because we achieved close to a 100 per cent response rate from the employees we selected to interview, other biases were minimised (many postal questionnaires achieve response rates below 10 per cent). Our data has its limits – in terms of size and diversity – but it is more than adequate for the statistical analyses included in the empirical chapters in this book.

The selection of employees was done in collaboration with managers, to get a wide cross-section of employees at all levels within the organisation. In some cases we were able to timetable the interviews to spread them evenly through the day. In other cases, where employees had to be prepared to respond to unpredictable demands (such as on birthing units) the researchers often had to wait around in the workplace, interviewing the selected respondents as the opportunities arose.

An unusual feature of the research was that the employee interviews were not conducted by a market research organisation, or by junior research assistants. Everyone in the research team took part in these interviews. Although this was a very time-consuming task, we are of the opinion that by immersing ourselves so fully in the data we got a more detailed feel of the workplaces and the lives of the employees than if we had subcontracted out the data-collection phase of the research. When several of us had spent several days each in a workplace we felt that we understood the phenomena that we were studying in a way that one never achieves in secondary data analysis.

Finally, twenty-six of the employees were re-interviewed, usually in their own homes. This interview was considerably less structured than the initial interviews. A wide variety of employees was again selected for re-interview, but with a moderate over-sampling of the less secure employees. The topics covered in these interviews included empowerment, representation, work, family life and social support. These interviews also gave the researchers (usually the same one who conducted the initial structured interview) a chance to explore changes over the time-period between interviews, which ranged from over a year to just a few months. These interviews were tape-recorded and transcribed for later analyses using ATLAS, a qualitative data analysis package.

The scope of our analysis

The scope of our analysis has widened considerably since the publication of our report to the Joseph Rowntree Foundation in September 1999 (Burchell *et al.* 1999). The main thrust of that first phase of dissemination was to put our findings and conclusions into the public domain, and bring them to the attention of as many policy makers as possible. Satisfyingly, the conclusions of the research quickly found their way into trade union newsletters, government reports and academic articles. Our findings were also widely reported on UK television and radio broadcasts, and in scores of articles published by the broadsheet and tabloid newspapers. The reactions to our research have been overwhelmingly positive, with both employees and employers resonating to our findings, although we also had a few fierce critics.[2]

This book builds upon those early findings but we have used the intervening period to analyse the data in more detail and set our research in the context of wider academic and policy debates. Where possible, we have compared the information contained in the JIWIS data with the evidence obtained from larger, more representative, surveys such as the British Household Panel Survey, the Workplace Industrial Relations Survey, the British Social Attitudes Survey and the various surveys conducted by the Institute for Personnel and Development. Our analysis of job insecurity and work intensification has also been extended to include other countries besides the UK. We have conducted a broad review of the international literature on job insecurity and occupational stress together with a more detailed analysis of the data contained in the European Survey of Working Conditions and the US General Social Survey.

The contents of the book

We have arranged and edited the chapters so that the book can be read in a linear narrative fashion. But because each chapter addresses a particular aspect of job insecurity and work intensification, the reader is free to engage with our analyses in a thematic (non-sequential) fashion.

In Chapter 1, David Ladipo and Frank Wilkinson examine the competitive pressures imposed upon employing organisations by technological innovations, trade globalisation, and the growth (and deregulation) of the capital markets. They show how these pressures are passed on to the labour force through the demand for increased 'flexibility' and they chart the erosion of some of the laws and institutions which had traditionally protected workers from the threat of unfair dismissal or excessive workloads.

In Chapter 2, Maria Hudson investigates the measures adopted by employers in response to the demand for flexibility. She shows how redundancies, lay-offs, natural wastage and other forms of 'downsizing' are viewed – by even the most secure and profitable companies – as an opportunity to reorganise traditional working practices and transform the attitudes, values and organisational culture of the core workforce. But she also reveals that, for many organisations, the impact on productivity, costs and managerial control has proved less favourable than initially anticipated. The stress and insecurity generated by these initiatives has damaged the psychological contract between employers and employees and made it increasingly difficult for managers to retain the goodwill and cooperation of their workforce.

In Chapter 3, Brendan Burchell examines the rise in job insecurity in the UK and the US and identifies the groups that have been most affected. He also charts the growth in the proportion of workers, in each of the EU member states, who spend 'most' or 'all' of their time working at speed or to tight deadlines. For some countries (e.g. Greece and Luxembourg) this growth has been negligible. But, for other countries – and the UK in particular – the past ten years have witnessed a worrying increase in the percentage of the labour force employed under intense working conditions.

In Chapter 4, Maria Hudson suggests that the anxieties triggered by the drive towards flexibility are not restricted to the fear of job loss or the intensification of work. Citing evidence from both the UK and the US, she argues that many employees are worried not because they might lose their jobs *per se* but because they are threatened with the loss of valued job features. Faced with the de-layering of occupational hierarchies, they are scared of losing their promotion opportunities. And, confronted with a rapid growth in wage disparities, they are anxious about their pay relativities and frustrated at the emergence of inequalities which they perceive as unjust and unmerited.

In Chapter 5, Ines Wichert explores the impact of job insecurity and work intensification on the individual's psychological health and well-being. Her analysis suggests that it is not just the *transition* from secure to insecure work (and from challenging to overtaxing workloads) that employees find stressful. Having made the transition, our minds and bodies do not 'adjust' to higher levels of job insecurity and work pressure. On the contrary, the longer we remain subject to these phenomena, the more we exhaust our capacity to cope with stress. This is not to say that insecurity and pressure affects everybody in the same way and to the same extent. Each of us is subject to a range of personal, social and environmental 'moderators' that influence our resilience and vulnerability, and thus our susceptibility to the adverse effects of job insecurity and work.[3] And, in considering the role of these moderators, this chapter pays particular attention to the moderating role of social support, that is, the help received from 'significant others'.

In Chapter 6, Jane Nolan shows how the stress associated with job insecurity and work intensification spills over into people's family lives. She examines the various factors which moderate (or exacerbate) this process, for example, the gender of the respondent and their responsibility for young children. Her analysis suggests that the achievement of an equitable 'work–life' balance depends upon the willingness of organisations to offer clearly defined family-friendly policies and the active support of managers and colleagues. But her research also indicates just how difficult it can be to secure this support when managers are, themselves, under intense performance pressure.

In Chapter 7, Roy Mankelow considers the impact of job insecurity and work intensification not on individuals (or their families) but on the health and efficiency of the organisations by whom they are employed. His analysis suggests that the costs of workplace stress are not restricted to sickness and absenteeism. Excessive work pressures, as with job insecurity, damage one of the principal sources of profitability and competitive advantage, namely the goodwill of the workforce.

In Chapter 8, Ines Wichert describes some of the steps which employers can take in order to tackle the stress caused by overwork and job insecurity. She argues that managers and supervisors need to lead by example. If they themselves accept high levels of stress (and suffer from them) they will have neither the time nor the emotional resources with which to support their staff. Her analysis also suggests that a genuine commitment to reducing workplace stress must involve a widespread acceptance that stress is real, that it needs to be monitored and managed systematically and that it must not be ignored and written off as a sign of personal weakness.

In Chapter 9, Frank Wilkinson and David Ladipo endorse the claim that managers can do a great deal to improve the working lives of their employees. But they also recognise there are limits to the extent to which the individual organisation can provide a credible, and long-term, commitment to the health and security of its employees. They argue that the employer's 'duty to care' needs to be supported by the statutory protection of social rights. And they point to the vital role played by government regulation in protecting, not just the health of the individual worker, but the effective operation of the economy as a whole.

1 More pressure, less protection

David Ladipo and Frank Wilkinson

Much of this book is concerned with the impact of job insecurity and work intensification on the health and well-being of workers and their families. But in this chapter our attention will focus on the causes, rather than the effects, of stress and insecurity. In the product markets, we look at the competitive demands imposed on firms by technological innovations, trade globalisation and the commercialisation of the public sector.[1] In the capital markets, we witness the pressures exerted by dominant stakeholders, anxious for a quick and profitable return on their investments. We watch these pressures being passed on to the labour force through the demand for increased 'flexibility' and the acceleration of the pace and flow of work. We observe how the supply of labour continues to outstrip the availability of jobs, long after the economy has recovered from the recession of the late 1980s and early 1990s. We chart the erosion of some of the laws and institutions which had traditionally protected workers from the insecurities of the market; and we note, in particular, the declining power of trade unions, the weakening of employment laws and the reduction in unemployment benefits.

Technological innovation

> The world is changing very fast. We are moving from an old model economy to a new one, and every business has to find a way of transforming itself for this new economy which is coming upon us with lightning speed. Big will not beat small any more. It will be the fast beating the slow.
>
> (Rupert Murdoch, 1 July 1999)[2]

Over the past twenty years the new technologies of information and communication have accelerated the speed at which goods and services are produced. More importantly, they have increased the flexibility with which organisations source, produce and distribute their products. For example, in manufacturing industries the flexibility of electronically controlled technology means that far-reaching changes in the process of production are no longer dependent upon the increased scale of production. On the contrary, one of the major results of the new electronic and computer-aided production technology is that it permits rapid switching from one part of a process to another and allows 'the tailoring of production to the requirements of individual customers'.[3] In the Job Insecurity and Work Intensification Survey (JIWIS) sample this effect was particularly noticeable in the organisation which manufactured components for the telecommunications and IT markets. As described to us by one of the senior managers, the introduction of flexibile automation had led to a 'a dramatic change in lead times, from thirteen days to one or two days'. And in the food and drinks sector, the managing director of a large production plant told us how the introduction of computer-controlled technology was helping them to 'build to orders . . . so that we can replenish stocks as we get the signals from the retailers'.

Meanwhile, in the financial and insurance sectors the introduction of new data-processing technologies has enabled firms to automate the lower end of clerical jobs where the routine tasks 'because they can be reduced to a number of standard steps' can be easily programmed.[4] In the JIWIS sample, the two companies which worked in this sector had used these technologies to de-layer their occupational hierarchies. In both cases they had centralised and automated much of their data-processing activities and had reduced the need for middle-management supervision by introducing computerised decision-making with respect to loan agreements, underwriting and other 'risk assessments'.[5] As one of their senior managers put it: 'the new technologies give lower level staff increased autonomy so they can make decisions on the spot, on lending limits for example'.

And, across all industries, the introduction of electronic point of sale (EPOS) technology has enabled firms to produce instant updates to their stock records.[6] The result is a product market in which daily and hourly fluctuations in customer demand can be instantly fed down the supply chain thereby making it much easier for firms to operate just-in-time supply systems. In the JIWIS sample, the company most dependent on such systems was the large retailer of food and household products whose operations relied upon 'the use of information technology to feed back information so facilitating the constant flow of goods'.

Since the JIWIS survey was completed the rapid expansion of 'business-to-business' e-commerce will have accelerated the move towards just-in-time inventory management. At the time we conducted the interviews few of the companies we visited had started managing their supply chain over the Internet. But figures published by the *Financial Times*[7] suggest that by the start of the year 2000, one in four British firms were already using the Internet in their 'business-to-business' transactions, cutting the average cost per transaction from £50 to £5. As the paper dryly observes, 'using the internet for purchasing and supply enables better inventory control, and sharpens competition between suppliers'.[8]

Besides their impact on business-to-business transactions, the new technologies have also transformed the relationship between businesses and consumers. Among the JIWIS sample, several firms suggested that their customers were better informed as a result of the new information technologies and were, as a result, much more demanding. In a large financial services organisation, one of the senior managers told us that: 'our ability to control the pricing of services has to a considerable extent been eroded by competition and the ease with which customers can avail themselves of information about the products and prices of our competitors in this market'. He also noted that 'competition has come increasingly from direct tele-sales services'. Of course, the impact of telephone and Internet sales is not restricted to financial and insurance services but is noticeable across a range of different sectors. For example, when we visited a large retailer of financial and insurance services, we were told that:

> Our customers now require 'just-in-time' delivery from us in as much as they want real-time access to the booking system. People want to get it sorted out right away – a large proportion of our customers want to book when they come in . . . and customers have started to flex their muscles a little bit because they've become more savvy about the supply procedures of the operators.

But, as we discuss in Chapter 2, the organisational flexibility demanded by the new information technologies calls for a corresponding flexibility in the workforce. For when competitiveness increasingly requires higher quality, better design *and* more frequent changes in products, senior managers require more involvement and cooperation from their employees. The emphasis then, is on a combination of measures to increase the range of tasks individuals perform, improve their skills and increase their involvement by making them more responsible for quality control, coordination and management. Hence, the pressure is on to modify one or all of: the task content of jobs, the intensity of work, the number of hours worked and the timing of these hours. Or, as Castells puts it:

> Because the value-making potential of labour and organisations is highly dependent upon the autonomy of informed labour to make decisions in real time, traditional disciplinary management of labour does not fit the new production system. Instead, skilled labour is required to manage its own time in a flexible manner, sometimes adding more work time, at other times adjusting to flexible schedules, in some instances reducing working hours, and thus pay. This new time-oriented management of labour could be called 'just-in-time labour'.[9]

Globalisation

As Standing reminds us, 'globalisation is not something that suddenly happened'.[10] Many commodities have had an international character for centuries and the acceleration of international trade relative to national consumption was visible in both the 1890s and the 1990s. But, as Kitson and Michie have shown, the 'disintegration' of the world economy triggered by the Great Depression and the Second World War ensured that it was not until 1968 that the openness of the world economy returned to the level achieved in 1913. The OPEC shock of 1973 and the collapse of the Bretton Woods system temporarily slowed down the move towards a more open world economy, as did the 'monetarist' shock that introduced the deflationary policies of the early 1980s. But, unlike the 1930s, the growth in world trade continued to outpace the growth in output, albeit at a slower rate than in the 'golden era' of 1950–73. And by the last decade of the century, the globalisation of the world's product markets was accelerating faster than ever before (see Figures 1.1 and 1.2).

To a large extent the globalisation of the world's economy has been driven by the international trade in manufactured products. Indeed, the share of manufactures in world merchandise trade has increased dramatically,[11] from 52 per cent of the total in 1963 to 77 per cent in 1997. And, as a result of this globalisation of trade, the UK's manufacturers – alongside most of their OECD counterparts – found that their fortunes were increasingly dependent upon the export market. But, of course, the growth of

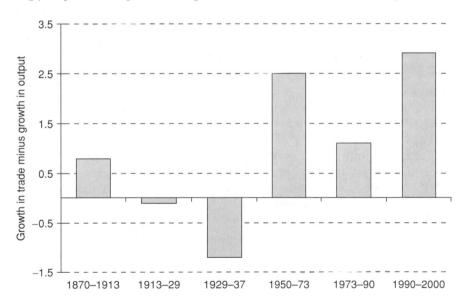

Figure 1.1 The globalisation of trade, 1870–2000

Sources: Kitson and Michie (1995, Table 1.1) and IMF (1999)

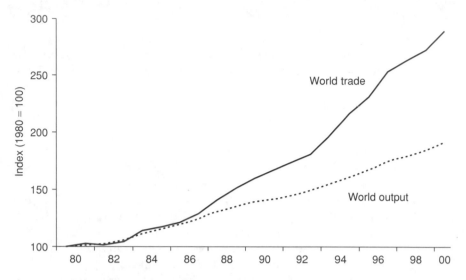

Figure 1.2 The growing interconnectedness of the world economy,* 1980–2000
* World trade represents the growth in the trade volume of goods and services.
World output represents the growth in real gross world product.

Source: IMF (1999)

international trade in manufactured goods was only possible because of
the parallel development of a whole variety of commercial, financial and
business services. As Dicken puts it, 'these are the services which lubricate
the wheels of production and trade' and what is striking about the 1980s
and 1990s is the extent to which *they themselves* became traded on the
international market.[12] In the 1970s, such trade grew more slowly than
manufacturing trade but, in the 1980s and 1990s, the information technology revolution and the development of off-shore information processing increased the percentage of world trade accounted for by commercial
services (see Table 1.1).

Not surprisingly, the globalisation of services has placed considerable
demands on the employees who work in this sector. For example, in the
JIWIS, we were told by the senior manager of a large financial services
organisation that his company needed 'increased flexibility' from its
workforce 'at a time of increasing external competition'. But the competitive pressures exerted by globalisation are only partly reflected in the
growth in transnational *trade*. Indeed, for many British workers, it was the
growth in transnational *production* which proved to be the most disturbing
development. Between 1970 and 1997, the number of TNCs grew from
7,000 to more than 60,000 with 500,000 affiliates around the world.[13] And,
although TNCs still employ only a small fraction of the world's workforce,[14]
they are particularly important in some sectors and nations. By the start of

Table 1.1 The growing dependence on foreign trade

	Trade in merchandise* as % of GDP		Trade in services** as a % of trade in merchandise	
	1987	*1997*	*1985*	*1997*
UK	36	48	27	33
EU	38	51	24	25
Japan	21	25	12	16
US	14	20	29	34
World	21	30	20	24

* Trade in goods is the sum of merchandise exports and imports measured in current US dollars divided by the value of GDP converted to international dollars using purchasing power parity conversion factors.
Source: World Bank (1999, Table 6.1)
** Trade in services is the value of world exports of commercial services divided by the value of world merchandise exports.
Source: WTO (2000)

Table 1.2 Global trends in FDI and international production

	Annual growth rate (%)		
	1991–6	*1997*	*1998*
FDI inflows	17.9	29.4	38.7
FDI outflows	14.2	25.1	36.6
Gross product of foreign affiliates	7.2	12.8	17.1

Source: UNCTAD (1999, Table 5)

the 1990s, transnational corporations already accounted for one-fifth of the world's paid employment in the non-agricultural sectors[15] and as early as 1989 more than 40 per cent of the UK's manufacturing workers were employed by multinational enterprises.[16]

Although the growth in transnational production is nothing new,[17] the first rapid acceleration of transnational production took place between 1983 and 1987 when the flow of foreign direct investment (FDI) grew at an average rate of 35 per cent.[18] The rate slowed down during the early 1990s as a result of the global economic downturn but, by 1993, the dramatic increase in FDI flows had resumed (see Table 1.2). According to the 1999 *World Investment Report*,[19] by the end of the decade the value of output under the common governance of TNCs (parent firms and foreign affiliates) amounted to approximately 25 per cent of global output. The report also notes that while most international production in developing countries is in manufacturing, most of the transnational production in developed countries is in services.

Table 1.3 Gross FDI as a % of GDP

	1987	1997
Sweden	4.3	12.2
Netherlands	5.8	8.8
UK	5.9	8.0
Norway	3.0	7.0
Denmark	0.9	5.2
France	1.7	4.5
EU	1.6	3.1
US	2.1	2.9
Spain	1.4	2.7
Germany	na	2.2
Italy	0.8	1.2

Source: World Bank (1999, Table 6.1)

Gross foreign direct investment is the sum of the absolute values of inflows and outflows of foreign direct investment calculated as a ratio of GDP converted to international dollars using purchasing power parities.

To measure the extent to which a particular host country is involved in international production UNCTAD statisticians have calculated an 'index of transnationality'. It measures the average of the following four ratios: FDI inflows as a percentage of gross fixed capital formation; inward FDI stock as a percentage of GDP; value added of foreign affiliates as a percentage of GDP; and employment of foreign affiliates as a percentage of total employment. Among the developed countries, New Zealand has the highest 'transnationality' score and Japan the lowest, with the UK ranked in sixth place – well above most of its EU competitors. Figures published by the World Bank also indicate the extent of the UK's involvement in international production. As shown in Table 1.3, by 1997 the flow of foreign direct investment into and out of the UK amounted to 8 per cent of the country's gross domestic product.

For many British workers, this acceleration of international production was deeply unsettling. For, as Dicken puts it, the defining characteristic of a transnational corporation (TNC) is its 'geographical flexibility . . . its ability to shift its resources and operations between locations at a global scale'.[20] In other words, their employees are subject to two kinds of competitive pressure. There is the *inter-firm* rivalry between 'parent' companies which is exacerbated by technological innovation and trade globalisation. But within the parent company there is also the *intra-firm* rivalry which takes place between its foreign affiliates, the managers of which are conscious that the multiplicity of production sites allows the 'parent' company the flexibility to relocate production according to shifts in relative costs and the availability of suitable labour. The pressures generated by *intra-firm* rivalry were apparent in all eight of the TNCs which participated in the JIWIS survey but they were especially noticeable in the financial services

Table 1.4 National regulatory changes, 1991–8

	1991	1992	1993	1994	1995	1996	1997	1998
No. of countries that introduced changes in their investment regimes	35	43	57	49	64	65	76	60
Number of regulatory changes								
more favourable to FDI	80	79	101	108	106	98	135	136
less favourable to FDI	2	0	1	2	6	16	16	9

Source: UNCTAD (1999, Table 4)

sector. In one case, the employees we interviewed belonged to an international financial services group which had subsidiaries in over fifty countries around the world. The bulk of its employees are located outside the UK and three-quarters of its total income was generated by its foreign affiliates. Within this firm, the managers that we spoke to were acutely conscious of their organisation's ability to switch production from one site to another, or even from one country to another.

But the globalisation of trade and production has not been an *automatic* response to technological innovation and geographical differences in costs. On the contrary, it has been actively promoted by the dismantling of tariff and non-tariff barriers under the General Agreement on Tariffs and Trade (GATT) and the World Trade Organisation (WTO). National governments (the UK's in particular) have also promoted the globalisation of trade and investment. In 1998, for example, of the 145 regulatory changes relating to foreign direct investment made during that year by sixty countries, 94 per cent were in the direction of creating more favourable conditions for FDI. And, if one takes the period 1991–8 as a whole, only 52 out of 843 FDI policy changes went in the direction of greater control (see Table 1.4). These unilateral national efforts at liberalization were also complemented by a growth in bilateral investment treaties (BITS). By the end of 1997, there were 1,794 BITS in existence, two-thirds of them concluded during the 1990s.[21] As Burbach and Robinson put it, during the 1980s and 1990s, nation-states restructured their markets not simply because they were 'powerless' in the face of globalisation but because of 'a particular historical constellation of forces' that presented 'an organic social base for neoliberal restructuring'[22] – an observation which we will return to at the end of this chapter.

The commercialisation of the public sector

The impact of new technologies and the spread of globalisation are not the only factors responsible for the increase in market pressure. Other factors include the privatisation of public industries. Although this development took place across the OECD, the scale of the privatisations varied

Table 1.5 Major UK privatisations

Cable and Wireless	October 1981
Amersham International	February 1982
Britoil	November 1982
Associated British Ports	February 1983
Enterprise Oil	June 1984
Jaguar	July 1984
British Telecom	November 1984
British Gas	December 1986
BA	February 1987
Rolls Royce	May 1987
British Airports Authority	July 1987
British Steel	December 1988
10 Water Authorities	December 1989
12 Electricity Boards	December 1990
Electricity Generators (CEGB)	March 1991
Rail Rolling Stock	December 1995
Railtrack	May 1996

Source: Thornton (1998, Figure 1)

from country to country. In their review of public sector reform in Western Europe, Toonen and Raadschelders distinguish between 'timid', 'middle-range' and 'radical' privatisers.[23] They class Sweden and Greece as timid privatisers; Belgium, Spain, Italy and the Netherlands as middle-range privatisers and Germany, France and Portugal as radical privatisers. But the most radical of them all was the UK, which sold off more than eighty public enterprises[24] during the 1980s, including some of the country's biggest employers of labour (see Table 1.5). They also included three of the organisations participating in the JIWIS, all of which had engaged in downsizing or other forms of workforce restructuring in the wake of their initial exposure to the commercial market.[25]

Although privatisation was the most dramatic example of the 'marketization' of economic activity, the services which *remained* in the public sector were also exposed to the pressures of 'market forces'. Nowhere more so than in the UK where, by the mid-1990s, the bulk of its public services had been subjected to some form of 'contractual or quasi-contractual' market mechanism.[26]

Although contracts had long been used for the provision of certain services by smaller rural authorities, until the 1980s, the 'normal assumption' had been that most services would be provided through directly employed staff. But this assumption was soon to be discarded. In 1983, the Department of Health and Social Security required competitive tendering for ancillary functions in the National Health Service i.e. catering, laundry and domestic work. The expansion of contracting and competitive tendering was given a further boost by the Local Government Act of 1988, which required local authorities to subject a range of manual services to competitive tender. And from 1993, competitive contracting was extended throughout the civil service to include professional services such as engineering, law, finance, personnel, housing management and computer services.[27]

Of course the exposure of public services to private sector competition is not the only means by which market mechanisms have been introduced into the British public sector. The creation of *internal markets* – through the separation of purchaser and provider roles – ensures that the services which remain within the public sector 'are gradually being moved onto a trading basis' where they must 'earn their income from the sale of services to the client side of the organisation'.[28] The operation of such markets is clearly visible within the restructured National Health Service but internal markets are also important in the purchase of further education courses by Training and Enterprise Councils. The development of local management of schools also encouraged the internal trading of services as the local education providers transformed themselves into business units selling services to schools.

The UK was not the only country to have exposed its public services to market 'testing' during the 1980s and 1990s. America had already seen a rapid increase in contracting out during the 1970s but the trend continued over the next twenty years, spreading to a wide range of services including those located in politically sensitive sectors such as the management of prisons and mental health facilities.[29] Internal markets (primarily in health services) were introduced into the public sectors of New Zealand, Sweden and the Netherlands and the growth in competitive tendering and contracting out was a feature of most OECD countries during this period.[30]

By the end of the 1990s, the drive to introduce market mechanisms into the public sector was stronger than ever and both the World Trade Organisation and the World Bank were determined to expand private sector involvement in the traditional areas of public provision. In their review of the WTO's General Agreement on Trade in Services (GATS), Price *et al.* note that 'with the backing of powerful coalitions of transnational and multinational corporations, the race is on to capture the share of gross domestic product governments currently spend on public services'.[31] By way of illustration, they cite the following quotation from the US trade delegation:

> The United States is of the view that commercial opportunities exist along the entire spectrum of health and social care facilities, including hospitals, outpatient facilities, clinics, nursing homes, assisted living arrangements, and services provided in the home.[32]

Price *et al.* also note that when GATS was first introduced in 1995, only 27 per cent of WTO members agreed to open hospital services to foreign suppliers. But that was partly because the previous round of WTO ministerial talks (the Uruguyan round) allowed governments to protect health and social services from GATS treatment by defining them as government services which are provided 'neither on a commercial basis nor in competition with one or more service suppliers'. But the WTO secretariat now argues that for services to be classified as such, they must be provided free of charge and that whenever there is a mixture of public and private funding – as is the case in most European countries – the service sector should be open to foreign corporations. As stated in Article 19 of GATS: 'members shall enter in successive rounds of negotiations . . . with a view to achieving a progressively higher level of liberalisation'.[33]

But if the multinational service providers – including the pharmaceutical companies and the 'health maintenance organisations' – hope to profit from the liberalisation of public services, the workers employed in these services may find themselves uncomfortably exposed to increased levels of job insecurity and work intensification. As described in Chapter 2, the pressures exerted by the commercialisation of public services were certainly visible in all the public sector organisations that participated in the JIWIS survey.

The stock markets

In most of the organisations we visited, the pressure of an increasingly competitive product market was exacerbated by the impatience of their dominant stakeholders. In the private sector, managers and employees were conscious of the increasingly 'contingent' commitment of their investors. And in the public sector, the demands imposed by the stock market were being simulated through the introduction of commercial accounting practices.

As described in Hutton, and in Akyüz and Cornford,[34] the commitment of investors is directly related to the liquidity of their assets. As Hutton puts it:

> The more liquid a financial asset, the less committed the owner must be to the longterm health of the underlying investment. If the going gets tough or conditions change the investor has already made provision for his or her escape: sell the financial asset, withdraw the short-term loan, rather than share the risk of restructuring and of managing any crisis.[35]

This desire for liquidity is reflected in the rapid 'capitalisation' of the world economy and the corresponding growth in the number of employees working for organisations whose shares are auctioned, daily, on the world's stock exchanges. If their profits dip, or if the returns look more favourable elsewhere, their shareholders can 'disinvest' almost immediately. Figures released by the World Bank show a two-fold increase in the size and liquidity of the British stock market between 1990 and 1997.

Table 1.6 The growing importance of the stock market

	Capitalisation as a % of GDP		Value traded as a % of GDP	
	1990	*1997*	*1990*	*1997*
UK	87.0	155.2	28.6	64.4
US	55.1	144.4	55.1	144.4
Netherlands	42.2	130.1	14.2	79.1
Sweden	42.6	119.8	7.6	77.4
Belgium	33.4	56.5	3.3	12.3
France	26.3	48.4	9.8	29.1
Norway	22.6	43.4	12.1	30.3
Germany	22.9	39.4	22.1	49.2
Italy	13.6	30.1	3.9	17.3
EU	22.4	46.5	7.5	39.8
World	51.8	84.6	29.0	69.9

Source: World Bank (1999, Table 5.2)

Market *capitalisation* measures the overall size of the stock market as a percentage of GDP. Market liquidity, the ability to easily buy and sell shares, is measured by dividing the total *value traded* by GDP.

During the same period, the US witnessed a three-fold increase in the size of its stock market and a four-fold increase in its market liquidity. In Continental Europe, the story was much the same (see Table 1.6).

Since then, the trend has continued to accelerate. At the time this chapter was written, the 'tradeability' of corporate control was being pushed still further by the rapid diffusion of on-line share trading and the accompanying reduction in dealing fees.[36] In less than four months – between November 1999 and March 2000 – the number of trades on the London Stock Exchange ballooned from around 50,000 a day[37] to an average of 100,000. In Europe as a whole there were 1.26 million online trading accounts by the end of 1999, a figure which is set to rise to more than 14 million by 2004.[38] The liquidity of the world's financial markets is also reflected in the volume of cross-border share trading. In America, overseas investment by pension funds increased from less than 1 per cent of their assets in 1980 to 17 per cent in 1997 and,[39] over the same period, the percentage of UK shares held by foreign investors rose from 4 per cent to 24 per cent (see Figure 1.3). And, with the launch of 'single access' trading points such as the JIWAY Exchange,[40] the volume of cross-border trading has continued to expand, with current estimates[41] suggesting that the volume of cross-border share trading will triple between 2000 and 2003.

Another indicator of the pressures imposed by the globalisation of the world's capital markets can be found in the pattern of mergers and acquisitions (M&A). In the year we conducted the JIWIS survey, the value of cross-border M&A reached a record US$468 billion.[42] The UK alone attracted $86 billion worth of foreign acquisitions making it the 'most powerful

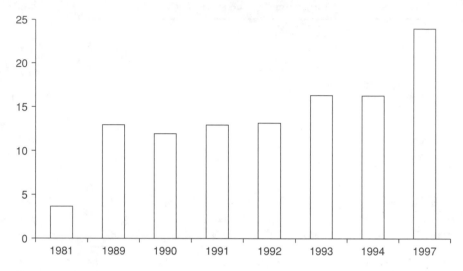

Figure 1.3 Foreign ownership of UK shares

Source: Hill (1999, Table A)

Table 1.7 Top ten buyer and seller countries in global M&A

| | Seller | | Buyer | |
	Deals	Value	Deals	Value
US	849	201.2	1,440	124.8
UK	560	86.1	658	127.7
Germany	364	36.7	369	60.9
France	320	23.1	356	40.5
Canada	240	15.3	403	40.7
Netherlands	165	18.3	358	38.7
Australia	143	7.4	70	7.5
Sweden	102	6.1	146	14.0
Japan	88	6.9	159	7.2
Switzerland	83	6.3	145	12.1

Source: Miyake and Thomsen (1999, Table 3)

magnet in Europe for foreign businesses', with US buyers accounting for a large proportion of the deals. But Germany, France and the Netherlands were also popular destinations for corporate buyers, attracting US$78 billion of deals between them (see Table 1.7). And what makes the current wave of M&A particularly interesting is that it 'does not seem to be deterred by the relatively poor results that have been observed with respect to M&As, particularly in some industries'. According to UNCTAD, the phenomenon has been driven by the fiercer competitive pressures brought about by globalisation and technological changes:

Size puts firms in a better position to keep pace with an uncertain and rapidly evolving technological environment, a crucial requirement in an increasingly knowledge-intensive world economy, and to face soaring costs of research . . . furthermore, the dynamics of the process feed upon itself, as firms fear that, if they do not find suitable partners, they may not survive, at least in the long run.[43]

The UNCTAD commentary, however, provides only a partial explanation of the forces that are driving the massive expansion of M&A activity. As described by John Clancy, instead of expanding their operations and innovating, industry today uses cost-cutting through redundancies and work intensification as a quick-fix strategy for increasing profitability. Such strategies are greatly facilitated by setting up mergers. Given the generally poor longer-term record of success by merged enterprises, it seems more convincing that many of these operations are indeed set up for the purpose of rewarding top management through share options and bonuses, than for the need to remain competitive in a globalised market.

But technological change was not the only factor responsible for the capitalisation of the world economy and the growth in cross-border financial transactions. As described in Akyüz and Cornford (1995), the consensus which prevailed throughout the Bretton Woods era was that capital flows unrelated to foreign direct investment or trade should be discouraged (or even prevented). By contrast, since the early 1970s, freedom of capital movements has been increasingly viewed as a desirable policy objective. As a result, in most of the major financial centres foreign exchange transactions are now virtually unrestricted and the controls governing the trade in financial assets are being rapidly dismantled. Symptomatic of this trend was the repeal, on 20 November 1999, of the Glass Steagall Act, which had separated the US's banking and securities business for more than sixty years.[44] In Europe, meanwhile, the major stock exchanges ('anxious to be seen as innovative and scared to be left behind by rivals')[45] were busy relaxing their listing rules. By the end of the 1990s, the London Stock Exchange (LSE) had largely dropped its requirement that a company have a three-year trading record before admission to its main market. And, in March 2000, it allowed the initial public offering of the infamous Lastminute.com to proceed just 18 months after the company first started trading.[46]

Perhaps the best illustration of the *active promotion* of 'stock market capitalism' is that provided by Stephen Wilks in his analysis of the UK's Monopolies and Mergers Commission (MMC). He notes that although mergers have always aroused criticism (on the grounds that they 'encourage short-term financial opportunism' and impose 'great frictional costs') the government's position throughout the 1980s and 1990s has been that mergers are desirable. As the Deputy Director of the Office of Fair Trading (OFT) observed to a business audience in 1983, 'We frequently point out to firms that British law is basically favourable to mergers.' And over the past two decades, 'neither the OFT nor the MMC has been inclined to stand against this presumption'.[47]

And in the public sector, Price *et al.* note that the impatience of the stock market has been mimicked by the introduction of commercial accounting practices. To such an extent that, by the end of the 1990s, Price *et al.* were able to state that:

> The sole statutory duties of National Health Service provider trusts (hospital and community services) are financial and not health-care duties; NHS bodies must break even after having made a profit for their owners (the Government) equivalent to a 6% return on capital. The same will apply to primary-care trusts, which will also be made to behave commercially as if they have shareholders.[48]

Unemployment

In addition to the competitive pressures exerted by the globalisation of the world's product and capital markets, most OECD countries also had to contend with the persistence of mass unemployment throughout the 1980s and 1990s. Although there was a steady growth in the demand for labour, in many countries it was not sufficient to compensate for the simultaneous increase in the supply of labour. Helped along by the rapid growth in rates of female labour force participation, in European nations, such as France and Italy, the rate of 'open' unemployment continued to rise throughout this period (Figures 1.4 and 1.5). In the UK, unemployment

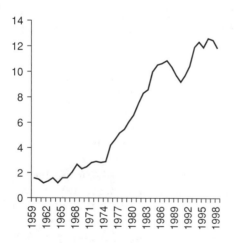

Figure 1.4 Unemployment rate (%) in France

Source: BLS (1999)

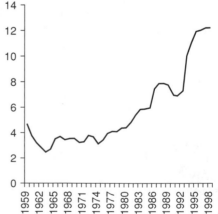

Figure 1.5 Unemployment rate (%) in Italy

Source: BLS (1999)

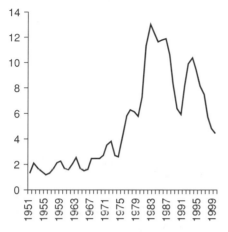

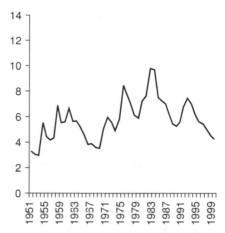

Figure 1.6 Unemployment rate (%) in the UK

Source: Denman and McDonald (1996); StatBase (2000)

Figure 1.7 Unemployment rate (%) in the US

Source: BLS (2000)

rocketed during the early 1980s and, despite two periods of sustained economic recovery (1985–90 and 1994–9), the country ended the century with an official unemployment rate still well above that which prevailed during the 'golden age' of the 1950s and 1960s (Figure 1.6). Even in the US, where the rise in open unemployment has been contained by the low level and short duration of benefits (and the difficulty of obtaining them),[49] unemployment rates averaged 7.1 and 5.8 per cent respectively during the 1980s and 1990s compared to 4.5 and 4.7 per cent during the 1950s and 1960s (Figure 1.7).

In fact, there is plenty of evidence to suggest that the official figures described in Figures 1.4–1.7 *underestimate* the growth in 'labour slack' which occurred during this period. As Guy Standing notes, although regular full-time employment has ceased to be the overwhelming norm, the official unemployment statistics continue to treat part-time and full-time jobs as identical, despite the fact that many of the people now engaged in part-time employment would prefer to be working full-time. Moreover, many of the OECD countries have also witnessed a growth in 'discouraged job-seekers', that is, people who have dropped out of the 'active' labour force but who continue to want (and remain available for) employment.[50] In the UK, for example, the claimant unemployment data used by the Treasury leaves out of account those who are actively seeking work but are not claiming benefits. These are included in the ILO definition of unemployment but the ILO measure still excludes many people who say they want to work but do not meet the criteria for inclusion.[51] By adding together

Table 1.8 US unemployment indicators, 1995

Official unemployment rate (= U3)	5.6%
U3 plus discouraged workers (= U4)	5.9%
U4 plus all marginally attached workers (= U5)	6.7%
U5 plus involuntary part-time workers (= U6)	10.1%

Source: BLS (2000)

According to BLS definitions: marginally attached workers are persons who currently are neither working nor looking for work but indicate that they want and are available for a job and have looked for work sometime in the recent past. Discouraged workers, a subset of the marginally attached, have given a job-market related reason for not currently looking for a job. Involuntary part-time workers are those who want and are available for full-time work but have had to settle for a part-time schedule.

the 'ILO unemployed' and others who want to work as revealed by the Labour Force Survey, the TUC has produced what it calls a *want work* rate. In Autumn 1999 the claimant unemployment rate was 4 per cent, the ILO unemployment rate was 6 per cent and the want work rate was 13 per cent (ranging from 17.5 per cent in the North East to 9.6 per cent in the South East).[52] The same goes for the US where the Bureau of Labor Force Statistics publishes a range of 'alternative measures of labor underutilization' which suggest that the 'real' index of labour slack could be as much as twice the official rate of unemployment (Table 1.8).

However, if the standard measures of unemployment underestimate the true extent of labour slack they are still a good indicator of the *direction* in which the labour market is moving. For example, if we look at the UK and the US, it is clear that, although the figures were still well above those recorded during the 1950s and 1960s, rates of unemployment were actually falling for much of the 1990s – a trend which should have *reduced* people's feelings of job insecurity. And yet, as described in Chapter 3, by the late 1990s the people in the workforce in both countries felt slightly *more* insecure than they had done during the height of the 1980s recession. As we shall see, this was partly because of a rise in the cost of job loss. But it was also a reflection of a more turbulent labour market wherein the threat of redundancies spread to a far wider range of industries and occupational sectors than had hitherto been the norm.

In the UK, for example, the analysis undertaken by Turnbull and Wass shows a secular increase in the number of involuntary job losses, in both absolute terms and as a proportion of all job losses. Over the twenty-year period from 1977 to 1997, the number of redundancies rose and fell according to fluctuations in the business cycle. But the point to note is that in each cycle, the level of post-recession redundancies remained *above* the pre-recession level. For example, in 1997, when the unemployment rate (4.9 per cent) had fallen slightly below that in 1989 (5.3 per cent) the rate of redundancies was still well above that of the late 1980s.[53] As Turnbull and Wass describe it, 'the sheer scale of redundancy in Britain, when

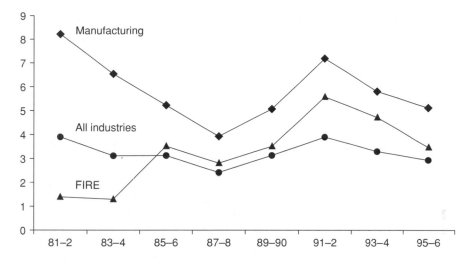

Figure 1.8 Displacement rates of long-tenured workers, US, 1981–96

Source: BLS statistics published in Hipple (1999, p. 18)

The statistics are limited to those who lost jobs they had held for at least three years on the assumption that these *long-tenured* workers have developed a more-than-marginal attachment to their jobs.

allied to ever greater recourse to redundancy during upturns (the ratchet effect), suggests that workers' fear of job loss is well founded'.[54]

In the US, the figures published by the Bureau of Labor Statistics (BLS) suggest that although aggregate redundancy rates did not 'ratchet' upwards during this period, the risk of displacement[55] was spread much more evenly across the workforce. And by the late 1990s, there were few industries or occupational sectors that could boast of their immunity to lay-offs or other forms of involuntary job separation. Reflecting this trend, displacement rates in the manufacturing industry fell from 8.2 per cent in 1981–2 to 5.1 per cent in 1995–6, although workers in this sector continued to be at greater-than-average risk. Meanwhile, displacement rates were increasing rapidly among many of the professions that had traditionally remained untouched by the threat of involuntary job loss. For example, during the early 1980s, the displacement rate for the finance, insurance and real estate sector (FIRE) was among the lowest of all industries; by the time of the 1990–1 recession, the rate for this sector had climbed well above the workforce average (see Figure 1.8).

The declining influence of trade unions

While the threat of redundancy was spreading from manufacturing to service occupations, many employees were also facing a loss of *representation security*, the most noticeable reflection of which was the decline in

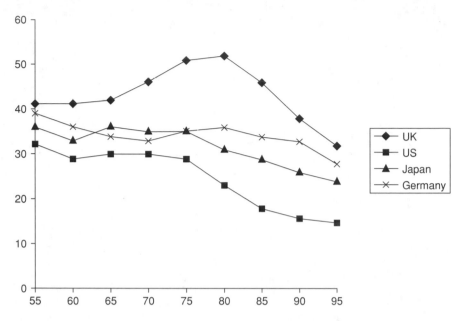

Figure 1.9 Union membership as a percentage of wage and salary earners

Sources: LRA (1999), Machin (2000), Chang and Sorrentino (1991), ILO (1998)

trade union membership. For example, between 1980 and 1995, the proportion of wage and salary earners belonging to trade unions fell by 38 per cent in the UK, by 35 per cent in the US and by 22 per cent in both Japan and West Germany (see Figure 1.9). But the most striking indicator of the decline in union influence was not the fall in union membership but the fall in union *coverage* (i.e. the proportion of workers whose pay was set by collective bargaining). In the UK, the proportion of workers whose pay rates were fixed by collective agreements fell from 71 per cent in 1984 to 41 per cent in 1998. In the US, the percentage of workers covered by collective agreements had fallen to less than 15 per cent by the mid-1990s. And in Europe and Japan, although the majority of workers were still covered by industry-wide pay agreements, the 1990s saw a growing recourse to 'open clauses' allowing works councils and employers to negotiate amendments to these agreements at the enterprise level.[56]

As described by Guy Standing, the widespread decline in unionization was attributable to several factors. Among other things, it reflected the changing composition of the labour force and, in particular, the growth in 'flexible' and 'non-standard' forms of employment.[57] In some cases, it also reflected the passage of anti-union legislation, such as that introduced by the British government during the 1980s and early 1990s. More generally, unions throughout the OECD have found their room for manoeuvre increasingly restricted by the internationalization of trade and production. As Standing puts it:

> Strikes are less successful in globally integrated production systems. If the union prevails, the firm's competitiveness is weakened, leading to job losses, or to job transfers within a geographically diversified enterprise, or to bankruptcy.[58]

Of course, the declining influence of the trade unions does not *necessarily* imply a loss of representation security. For, although trade union representation constitutes the traditional mechanism through which the concerns of workers are 'voiced' to management, it is not the only form of collective representation and expression. Other forms of participation, such as consultative committees and works councils, can serve the same function. Nevertheless, as the UK discovered during the 1980s and 1990s, the slow development of these alternative forms of representation has done little to counteract the rapid decline in the strength of its unions.

In fact, the evidence from the latest Workplace Industrial Relations Survey (WIRS) reveals that the proportion of British workplaces with a functioning joint consultative committee of managers and employees has actually been falling: from 31 per cent to 23 per cent between 1984 and 1998.[59] In some of the larger organisations, the reduction in *workplace* consultative committees was partially offset by the growth in *higher-level* consultative committees. But if we take as our indicator of employee representation the extent to which their workplace has *either* a functioning consultative committee *or* a representative on a higher-level committee, we find that the proportion of workplaces with such consultative machinery remained unchanged between 1984 and 1998.[60] As described by the authors of the WIRS report: 'If legislative developments at the European level in the 1990s were expected to have a pervasive influence on the extent of consultative arrangements in Britain, such an expectation has yet to be fulfilled'.[61]

In contrast to the decline in *representative* forms of consultation – through trade unions and joint committees – there has been a sharp increase in forms of communication which are not reliant on employee representatives acting as intermediaries between workers and management. They include such things as quality circles, improvement groups, focus groups, suggestion schemes, opinion surveys and 'upward appraisals'. As Maria Hudson describes in Chapter 2, nearly three-quarters of the employees who took part in the JIWIS survey indicated that their organisation had introduced one or more of these programmes during the 1990s. Nevertheless, although many of the JIWIS employees welcomed these schemes and viewed them as an opportunity to air their views and learn about other sides of the business, few of them felt that such initiatives could provide an adequate substitute for the protections traditionally afforded by their trade unions and staff associations.[62]

Of the JIWIS employees we spoke to, one-third said they did not belong to a trade union or staff association. But, of these, only a handful suggested that their lack of membership was due to the presence of adequate *alternatives*.[63] Instead, the most frequently cited explanations for non-membership pointed to a lack of recruitment effort on the part of trade unions or a lack of interest on the part of the employee. Other responses referred to the unions' 'lack of clout' or the fact that unions were not recognised within the employee's organisation. As one employee put it:

> I fell out with the union representative. I didn't believe in paying £8 a month for nothing – they weren't helping with the pay increases – they were only making things worse. When I first joined they were really strong, but now they are useless.

The rest of the JIWIS sample (67 per cent of the total) did belong to a trade union or staff association and the most frequently cited reason for membership was for 'support, security and protection', closely followed by the need for 'legal services and insurance'.[64] Moreover, 53 per cent of union members felt that it had become more important to be a trade union member in the last five years, compared to only 14 per cent who felt that it had become less important. On the other hand – and precisely because of the value that they placed on independent representation – many of these employees were deeply concerned about the erosion of trade union influence.[65] In the words of a machine operator working for a large building components manufacturer:

> They say unions but I don't know . . . Even if you say fair pay rates or anything and if everyone refuses to work, still the management refuses it, you can't do anything . . . The union should do something you know because when the redundancy comes the management takes people, it's not last in first go, it wasn't like that. Who they didn't want they just finished them, it was like that . . . [The union] should be doing more, but they are doing what the management say.

Changes in employment law

While the protections afforded by the trade unions were diminishing in most of the OECD states during the 1980s and 1990s, some of the changes in employment law which took place during this period were also responsible for the growth in job insecurity and work intensification. And whilst the reforms were particularly noticeable in the UK, most of its competitors also experimented with some form of employment 'deregulation'.[66] In countries such as France and Germany, we find a mixture of reforms, with some protections removed and others restored. In the more heavily regulated economies of Spain and Italy, the direction of change was more consistent, with most of the reforms tending to reduce the legal restrictions on workforce recruitment and dismissal. At the other end of the spectrum, the US retained its position as the country with the least protected labour market despite numerous lawsuits challenging the right to 'employment-at-will'.

Taking France as our first example, we see a relaxation, during the mid-1980s, of the laws protecting workers from redundancy. In 1986, the government ended the requirement for firms to obtain official permission before dismissing their staff on 'economic grounds' and it abolished the list which limited the circumstances in which the use of temporary and fixed-term staff was permissible. However, it is worth noting that many of the protections removed by these reforms were then restored in the subsequent decade. Thus, in 1989, the government introduced new regulations specifying that collective redundancies had to be accompanied by a social plan. In 1990, it reintroduced the list limiting the permissible use of temporary and fixed-term contracts. And, in 1993, it introduced a new law empowering the administrative authorities with the right to control the quality of the social plan.

A similar pattern occurred in Germany where the legislative reforms of the late 1980s reduced the proportion of the workforce covered by legislative protection against unfair dismissal. These reforms included the 1985 Employment Promotion Act (EPA) which partly exempted newly established small enterprises from the obligation to prepare a social plan when introducing collective redundancies. The Act also increased the number of small establishments not covered by statutory dismissal protection by excluding apprentices and marginal workers from the formula which calculated the minimum number of employees required for the application of the procedures of dismissal law. Other provisions of the EPA reduced employment protection on the hiring side by extending the maximum period for the use of fixed-term and agency workers and by allowing firms to prolong the probationary period for newly hired workers. Nonetheless, some of the protections lost during this period were recovered during the 1990s with the introduction of new laws which increased average notice periods (for workers with over ten years tenure) and raised the employment threshold for protection against 'socially unwarranted dismissal' from five to ten full-time employees per establishment.

In Spain, the laws governing recruitment and dismissal were relaxed in 1984 when the government increased the range of permissible fixed-term contracts thereby enabling employers to escape redundancy payment obligations (and cumbersome dismissal procedures) by substituting contract workers for permanent employees. As Spanish employers increased their reliance on temporary workers – to the point where they accounted for 90 per cent of all contracts agreed annually – the government decided to tighten the restrictions on fixed-term contracts and make it easier for employers to hire and fire their permanent workforce. Accordingly, in 1994, a new law was passed extending the permissible grounds for collective redundancies from economic and technological exigencies to production and organisational causes.

Akin to that of its Spanish neighbour, the Italian labour market has traditionally been regulated by strict laws on the recruitment and dismissal of permanent workers. Most of these restrictions remained in place throughout the 1980s and 1990s but a succession of employment reforms helped employers to circumvent these laws by expanding the proportion of the workforce employed on temporary contracts. The reforms of the late 1980s allowed for more extensive use of fixed-term contracts and, in 1997, the Italian government passed a new law legalising temporary work agencies and limiting the circumstances under which employers could be forced to convert fixed-term contracts into open-ended ones. Nonetheless, in contrast to the situation prevailing in the UK and the US, the laws protecting Italian workers from unfair dismissal and involuntary redundancy still appear remarkably strong.

As described by Sandra Brandão, US workers have rarely enjoyed the same legal protections as their European counterparts. Whilst some unionised employees have been safeguarded under enforceable union contracts or collective agreements which specify that dismissals must be for a valid reason or 'just cause', the majority of US employees are governed by the doctrine of employment-at-will. The doctrine asserts that 'employers can dismiss their employees at any time, for any reason, under any circumstance'. Recent years have seen this doctrine challenged by State court rulings in several jurisdictions and by the passage of the 1988 Worker Adjustment and Retraining Notification Act (WARN). The latter requires that employers provide workers or their representatives and local government officials sixty days written advance notice before closing a plant or embarking on mass lay-offs. But employers are under no obligation to consult with or inform workers about operational modifications or strategic decisions upon which the redundancies are based. Moreover the coverage of the WARN legislation is restricted by the numerous exemptions contained in the statutes. For example, the Act only applies to employers with 100 or more employees, and employers are not obliged to provide advance notice if the reductions are a result of business circumstances that could not be 'reasonably foreseen'.[67]

By the end of the last century, the US still possessed the least restrictive employment laws in the developed world. But the reforms implemented in the UK during the 1980s and 1990s meant that the legal protections offered to British workers were not much stronger than those enjoyed by their American counterparts. In respect of collective redundancies, the government retained the statutes laid down in the 1965 Redundancy Payments Act, which restricted the provision of statutory redundancy payments to workers with at least two years of continuous service.[68] But the regulations protecting individual workers from arbitrary dismissal or redundancy were relaxed when the government raised the qualification for unfair dismissal from six months to one year in 1979, and then to two years in 1985. These changes had a significant impact on the proportion of the working population protected by basic employment rights. In 1975, when the basic qualifying period for unfair dismissal protection was six months (one year for those working between eight and sixteen hours per week), 91 per cent of employees of working age had sufficient tenure to qualify for protection. The remainder of the employed labour force were excluded from this right along with 1.8 million self-employed workers. In 1990, when two years' service was required (five years for those working between eight and sixteen hours per week), only 62 per cent of employees qualified and the number of self-employed had risen to 3.4 million. In 1995, having lost a historic battle with the House of Lords, the government was forced to remove the working hours qualification for all employment protection rights. Nonetheless, even though the qualification period for part-time workers fell from five years to two years, the proportion of the total workforce qualifying for employment protection (70 per cent) still remained well below the levels that prevailed during the 1970s.[69]

If the UK and the USA were united in their opposition to laws protecting workers from redundancy and unfair dismissal they were equally opposed to legislation designed to safeguard employees from excessive working hours. And while France and Italy were passing laws to reduce the statutory working week, the UK was moving in the opposite direction. The legislation which it had inherited form the nineteenth-century Factories Act, which set maximum working hours for women and young children, was repealed in 1989[70] and, thereafter, the government refused all attempts to reintroduce an upper limit on working time. Indeed, it was not until 1999 that the provisions of the 1994 EC Directive on Working Time were finally incorporated into UK labour law. And, even then, the government insisted on the maximum use of the exceptions and derogations allowed by the directive, thereby limiting the effectiveness of the protection afforded to workers. Meanwhile, the US labour market continues to operate in the absence of any general restrictions on the normal working week. Faced with such lax regulation, it is not surprising that the UK and the US were among the countries that experienced the sharpest increase in average working hours during the 1980s and 1990s (as described by Burchell in Chapter 3).

Benefit reforms

Anxiety about the *risk* of job loss has been fed by an increasingly competitive labour market, the declining power of trade unions and the erosion of employment legislation. But workers' insecurities have also been fed by the rising *cost* of job loss as reflected in lower benefits and greater conditionality for access to such benefits.

By way of illustration, consider the evolution of the UK's benefit system. The UK's post-war system of social security was based on the contributory principle laid down by the Beveridge Report of 1942. It was designed to protect living standards from the effects of unemployment, sickness and old age through the provision of low, flat-rate, benefits paid for through flat-rate contributions. And, although it was initially less generous than the benefit systems developed elsewhere in Europe – where payments were more usually linked to earnings – it was made more generous in the 1960s and 1970s by the introduction of earnings-related supplements to unemployment and sickness benefit and the State Earnings Related Pension Scheme (SERPS). During this period, it also became the convention to upgrade benefits in line with average earnings.

From 1979, however, this progress was reversed under the political imperative to cut taxes and the growing insistence by policy makers and their advisers that joblessness results from fecklessness or 'unemployability' rather than a shortage of work. The level of support was reduced, the contributory principle was diluted and the unemployed were subjected to increasing degrees of monitoring and coercion. The government cut the link between earnings and benefits and allowed the relative value of the latter to decline by linking them to prices (which rose more slowly than average earnings). The earnings-related top-up and the supplementary allowances for dependent children in unemployment and sickness benefit were also abolished in the early 1980s. As a result of these changes, the basic pension for a single person fell from 47 per cent to less that 36 per cent of average income between 1983 and 1995 and over the same period unemployment benefits fell from around 36 per cent to 28 per cent of average income. Subject to this downward pressure, more and more of the poor turned to means-tested benefits, the operation of which tended to ensnare them in poverty and unemployment 'traps'.[71]

Meanwhile, entitlement to unemployment benefit was restricted by more stringent contribution requirements and longer periods of disqualification for rule infringements.[72] For example, a person judged by local officials to have left a job without good cause was initially disqualified from benefit for six weeks but this was lengthened to thirteen weeks and then extended to twenty-six weeks.[73] Availability for work, as a condition for benefit payment, was transformed into a growing insistence that benefit claimants should participate in government training and 'make-work' schemes and accept unskilled, low-paid and casual work or risk losing benefits. Claimants were increasingly required to be 'actively seeking work', as defined by a state official, and to attend interviews at which their availability was continuously monitored. Additional requirements were introduced in October 1996 when, symbolically, unemployment benefit was defined as a *jobseekers'* allowance and made available for only six months, after which point means testing begins. Under the Jobseekers Act, a claimant is required to enter a 'jobseeker's agreement' with a local officer of the Employment Department, which could specify the lowest wage for which the claimant would be willing to work, but which also imposes a duty on the claimant to comply with any *reasonable* jobseeking direction. Failure to comply carries the threat of benefit reduction or complete withdrawal.

In turn, the Jobseekers Act provided the foundation for the Welfare to Work strategy adopted by the Labour Party when it returned to power in 1997. The purpose of Welfare to Work is 'to forge an entirely new culture which puts work first'. In pursuit of this objective, wage subsidies are used to encourage employers to participate in the scheme whilst legal minimum wages and other labour standards are set at a minimum to ensure labour market flexibility and to encourage employers to create jobs. Nonetheless, the striking feature of Welfare to Work is not the inducements that it offers to employers but the sanctions that it levies upon the unemployed. It is designed to oblige out-of-work benefit recipients to take any job on offer; and any employees who refuse to participate in the scheme risk loss of benefit.

The UK, however, is not the only country where changes in the level and conditionality of benefits have increased the cost of job loss. According to OECD estimates of benefit 'replacement rates' (i.e. benefits relative to average earnings), the three European countries which experienced a significant increase in their average replacement rates[74] in the 1980s were France, Finland and Sweden. In Austria and Spain, they remained relatively unchanged; whilst the UK, the US, Denmark, Germany and Ireland all witnessed a significant decline in the generosity of unemployment benefits during this decade.[75] During the 1990s, the downward trend in benefit rates could be observed in most of the OECD countries, including those which had previously bucked the trend.[76]

Besides reducing the average value of their benefits, many of the OECD countries have also followed Britain's example by tightening up their eligibility criteria and reducing the duration of benefit payments. According to OECD reports, during the first half of the 1990s, eligibility requirements were tightened in Germany, France, Italy, the UK, Canada, Austria, Belgium, Denmark, Finland, Ireland, Norway, Spain, Sweden and Switzerland.[77] And the trend continued through to the end of the decade as politicians across the industrialised world redoubled their efforts to combat 'welfare dependency'. For instance, until the mid-1990s, a Danish worker had to have worked a minimum of twenty-six weeks in the three years prior to becoming unemployed to qualify for unemployment benefit; now they have to have worked for fifty-two weeks.[78] A similar change also took place in Finland where workers are now required to work forty-three weeks in the two years before becoming unemployed, compared with twenty-six weeks prior to 1997. Across the Atlantic meanwhile, both Canada and the US have been reforming their benefit system in attempt to reduce 'welfare dependency'. In Canada, several provinces have recently reduced social assistance benefit levels, most notably during 1996 and the early part of 1997 when the government of Ontario made the receipt of basic assistance dependent upon participation in mandatory work programmes. In the United States, a cash welfare block grant called Temporary Assistance for Needy Families (TANF) has replaced Aid for Families with Dependent Children (AFDC).[79] The AFDC was one of the only federal benefits in the United States available to families on the basis of financial need. A 'last resort' benefit, it was never very generous but at least its receipt was not subject to a time limit. By contrast, the recipients of the TANF now have to return to work and become self-sufficient within a given time limit determined by the state.[80]

The strength of neo-liberalism

In the UK, as in many of its OECD partners, the declining generosity of unemployment benefits symbolises the rejection of the ethical and ideological principles that underpinned the post-war commitment to 'social citizenship'. As described by T.H. Marshall, the idea of social citizenship rights encompassed 'the whole range . . . from the right to a modicum of economic welfare and security to the right to share to the full in the social heritage and to live the life of a civilised being according to the standards prevailing in the society'.[81] It was an idea that developed out of the experience of unemployment and poverty during the inter-war years, was put into practice during the Second World War, and found full expression in the post-war 'consensus' which emerged during the 1950s and 1960s.

During these post-war decades, the idea of social citizenship involved a full-employment macro-economic policy based on Keynes's argument that the recession of the 1930s was due to a lack of 'effective' demand,[82] a reorganisation of education allowing more general access, the introduction of a National Health Service with health care free at the point of delivery and a benefit system rooted in the contributory principle. Of course, the benefits it provided carried with them a duty to work, as was recognised in the norm that recipients of unemployment benefit should make themselves available for work. But the principle of social citizenship also required that the unemployed not be pressed into employment on any terms. The credibility of the contributory principle, its effectiveness as a tool for job search, and the need to protect the labour market status of individuals suffering from involuntary job loss, required rules to prevent the undue harassment of benefit claimants and recipients. As full-employment policy guaranteed the right to work and therefore to earned income, the role of social welfare was to provide an income-replacement safety net against temporary unemployment, sickness, more permanent incapacity and old age. The expectations were that high employment, good education and health provision, and the elimination of the economic and social destabilising effects of mass poverty, would generate self-sufficiency and that the national insurance system would extend this to periods of temporary illness and unemployment, and into old age. Those who were incapable of securing and maintaining the customary standard of life, for example because of domestic and other commitments, or because of physical or mental incapacities – and it was expected that this would be a small minority – could be readily supported because of the general prosperity.

Expanding government expenditure and increased state intervention found wide justification among economists who encouraged the British government to expand education and training in the interest of a larger and better qualified labour force. Better social welfare provision, greater job security and improved labour standards were also welcomed because, it was argued, these measures contributed to human capital formation, facilitated job search and generally increased the efficient utilisation of human resources. The position of those that remained trapped in, or were drawn into, the lower reaches of the labour market was improved by an extension and strengthening of the regulatory framework. On the supply side, these policies improved the country's economic performance by enhancing its labour input. On the demand side, they encouraged the diffusion of new products, thereby raising the customary standard of life and providing extra impetus to the labour market upgrading process.[83]

But strains began to appear as the long boom came to an end in the early 1970s. Growing international competition and international capital flows led to increasing de-industrialisation whilst rising commodity prices fuelled a worldwide inflation, the policy response to which caused mass unemployment. Reinforced by a second round of oil price increases in the late 1970s, the long period of stagflation (the coincidence of inflation and high unemployment) seriously accelerated the de-industrialisation of British industry, thereby eliminating a wide range of 'middle-income' jobs the result of which could be seen in the growing polarisation of economic and social opportunities. In turn, the problems of high inflation, high unemployment and de-industrialisation were compounded by the fiscal pressures caused by the fall in tax receipts and the rise in government expenditure (as the government struggled to provide the benefit payments required by the rising tide of displaced workers).

Faced with these increasingly intractable problems, the economic orthodoxy retreated to its pre-Keynesian beliefs that money determines prices and the market determines everything else. Economists increasingly warned governments of the dangers of interfering with the laws of 'the market' and counselled against the regulatory framework which had been previously regarded as sustaining economic progress. In contrast to the orthodoxy that prevailed in the 1950s and 1960s, the neo-liberal economists of the late 1970s and early 1980s argued that inflation results from increases in the money supply induced mainly by expansionary macroeconomic policy. They claimed that unemployment was caused not by deficiencies on the *demand side* of the economy (as argued by Keynes) but by those on the *supply side*. In their opinion, the reason unemployment remained so high was because of the inflexibility of the labour market and, in particular, the failure of wages to make sufficient downward adjustment. Interventions by the state and trade unions were seen as exacerbating these 'wage rigidities' which could only be cured through the deregulation of terms and conditions of employment and the reduction of unemployment and other welfare benefits.[84]

These self-styled 'neo-liberals' also rejected the notion that economic progress was fostered by increased equality and job security. Instead, they embraced the idea that economic progress requires increased inequality and a more flexible labour market (i.e. lower pay and less job security). In sum, the essence of their argument was that the rights won during and in the aftermath of the Second World War had impeded the effective working of the economy and it was time to insist on a different set of rights, the policy applications of which would reflect the ideology not of 'social citizenship' but of 'individual economic freedom'. But the rejection of social citizenship came at a price. And it was a price paid by the weakest members of society, as the adoption of the neo-liberal perspective shifted responsibility for unemployment and poverty away from the government and on to the jobless and the poor. Under the influence of this perspective, the duty to work was transformed into a compulsion to work (by the manipulation of the scale and entitlement to benefits) whilst the right to work was seriously compromised by the government's abandonment of full employment as a desirable policy objective.

Of course, it should not be imagined that the UK was the only country to have experienced the attack on social citizenship. On the contrary, as described by Guy Standing, the neo-liberal nostrums advocated by the 'supply-side' economists have spread their way across the globe, 'beginning in the late 1970s in the UK and USA, being adopted by stages within western Europe and exported to Latin America, Africa and most recently South Asia'.[85] And they scored their biggest triumph in the early 1990s, when Russia and other parts of the former eastern bloc 'adopted the same prescription under the name of "shock therapy"'.[86]

Nor, despite the shift in terminology away from 'free market' to 'third way', should one underestimate the continuing strength of the neo-liberal philosophy. Over the past two decades, this philosophy has served as the basis for an opportunistic alliance between vote-seeking political parties offering tax cuts and market deregulation, and the rent-seeking contented classes, who stand to benefit from the tax cuts, the availability of low-paid labour and the opportunities for profits created by deregulation.[87] It is a powerful alliance, and one that has been strenghthened by four reinforcing processes.

First, the victims of the downward economic and social spiral triggered by policy change have become increasingly alienated from the 'democratic' process so that political exclusion has been added to economic and social

exclusion. Second, this political exclusion has been progressively reinforced as political parties of the left have abandoned their traditional class
allegiances and embraced the new economic and social orthodoxy to compete for the so-called political centre ground. Third, the growing problems
of long-term unemployment, poverty, crime and social dislocation over the
past two decades have increasingly polarised society and the contented
classes have found themselves more and more threatened by the *dangerous
classes*. Fourth, those promoting the conventional economic wisdom to
policy practitioners have continued to justify their failed predictions by
developing theories explaining unemployment, under-employment and
poverty in terms of labour market imperfections, welfare state dependency
and the low quality and poor motivation of the unemployed, the under-
employed and the working poor. By doing so they have provided continued
justification for economic and social policies by the age-old expedient of
blaming the victim.

Concluding remarks

The intensive exploitation of any resource cannot be continued indefin-
itely. It is a truth of which most Japanese and American farmers are all
too aware. Having enjoyed nearly 100 years of continuous productivity
growth, Japanese farmers have been unable to improve average rice yields
for more than a decade. Meanwhile, despite genetic re-engineering and
continuous applications of fertiliser, wheat farmers in the US have been
struggling to raise crop yields since 1983. In both countries, the soil erosion and soil exhaustion which have accompanied the intensification of
crop production appears to have imposed an 'optimal limit' beyond which
further intensification 'is no longer cost-effective'.[88] By analogy, if managers
in the manufacturing and service sectors continue to exhaust their human
resources – through job insecurity and work intensification – how long will
it be before such practices cease to yield further increases in productivity?
For, as Polanyi puts it:

> The alleged commodity 'labour power' cannot be shoved about, used
> indiscriminately, or even left unused, without affecting also the human
> individual who happens to be the bearer of this particular commodity.
> In disposing of a man's labour power, the system would incidentally,
> dispose of the physical, psychological, and moral entity 'man' attached
> to that tag.[89]

This book examines the costs incurred by organisations when their
workers are 'shoved' to the point where stress and insecurity feeds into
demotivation, sickness and absenteeism (see Chapter 7). But this book
also recognises that the negative feedbacks of stress and insecurity are not
confined to the workplace. As described in Chapter 6, the pressures we

absorb in our working lives spill over into homes and households. Thus, like environmental scientists who point out that many organisations fail to take account of the damage they do to the natural environment, what we as social scientists must stress is the extent to which job insecurity and work intensification damages the social environment. We accept that many of the organisations which took part in our survey claim to have profited from the downsizing and restructuring of their workforce (see Chapter 2). But the cost of these developments, in terms of greater insecurity and reduced physical and psychological well-being, do not appear on their balance sheets. The result is what economists refer to as the 'The Tragedy of the Commons'. Precisely because they can externalise the costs of their actions, firms which intensify the pressures on their workforce can obtain short-run advantages over their competitors. And, in an economy where managers are driven by the fear of hostile takeovers, the temptation for others to emulate their actions becomes hard to resist. The consequence of this is a form of Gresham's Law, as bad labour practices drive out good.

Admittedly, the current economic and political climate makes it especially hard to escape this law. All workers are consumers, most are taxpayers and many are shareholders in their capacity as savers and as recipients of private pensions. In their role as workers, parents and hospital patients their interests usually lie in policies which focus on the long term. But as shareholders, they are tempted to vote for the short-run productivity gains accompanying downsizing and restructuring. As taxpayers it is hard for them to vote against short-run reductions in income tax despite the long-term damage that this may impose on the viability of public services. And, as consumers, they may often vote for short-run price reductions over long-run quality improvements. Worse still, politicians and other 'vote brokers' are all too conscious of this. However, the acknowledgement of this political 'reality' is no excuse for apathy or resignation. For, as described in the following chapters, the rise in job insecurity and work intensification has worrying implications, not just for individual workers and their families, but for the health and efficiency of the economy as a whole.

2 Flexibility and the reorganisation of work

Maria Hudson

As described in the previous chapter, the 1980s and 1990s exposed many employers to an increase in 'market pressure'. The competition they faced increased as a result of privatisation, concentration and globalisation; their customers began to exercise their 'choice' more aggressively; their shareholders became increasingly impatient for a quick and profitable return on their investments; and taxpayer resistance required the government to cut the cost of public services. Not surprisingly, some of the organisations that participated in the JIWIS survey had attempted to offset these pressures by passing them on to their suppliers.[1] However, in most of the organisations we visited, the senior managers suggested that they had met with little success in their attempts to 'squeeze' their suppliers. Instead they had shifted the primary responsibility for ensuring the flexible delivery of goods and services onto the shoulders of their own workforce. But what kind of flexibility were these organisations demanding from their workforce? From the questions we put to the senior managers in the JIWIS survey, it seems that although most employers are pursuing a range of flexibilities, some of these flexibilities are more important than others.

Numerical flexibility

In the language of industrial sociologists, the extent of an organisation's numerical flexibility can be measured by its capacity to adapt the quantity of labour to changes in the level or pattern of demand. Employer practices which facilitate this include the use of temporary, casual and short-term contracts and the externalisation of work through contracting out. 'Local' flexibility (through commuting or relocating) can also be seen as a form of numerical flexibility in so far as it permits the movement of workers to fill a shortage of labour in the face of difficulties in meeting demand.

During the 1980s, the search for numerical flexibility attracted a good deal of scholarly attention, particularly from those working within or providing critiques of a 'core–periphery' model of the labour market. The model, as expounded by the researchers at the Institute of Manpower Studies (IMS), described a world in which employers were making dramatic job cuts in response to increased market uncertainty and volatility, the

Table 2.1 The changing composition of employment, 1979–97

	Percentage of all in employment			
	1979	*1984*	*1990*	*1997*
Full-time employees	76.7	69.7	67.1	65.2
Permanent		67.4	64.8	61.7
Temporary		2.3	2.3	3.5
Part-time employees	16.1	18.8	19.4	22.2
Permanent		16.5	17.2	19.2
Temporary		2.3	2.2	3.0
Full-time self-employed	6.5	9.4	11.3	9.9
Part-time self-employed	0.7	1.9	2.1	2.6

Source: Robinson (2000, Table 2.3)

increasing pace of technological change, and the constant pressure to reduce unit labour costs. And it suggested that, as employers reorganised their internal labour markets, they were tending towards the division of the workforce into core, peripheral and externalised components.[2]

Within this model, the core workforce was seen to enjoy secure, skilled, well-paid, cooperative and functionally flexible employment relations characterised by the mutual long term commitment of both employers and employees. By contrast, the peripheral workforce was described as insecure, sub-contracted, poorly paid, semi-skilled and increasingly exposed to the uncertainty of market forces.[3] But, in many respects, the evolution of the British labour market during the 1980s and 1990s did not follow the trajectory predicted by this core–periphery model.[4] Indeed the pattern that emerged in both Britain and the United States suggests that it has been the *core* labour market, not the peripheral labour market, that has served as the principal source of numerical flexibility.

It is true that 'peripheral' forms of employment have increased in both these countries but what is striking about this development is not so much the speed but the sluggishness with which these forms have grown. As described by Peter Robinson, the pattern of growth in the share of 'flexible' or 'non-standard' forms of employment suggests that 'the sharpest fall in the share of employment of full-time permanent employees took place in the early 1980s, since when the pace of change has slackened considerably'.[5] In Britain, for example, the share of full-time permanent employees as a proportion of the total workforce fell by about seven per cent between 1979 and 1984 compared to just three per cent between 1990 and 1997 (see Table 2.1).

As evidenced in the work of Kate Purcell *et al.*, data from the Labour Force Survey indicates that the proportion of the workforce in temporary employment rose steadily throughout the 1990s, led by the growth in fixed-term employment and the increase in temporary employees supplied

Table 2.2 Temporary workers as a percentage of the total workforce in 1999

United States	1.9
Luxembourg	2.8
Ireland	5.8[a]
Britain	5.9
Austria	6.5
Italy	7.0
Greece	7.4[a]
Belgium	8.5
Denmark	9.2
Switzerland	9.5
Norway	9.8
Netherlands	10.6
Germany	11.5
Sweden	12.2
France	12.2
Portugal	13.5
Finland	15.6
Spain	25.6

Source: Eurostat and US BLS

[a] 1998

by labour supply contractors.[6] Nonetheless, by the end of 1997, they still accounted for less than 7 per cent of the total workforce and, as revealed by the latest Workplace Employee Relations Survey, the use of temporary and fixed-term contract labour was *not* concentrated among the poorly paid and semi-skilled sectors of the British labour market. In fact, the highest incidence of temporary working was to be found where skilled workers were in the majority.[7]

Further evidence suggestive of the extent to which the British labour market departs from the kind of numerical flexibility emphasised in the core–periphery model can be found in Table 2.2. It shows that in 1998 the incidence of temporary employment was significantly lower in Britain than in most other countries whilst the OECD country with the lowest incidence of temporary employment was the United States. It is not that employers in Britain and the United States are less capable of adjusting their staff numbers to variations in labour demand than their European or Japanese counterparts. On the contrary, it is precisely because of the ease with which they can hire and fire the members of their core workforce with 'permanent' contracts of employment that British and American employers are less reliant upon temporary workers for the provision of their numerical flexibility. As Robinson puts it:

> The regulation of 'standard' forms of employment is relatively modest in Anglo-Saxon labour markets and always has been, so that employers have generally not had the incentive to switch to other forms of employment which allow them to avoid regulation.[8]

The freedom with which Anglo-American employers can exercise numerical flexibility without relying upon peripheral labour was clearly demonstrated by the employment strategies used by the organisations which participated in the JIWIS survey. Lay-offs and redundancies among the core workforce were implemented with little hindrance from employment protection legislation and with little (effective) opposition from the trade unions. By contrast, only a small proportion of the organisations (30 per cent and 20 per cent respectively) relied upon the 'buying-in' or 'putting-out' of labour when scheduling their production of goods and services. And the majority of employers (60 per cent and 73 per cent respectively) neither 'hoarded' nor 'dis-hoarded' labour when attempting to meet fluctuations in demand. Instead, these fluctuations were typically met through variations in the working hours of the core workforce and – if the shift in demand lasted longer than a few months – by downsizing the organisation through redundancies.[9] In addition, many of the organisations we visited were also requiring more locational flexibility from their workforce and some of them had begun to include redeployment and mobility clauses in the job contracts signed by their employees.[10]

In this respect, the JIWIS organisations reveal the extent to which Britain's labour market differs from that of many of its OECD counterparts and, in particular, from that which exists in Japan. As described by Manuel Castells and Peter Dicken, the *Shushin Koyo* system that provides assurance of long-term employment is restricted to Japan's larger companies (those with over 1,000 employees) and, in most cases, concerns only the male, core labour force. In other words, it is the flexibility of the Japanese labour market, *unlike that of Britian and the United States*, which best accords with the employment structures depicted by the core–periphery model. Castells estimates that long-term job security in the same company applies to only about one-third of Japanese employees, with the rest of the workforce consisting of part-time, temporary and dispatched[11] workers who have no job security and are 'fired and hired' according to their employers' convenience.[12] It is this large pool of 'peripheral' workers that has helped the country to maintain its country's highly developed domestic subcontracting networks.[13] However, Castells suggests that, in the face of rapid cultural and technological changes, Japanese employers may soon find themselves reversing their search for numerical flexibility – away from the periphery and back to the core. In his words:

> Japanese firms seemed to be able to cope with competitive pressures by retraining their core labour force and adding technology, while multiplying their flexible labour, both in Japan and in their globalised production networks. However since this labour practice relies essentially on the occupational subservience of highly educated Japanese women, which will not last for ever, *it is just a matter of time until the hidden flexibility of the Japanese labour market diffuses to the core labour force.*[14]

Indeed, there is evidence that this diffusion of flexibility 'to the core' is already occurring. The Japanese employers' federation has been looking at new ways of multiplying the supply of flexible labour. A central feature of the Nikkeren policy is its promotion of a further segmentation of the labour market to create a third group of highly skilled specialists who are highly rewarded on the basis of their performance – but remain on fixed-term contracts.[15] Labour flexibility has also been achieved through other means. For example, there is evidence that the *nenko* system of wages and promotions being determined by length of service is being usurped by the growth of an appraisal system:

> which stimulates employees to work hard, intensively and for long hours in order to achieve wage rises and promotion. Thus intensive labour and long working hours are characteristic of the Japanese labour process.[16]

Temporal flexibility

Adjusting the number of employees (be it through the hiring and firing of core workers or through the use of 'peripheral' temps) is not the only way that organisations can try to match the supply and demand of labour. As with many of the organisations that participated in the JIWIS survey, they can also attempt to vary the length and intensity of the hours worked by their employees. Indeed, more than half (60 per cent) of the organisations we visited were pursuing *temporal* flexibility through changes in their working hours.

These changes took a variety of different forms. Some organisations had increased their basic contracted hours; others had reduced them. Two manufacturing companies and the transport firm had harmonised their basic hours downwards whereas the providers of educational services had extended the working year for lecturing and other staff. Organisations employing a large number of women (e.g. the government agency) were also experimenting with a variety of part-time working hours packages. The train operator sought to accommodate workers who needed flexible working hours for family and other reasons. The range of hours worked by employees in the food retailer was widening as it moved towards seven-day and twenty-four hour trading and as it increased its reliance on students for weekend working. In the large utilities, the willingness of staff to vary their working hours was heavily stressed and managers frequently asked their employees to adjust their start and finish times as and when required. Other organisations had introduced term time only and other *carer friendly* employment contracts, while the retailer of travel services had experimented with the use of zero-hour contracts.

Functional flexibility

We have seen that the organisations in the JIWIS survey were keen to increase the numerical and, more commonly, temporal flexibility of their workforce. But, in many respects, the most far-reaching changes were those which they had introduced in order to increase the functional flexibility of their employees. In line with the nostrums propounded by the advocates of 'lean production', they had introduced a variety of workplace reforms aimed at flattening their organisational hierarchies, reducing their bureaucratic overheads, and introducing their employees to the technologies and philosophy of just-in-time production.[17] And the success of these reforms was heavily dependent upon the extent to which their employees were willing, and able, to undertake a wider range of functions and responsibilities.[18]

As described in Appendix B, most of the organisations we visited reported a significant increase in the functional flexibility of their workforce over the past five years. Traditional job demarcations have been eroded, job contents have been redefined along with customary methods of work, and peer and authority relations have also been transformed. These innovations in working practices were described variously as: multi-skilling, multi-tasking, skills flexibility, multi-roleing, multi-functioning and role-modelling. Some of the innovations were designed to increase the skills and 'competencies' of the individual employee;[19] others were more concerned with the promotion (and reorganisation) of *teamwork*. For example, nine organisations said they had introduced self-managing work teams and five claimed to have empowered their employees by delegating quality control and decision-making to the task level. And, in seven organisations, these changes were also accompanied by the de-layering of management grades. Other, closely related, initiatives were aimed at fostering an 'attitudinal' or 'culture' change among the workforce, particularly in service sectors.[20] For example, the retail company had introduced 'behavioural skills training' in an effort to raise the motivation and adaptability of its employees. And in the large utilities company, staff were encouraged to undergo 'personal qualities' training as part of their career development.

Previous studies of task flexibility and work reorganisation have shown that the erosion of job demarcations can increase the 'vertical loading' of tasks and responsibilities by expanding the scope for self-regulation and decision-making. Nonetheless, as revealed in survey and case study evidence from the 1980s, what many workers experience is not so much the 'vertical' but the 'horizontal' loading of tasks, that is, the fact that their job simply requires them to take on more tasks at the same skill level.[21] Both effects were apparent among the employers we interviewed, although the scope of change varied between organisations. For example:

- The food retailer required shelf-fillers to deputise as checkout operators to keep queue sizes down.
- In the government agency the reduction in the numbers of managers required the survivors to take on more of the same kinds of responsibilities.
- The components manufacturer required its operatives to rotate around different machines and, in addition, team leaders were given supervisory responsibility.
- In one of the further education providers, when managers were made redundant their responsibilities for public relations and marketing were re-allocated to teaching staff.

Of course, the way in which these changes were described varied according to the organisational status of the person whom we were interviewing. For example, whilst the senior managers often emphasised the vertical loading brought about as a result of the new work practices, their employees tended to stress the horizontal loading of tasks, that is, the extra tasks that they had to perform at the same, or even lower, skill level than that required by their previous responsibilities.

Across the employee survey, 80 per cent of employees reported an increase in the skills content of their jobs in the last five years, 78 per cent an increase in the variety of tasks and 75 per cent growing responsibility. We came across employee narratives which reflected these processes at work at a number of points in the JIWIS survey. For example, in the British-owned financial services company, the job content of clerical workers had shifted from administration towards providing customer care and a wider range of services. This was accompanied by on-going training because of higher skill requirements. For one cashier, a multi-skilling exercise meant that she was training her colleague to do her job while her colleague reciprocated. Another cashier described how she used to only deal with incoming and outgoing payments; now she is working in a team and does the banking of cheques, the input of direct debits, the termination of loans, cheque requisitions – as well as processing incoming and outgoing payments. An office worker in the large utilities company described how she used to run the print room; now she is part of a multi-functioning team which runs reception, covers the post room *and* runs the print room. And, in the food retailer, a customer assistant described what the erosion of demarcations meant for her:

> My job title changed from cashier to customer assistant . . . it just means that we can do the packing role as well if we see the red light go; cashiers and packers all have the same name now.

Production workers were also taking on a broader range of tasks. An engineering craftsman reported how there was now more flexibility as everyone 'mucked in' to the extent that fitters' and engineering work now overlapped. A process operator felt that people in his job now did 'practically everything'. Through the multi-skilling process he'd be trained not to craft level, but to the point where he can "get on and do the job". To take a further example from manufacturing, the components manufacturer had extended training so that production workers could operate different machines. One machine operator described the development thus: 'After they got rid of people they brought in multi-tasking. It used to be one man one machine, now two men look after seven or eight'.

Redundancy programmes and the reorganisation of work

If the pursuit of flexibility – numerical, temporal and functional – involves a reorganisation of traditional working practices, it also requires a catalyst strong enough to overcome the strength of these traditions. And, throughout the 1980s and 1990s, it was usually the force of redundancies, lay-offs, natural wastage and other forms of 'downsizing' which performed this catalytic function. As described in the work of Rinehart and MacDuffie, such measures were used by even the most secure and profitable companies. Not just because they were seeking to protect themselves from declining sales or market share but because they were looking for an opportunity to re-engineer the systems which governed the activities performed by their workforce.[22] Flexibility was pursued by design and default. Indeed, for some organisations, downsizing has become less of a short-term 'workforce reduction strategy' than a 'systemic', long-term, strategy, the principal aim of which is to transform the attitudes, values and organisational culture of the core workforce. In such cases, downsizing is best understood as a 'way of life, as an ongoing process, rather than as a program or a target'.[23]

The twenty organisations in the JIWIS revealed an eclectic mix of workforce reduction, redesign and systemic approaches to downsizing. Seventeen of the twenty organisations had made workers redundant in the five years prior to our survey. The group most affected by redundancies consisted of ten organisations which had seen job losses take place across all occupational grades. This group consisted of most of the manufacturers, both utilities, two financial service organisations, the transport company and one further education establishment. A second group of five organisations had experienced 'compartmentalised' redundancies (i.e. where job losses were limited to particular occupations). This group included the government agency, the retail company and the provider of health services, all of which had concentrated their redundancies on management grades. Also included in this group was a manufacturing company which had closed a plant employing manual workers, and a further education college which had concentrated redundancies on its 'casual' part-time lecturers.

Nor were redundancies the only means by which employers had reduced their staffing levels. Contracting out had been an important feature of workforce restructuring in the public and utilities sectors. In one of the further education colleges, downsizing had been achieved by making permanent teaching staff redundant and re-employing them as part-time agency workers and also by contracting out the catering and security functions. And in the government agency contracting out was an 'on-going' process extending from training and estates to facilities management.

The reasons given for redundancies by our organisations reflect the pressures outlined in Chapter 1. They were introduced as cost-cutting responses to downturns in demand and regulatory pressures on prices, for unspecified 'efficiency reasons', and as part of a general restructuring of employment relations. Many of our employers had gone through several waves of redundancy in the past five years, a process of continuous job loss which can be illustrated by three examples from the manufacturing sector and two examples from the financial services sector.

The components manufacturer had been under pressure from all directions. Its 1996 redundancies, mostly compulsory, resulted from the loss of a major customer to which management responded by cutting costs by 40 per cent in an attempt to keep the business viable. It did so by making 45 per cent of the workforce redundant. A further redundancy exercise came roughly eighteen months later and involved a voluntary scheme. Shortly afterwards, following its takeover and subsequent corporate reorganisation, the closure of the factory was announced. Our second and third examples are manufacturers in the food and drink and building materials sector. Both have had major redundancies, involving compulsory job losses, followed by assurances that, in the future, compulsory redundancies would be avoided. In both cases, the *planned nature* of the redundancies was emphasised. The building materials manufacturer was one of the organisations for which product market conditions were the least unfavourable; but it still cut its workforce by 21 per cent in 1994 and three-quarters of the redundancies were compulsory. Meanwhile, the organisation in the food and drinks sector, whose market position was somewhat less favourable, had experienced successive rounds of redundancies as part of a restructuring plan. In 1993/4, it reduced the size of the workforce by 17 per cent, with 86 per cent of people going voluntarily. Since then, between 6 per cent and 7 per cent of the workforce have taken voluntary redundancy each year. In the five years prior to our survey, its workforce size had been cut by 30 per cent overall and the number of its plants had fallen from seven to four.

A development common across the financial services sector has been merger and takeover activity and the rationalisation of branch networks. And our two financial services cases reflect these developments. In the foreign-owned organisation, there was a 17 per cent reduction in the size of the workforce between 1993 and 1998, achieved through a mixture of compulsory and voluntary redundancies. During this period, redundancy exercises occurred each year and were accompanied by the centralisation of work away from branches towards central processing units. In the other organisation the redundancies occurred due to closures across traditional branch networks, with the workforce size falling by 10 per cent.

While the policy of many of the organisations was to avoid *compulsory* redundancies as a means of downsizing, not everyone was able to do so. For example the foreign-owned financial services company had compulsory redundancies every year between 1993 and 1997. And in other organisations, the distinction between voluntary and compulsory redundancy was not always clear. In two organisations, workers identified for redundancy were offered alternative jobs which would have required relocating to different parts of the country; those who refused were then described as having made themselves 'voluntarily' redundant. And in one of these firms, the term 'voluntarily' would seem to be especially misleading in view of the fact that, out of 106 people affected by plant closure, only one person chose to relocate. More generally, throughout the organisations we visited it seemed that the avoidance of redundancy was usually conditional on the acceptance of flexible working and pay moderation.

This link between job *loss* and job *redesign* was made particularly apparent when we asked senior managers about the impact of redundancies on the flexibility of their operations. In their responses, they often found it difficult to separate the effects of redundancies from the broader changes they had initiated in the organisation of work. This is illustrated by the responses from the organisations which said they had achieved greater flexibility (Table 2.3).

The 'extensive' downsizers constitute six of the seven organisations reporting more flexible working practices. Workforce flexibility was achieved by job redesign including multi-skilling and team working innovations. To achieve individual flexibility, one of the financial service organisations carefully screened its candidates for redundancy (voluntary and compulsory) so that it could retain the 'right kind of people' to take the business forward. Likewise, plant closure provided the opportunity for a food manufacturer to secure changes in working practices by removing the people responsible for 'inflexibility'.

Of the two organisations reporting a decline in flexibility following redundancies, the components manufacturer indicated that although the redundancy exercise provided an opportunity to erode traditional job demarcations the immediate effect was a reduction in flexibility. Similar consequences followed when one of the further education colleges shifted managerial responsibilities to teaching staff when flattening its managerial structure. Likewise, the manager of the government agency said that employees anticipated that office closures would reduce the capability of remaining staff to provide an effective service. On the other hand, although the recent redundancies in the transport company had not increased flexibility, the senior manager to whom we spoke suggested that the building-in of flexibility requirements into conditions of service would signal to staff the behaviour expected of them.

Table 2.3 The impact of redundancies on flexibility

Organisation	Why did the redundancies give your organisation more flexibility in terms of its production/provision of services?
Case 1	because the redundancies were accompanied by a major programme of job redesign.
Case 2	there is a company agreement, signed fifteen years ago, covering manual work and requiring everyone to do any job that they are trained for.
Case 9	because there was an emphasis on training/multi-skilling. I tell my staff you can spend as much money as you like on multi-skilling.
Case 14	because now the focus is on customer care and sales rather than on administration.
Case 14	because I think we retained the individuals we required in order for the business to go forward and those who left were people who didn't necessarily fit the services we were seeking to provide.
Case 13	because we have changed from task-based to multi-functional team-based operations.
Case 8	the only way that you can cut the size of the workforce is if the flexibility of the existing workforce increases.
Case 11	the people we had in the glass bottling hall wouldn't work in other sides of the plant. Once they went, so did those practices.

Of the thirteen senior managers who were asked whether the redundancies had changed traditional occupational boundaries, nine reported that they had, four that they had not. Those responding positively again emphasised the importance of multi-skilling and the additional responsibilities taken on by the remaining workforce in securing these changes. As part of the work reorganisation which accompanied their redundancies, five employers had reduced the number of supervisors by introducing 'self-directed' teams and team working (in the manufacturing and financial service firms); by the 'empowerment' of multi-functioning managers (in the food retailer) and through empowerment of line managers (in the government agency) and empowerment of the whole workforce (in the large utilities). By contrast, the medium-sized utility told us that downsizing had replaced older but more experienced core workers with youthful but inexperienced contractors who required more supervision.

Even stronger evidence of the extent to which employers saw job cutting as a key to achieving job flexibility is to be found in the way they 'selected' candidates for redundancy. Generally, organisations had a clear sense of core areas of activity and the attributes (technical and social) which workers needed to make an effective contribution. In the components manufacturer, flexibility had become part of the redundancy criteria. A production manager spoke of how he made a foreman redundant because he wasn't capable of adapting to new working practices. While the staffing level in his section was cut from thirty-five to twenty people, he employed new people 'who had more intelligence, relatively speaking, rather than the other guys, because new plant was coming in, efficiency had to be kept high'. In the transport company, the 10 per cent of employees made redundant included those who wanted to stay, but whose needs could not be accommodated 'on skills or competency related grounds'. Similarly, in the food retailing company, skill levels, competencies, experience and 'adaptability' featured prominently in the criteria for compulsory redundancies. In the most recent round of redundancies at the foreign-owned financial services corporation, no invitations for voluntary redundancies were made because the organisation 'wished to retain people with strong skills'. Specific criteria were developed and those who did not meet these criteria were made compulsorily redundant. The greatest emphasis on careful selection for redundancy was found in the large utility where staff were required to reapply for their jobs and psychometric tests formed part of the assessment of their suitability.

Employers also retained a strong voice in defining which employees were eligible for *voluntary* redundancy. Only one firm, a manufacturer in the food and drinks sector, placed no obstacles to voluntary redundancy, on the grounds that they could train replacements. The others all had restrictions on eligibility for voluntary redundancy and although two mentioned selection criteria based on location (and one operated a policy of 'last in, first out') it was organisational skill requirements which featured most prominently in the decision about who could go. The government agency noted, for example, that 'people were not eligible if they held skills needed by the organisation'. Likewise, in one of the companies providing financial services, people with 'core skills' could only go 'when others have been trained to take over from them'. Even the organisations that encouraged voluntary early retirement made this conditional on their skill and business needs as well as the age of the individual. Employers clearly felt that it was important to exercise managerial prerogative in this area, and they did so.

The impact on productivity, costs and managerial control

In its promise to reap dividends for both product quality and productivity, and in turn the bottom line, the 'lean production' paradigm holds out a seductive set of practices for organisations in search of a competitive edge. Its advocates suggest that it will enable companies to run their businesses with half the human effort, half the person space and in half the production time. Although they acknowledge the stress created by systems which operate on the basis of 'just-in-time' labour, they believe the drive for flexibility will also provide workers with a sense of 'empowerment' – by allowing them to control their work within 'teams' instead of 'hierarchies'. All in all, they argue that the transition to lean production will deliver a 'win-win' situation and recommend that it is a model which should be 'spread to all corners of the globe for everyone's mutual benefit'.[24]

In practice, this 'mutuality' of benefit is often hard to detect. As Rinehart has shown in his commentary on Canadian corporate restructuring, lean production has usually meant fewer jobs, heavier workloads for all, over-time and constant 'speed up'.[25] Other critics suggest that lean production is a misnomer and that the practices it entails are better described as 'management by stress'.[26] And when the flexibility of the workforce depends upon their ability to absorb the pressures generated by just-in-time production it may be difficult for them to feel like winners. In this vein, a growing body of work addresses the negative attributes associated with organisational design. Even when hierarchy appears to be challenged, workplace innovations create new regimes of power and control over decision-making. As Quinn puts it:

> empowerment for workers in tightly coupled systems means being asked to act as if an order had been given rather than taking the time to reflect upon the course of action that would be most appropriate in those circumstances. This is the direct opposite of the notions of creativity, flexibility and individual responsibility implicit in other understandings of empowerment.[27]

Similarly, Sennett presents team working as an integral part of the process of shifting the burden of responsibility downwards in organisations *without eliminating underlying authority relationships*.[28] And Muetzelft describes the centralisation of *power* which accompanies the delegation of *responsibility* as 'devolutionism', a practice which serves as:

> An effective political strategy for those who wish to centralise organisational power and simultaneously incorporate workers . . . into those power relations. This is because it appears to devolve and disperse power throughout the organisation, giving the impression that it contributes to industrial democracy.[29]

Other commentators point out that if the drive for flexibility is taken too far, the result could be a lose-lose situation wherein employees lose health and well-being whilst the organisation loses 'essential competencies', capacities for innovation and *long-term* competitiveness.[30]

In view of these debates, we asked the senior managers in the JIWIS survey to describe the impact of redundancies and other forms of restructuring on productivity, costs and managerial control. Of the fourteen organisations responding to the question about the impact of the redundancies on productivity, nine felt that the impact was favourable, four said it had not had any effect and only one suggested that the impact was unfavourable. As for the impact on costs, twelve out of the fourteen felt that the redundancies had had a 'favourable' or 'very favourable' effect. Nevertheless, six senior managers said they now regretted some of the redundancies which had occurred. The communications company had failed to run checks on whether the skills of those made redundant could be re-deployed and one of the financial institutions, which had lost more people than anticipated through natural wastage, wished it had 'kept on a few good people'.

By contrast, the impact of the redundancies on the ability of organisations to control the pace and flow of work was found to be more neutral. Seven organisations reported a favourable impact, five said it had made no difference and one felt that the impact was unfavourable (this more neutral effect was replicated when we asked about the impact on the ability to control the quality of work). The food retailer noted that, with the introduction of multi-functioning managers, it had increased its control over the pace and flow of work via 'the erosion of organisational hierarchies, empowerment and improved communication'. And one of the financial services institutions noted that, although there is 'less controlling', there is 'more control'. On the other hand, several organisations spoke of the negative impact of workforce *restructuring* (as distinct from the impact of redundancies *per se*). For example, the senior manager of the government agency told us that:

> People have not been equipped to cope with the rate of change that has been occurring. With the introduction of IT, restructuring and successive de-layering such change has become the norm, but people don't want the norm . . . When you put the squeeze on people they get the work off of their desks . . . [but] . . . quality has suffered.

In order to gauge the success of our organisations' attempts to transform traditional norms and practices, we asked their employees about the benefits of programmes specifically designed to increase their involvement in decision-making. Not everyone saw having greater responsibility as a 'burden', at least not wholly. On the contrary, some of the most positive things that employees had to say about enrichment in their working lives emerged when they spoke about involvement programmes. Broadly speaking, such programmes were of two different kinds.[31] The first consisted of consultative programmes aimed at increasing employees' participation in the exchange of information and ideas. The second consisted of delegative programmes aimed at changing authority structures to encourage more autonomous working. Nearly three-quarters of the 340 employees we spoke to in the main survey said that they did have programmes for their involvement in decision-making at work. When people were asked to say what these practices were, a range of practices emerged (Table 2.4): 41 per

Table 2.4 Employee reports of involvement programmes existing at their place
(% of *total* responses)* of work

Consultative participation	
Permanent quality circles/improvement teams, etc.	21
Working parties/consultation groups/focus groups	8
Suggestion schemes	3
Delegative participation	
Self-managing teams/devolved responsibility	9
Formal consultation/negotiation committees	
Union recognition or consultation	4
Equal opportunities/safety/environmental committees	3
Meetings	
Team meetings	10
Staff forum/open forum	9
Company meetings	2
Other meetings (e.g. meetings with a manager)	10
Other	
Staff appraisals, peer review, auditing committees, etc.	5
Training/Investors in People	3
Questionnaires	2
Newsletters, bulletins, e-mail	1
Other (including no specific activity)	10

* Respondents could mention more than one programme (and did).

cent of responses consisted of task participation changes, most involving consultative participation (32 per cent), and the remainder (9 per cent) involving delegative participation. It is important to stress that these are employee *perceptions* of whether they had experienced 'involvement programmes', rather than an indication of what actually existed in their places of work. Moreover, as found in the Workplace Employment Relations Survey (WERS), not all the workforce is likely to participate in all practices.[32] Nonetheless, it is also worth noting that employee reporting of consultative programmes in the JIWIS survey reflects their relative prevalence in the WERS.

Employees reporting that they had involvement programmes were also asked what they had gained from them (Table 2.5). Employee responses indicated both personal and organisational gains. As illustrated by the quotations in Boxes 2.1 and 2.2, many of them welcomed the opportunity to air their views, to learn about other sides of the business, and to take more control over the day-to-day exercise of their responsibilities. And some of the most positive responses came when people spoke of their involvement in self-managing work teams, particularly where these innovations had been taken furthest: in the building materials manufacturer and British-owned financial services institution.

Table 2.5 What employees said they got out of involvement programmes
(% of *total* responses)*

Information and communication	
I learn about other people's work experiences, stops you being insular	8
Become better informed about the company	9
Feel listened to/involved	12
Job satisfaction	
Job satisfaction, makes me feel more confident, more motivated, work better as a team, learn to do my job better	9
Valuable experience/skills	4
Improves working conditions, pay, job security, promotion prospects	6
Active involvement benefits company/organisation	4
Brings change	
Opportunity to change things	14
Secure small changes, not major ones	1
Us and them	
Good for managers to hear how things are perceived, you can talk to them directly, improves relations with managers, moves away from them and us	5
Negative effects	
Nothing really changes, difficult to get things done	1
Senior management don't implement recommendations/block changes, can't really speak in front of managers, decisions already taken	5
You're never really empowered, don't get anything out of it	8
I don't get involved	7
Other (generally positive)	2
Other, including no comment	5

* Respondents could mention more than one thing (and did).

Box 2.1 Examples of positive responses to consultative involvement programmes

Business improvement teams/working groups . . . have expanded my awareness of other business unit issues. I've gained problem-solving experience – and also job satisfaction, that you are achieving something in the short term, fixing it in the short term.

(White-collar worker, utilities company)

Quality circles and quality improvement teams . . . it's great. On the team, we are all equal and all get a say. Managers, [health professionals], members of the public will say what they want to say.

(Health professional)

Box 2.2 Examples of positive responses to delegative involvement programmes

The satisfaction that we can do what we want, how we want. We've had more say in the running of the job for the better – on both sides, ours and management's.

(Blue-collar worker, building materials manufacturer)

I got a lot more power from being in one. Support from colleagues is greater. More likely as a team to challenge the management and its decisions than as individuals.

(White-collar worker, financial services sector)

Box 2.3 Examples of negative responses to involvement programmes

Business improvement teams . . . There were a lot of managers on the team – this weakened it – you couldn't really say what you wanted to say even though they said you could.

(Technician, utilities company)

Self-managing teams. They've said that there's to be a no blame culture, that there are to be no shift managers, but the coordinators think that they are shift managers. They are sliding back to the old culture and no one is keeping a check on it.

(Manual worker, manufacturing industry)

Empowerment . . . it empowers you to do what you think you should do after you've been asked to do it . . . It's a load of rubbish. It's OK when you're there [at the training centre], but as soon as you get back you realise that you are not empowered at all. It's different for the top bosses.

(Office worker, utilities company)

Business improvement team . . . That this is about a reduction in numbers, everyone knows. You're invited to make a contribution, but you must understand that the new MD has to impress the City.

(Manager, utilities company)

Nevertheless, we also found that – across the JIWIS sample – senior management reports of self-managing teams and devolved responsibility for quality were more pervasive than those of employees. And, as illustrated in Box 2.3, there were negative as well as positive responses to the introduction of involvement programmes. Some employees complained that the new systems soon generated new forms of hierarchy whilst other employees felt that the 'empowerment' programmes had forced them to make them work harder without giving them any *real* power.

The importance of partnership

As we studied the experiences of the JIWIS organisations, we were reminded of the extent to which the attainment of flexibility depends upon what happens to the *psychological contract*. As described by Rosenblatt and Ruvio, the term refers to the implicit commitments made between people and their employers and it draws out the kinds of informal dynamics which employers may affect as they change formal work structures. An important role of the psychological contract is that of helping to secure cooperation at work. The operation of this contract may be demonstrated by individuals staying with their organisation when there are opportunities elsewhere, and also by their willingness to be adaptable to changing performance requirements. In return for their loyalty, hard work and commitment, the employee expects to be 'looked after' through the course of their employment. In other words, employees expect employers to fulfil their side of the 'bargain'. By contrast, where expectations are not met, the likelihood of negative work attitudes and turnover may rise.[33]

Hence, the introduction of team work and 'involvement' programmes, with an underlying emphasis on shared aims and responsibility, can help to boost the morale and productivity of the workforce if they are seen as a part of a genuine commitment to the health and well-being of the workforce. But if they are perceived as a device by which the firm reduces its employment and intensifies the work of those remaining, they are likely to damage, rather than strengthen, the psychological contract between the organisation and its employees. It was a paradox neatly described by two of the organisations in our survey, both of which had significantly worsened the terms and conditions of their workforce in the process of introducing new forms of work organisation. In the first of these organisations, the senior manager told us that 'flexibility requires a higher degree of professionalism and mutual trust than did the old contracts'; and in the second case, the senior manager stressed that 'the system needs the goodwill of the employees'.

However, the goodwill required by these managers is difficult to gain, when – as was the case among many of the employees we interviewed – people do not trust their managers to look after their best interests. As shown in Table 2.6, although 55 per cent of employees said that they trusted managers at least 'somewhat' or 'a lot', 44 per cent held to the view that management could be trusted 'only a little' or 'not at all', and there was little difference between union members and non-union members in this respect. Trust emerged when there was a good working climate and

Table 2.6 The percentage of employees who trust management to look after their best interests

Degree of trust	All employees	Union members	Non-union members
A lot	12	9	16
Somewhat	43	42	48
Only a little	31	35	23
Not at all	13	13	12
Don't know	1	1	1

Table 2.7 Why do you trust (or not trust) management to look after your best interests? (% of total responses)

Distrust	Reason	
	because they are manipulative/self-interested	15
	because they are powerless	11
	because they put business first	11
	because they have a 'them and us' attitude	10
	because they don't support career development	6
	because of previous bad experiences	5
	because of poor communication	4
	because I never expected anything in the first place	4
	because they don't support us generally	2
Trust	because the working climate is good	12
	because I've not had any bad experiences	11
	because they've supported my career progress	3
	because it's worth their while to look after our interests	3
	because the working conditions are good	2

when people had always been well treated by their employer (Table 2.7). However, it is also evident that, even where there is said to be trust, it is far from total or unqualified. Again, despite positive feelings about involvement programmes, a large number of the statements of lack of trust referred to management as 'manipulative', 'self-interested', 'insincere and untruthful'. Management were also accused of focusing on the interests of shareholders at the expense of employees. Reinforcing the perception of a difference in employee and employer priorities was the tenacity of 'them and us' attitudes – and again there was little difference between union and non-union members in this respect (Table 2.8).

The persistence of 'them and us' attitudes, among both union and non-union members, reflects the traditional relationship between management and the representatives of organised labour. As described in Will Hutton's account of the history of collective bargaining, Britain's trade unions were founded 'in corporate opposition' to capital and were 'never organised to do other than champion a very narrow conception of working-class interest'.[34] It was a relationship that was maintained well into the late

Table 2.8 The percentage of employees who agreed with the following statement:
'In this organisation, management and employees are on the same side'

Response	All employees	Union members	Non-union members
Strongly agree	4	4	5
Agree	22	20	24
Neither	40	39	44
Disagree	27	30	19
Strongly disagree	7	7	8

1970s, when the trade unions were noticeably reluctant to help employers
run their businesses by engaging with them in joint decision-making – a
fact which suited British employers who were more than happy to bargain
through the 'antagonistic confrontation of rival interests' so long as they
retained their unchallenged 'right to manage'. During the 1980s, and at
a time when many were trying to broaden their constituency of interest
representation, the trade unions suffered an extraordinary restriction of
their ability to fund their activities, to organise their members and engage
in industrial activity.[35] Indeed, by 1993, nine major pieces of legislation
had been enacted, all of which were aimed at weakening the power of
organised labour and strengthening the hand of 'management'. By the
end of the 1990s less than a third of the workforce was covered by collective bargaining arrangements and there was evidence that new-style
employment contracts were being used as instruments of unilateral
management control both in organisations that had shifted away from
collective bargaining and those which had retained it.[36]

Not surprisingly, strikes and other collective forms of industrial action
declined in the context of these reforms, and as a result of changes in the
socio-economic environment. This was illustrated by the fact that none of
the JIWIS organisations had suffered any serious form of industrial action
in the five years prior to the survey. Nonetheless, although many of their
senior managers were glad that the unions had become 'more compliant'
and 'less militant', only four of them had made any progress towards the
kind of 'social partnership' which would have involved these bodies in joint
decision-making or profit-sharing (see Table 2.9). And yet, many commentators are increasingly convinced that the development of a skilled and
flexible workforce can only be achieved through the development of 'genuine' partnerships.[37] For example, the authors of the European Commission's
Green Paper on 'Partnership for a New Organisation of Work' stress that:

> A co-operative approach to a different organisation of work within the
> firm will improve industrial relations and allow greater worker participa-
> tion in decisions and potentially lead to better product quality. The
> latter in fact represents an essential component in any strengthening
> of the competitiveness of the European economy.[38]

Table 2.9 Senior management perceptions of how relations with unions/staff associations have been changing in the last five years

Move towards 'greater' social partnership	Case 13 Case 5 Case 9 Case 8
Unions have become more 'compliant', more realistic, less militant, less effective, 'never see the union', moved from negotiation to 'consultation'	Case 4 Case 10 Case 16 Case 2 Case 7 Case 3
Overall been good	Case 15
Overall good, but some deterioration	Case 1 Case 14
Continue to/currently have a difficult relationship	Case 11 Case 6

Moreover, when considering the relationship between flexibility and social partnership it is worth studying the experiences of some of Britain's economic competitors. For, as described by Wilkinson and Biracree *et al.*, cooperative partnerships between management and labour have been crucial to the success of the firms – in northern Italy, Germany, Japan and Sweden – which boast the world's most flexible production methods.[39] But even within Britain, current research suggests the adoption of a partnership approach can result in improved flexibility and competitive performance. Take, for example, the findings which emerged from a recent survey conducted by the Industrial Society (IS) based on fifteen case studies spread across a wide range of industries. The aim of the survey was to identify businesses in which a successful partnership approach had been established, to examine the arrangements and processes involved and to study the outcomes. Comparing the findings of this study to the 1998 Workplace Employment Relations Survey, John Knell was struck by the much greater incidence of flexibility innovations in the IS sample. The IS firms contained some of the leading examples of semi-autonomous team working, all of whom felt that the adoption of a partnership-based approach had enhanced their competitive performance.[40]

Summary

The organisations in the JIWIS sample were trying to redraw the boundaries of work, changing employees' past, present and future roles in their organisations. They were challenging labour standards by cutting across the grain of existing norms and practices. To this end they were introducing elements of high-performance work systems and pursuing flexibility by design (and default) in leaner organisations. Not only had they been integrating trade unions into their human resource strategies, they had also introduced a number of workplace innovations aimed, in part, at decentralising responsibility and collectivising effort. These moves echo the post-war 'quality of working life movement', which advocated autonomous group working, job enrichment and vertical loading techniques to counter the ill effects of scientific management.[41] However, whilst the intention of these early experiments was to improve the work environment, the primary purpose of the practices surveyed here was to raise business, and especially financial, performance and to improve the *bottom line*. Often through a combination of redundancies and work redesign, senior managers reported lower costs and productivity gains. Functional and temporal flexibility for the 'permanent' workforce featured prominently in this process.

The employers in our survey were also trying to instigate a cultural change within their workforce by changing the behaviour and attitudes of their employees. Their emphasis on selectivity, replacement and re-educational strategies reflected their understanding of the extent to which business restructuring is dependent upon securing (and retaining) the 'right sort' of human capital. And yet, despite the widespread introduction of employee involvement programmes, many of their employees exhibited feelings of fear, distrust and alienation. Moreover, even on the criteria of costs and productivity, downsizing and work reorganisation had not been a universal success. The organisational costs of these developments will be examined again in Chapter 7. But, before that, Brendan Burchell, Ines Wichert and Jane Nolan will examine the impact of these developments on the job insecurities, work pressures and family tensions experienced by employees.

3 The prevalence and redistribution of job insecurity and work intensification

Brendan Burchell

The preceding chapters have described the way in which the demand side of the labour market has changed for our organisations. But, more generally, there has been much concern and argument, among policy makers as well as academics, about the level of insecurity at work that has accompanied these changes. The JIWIS project was conceived against this backdrop, with a widespread worry that a higher level of job insecurity would bring with it a range of social problems for individuals, families, employers and the wider society. But before presenting the details of this project's extensive and detailed studies of secure and insecure employees and workplaces we will set the scene by exploring changes in the level of insecurity in the British, American and European labour forces over the past three decades. Has job insecurity, as is widely believed, increased massively over the recent past, or is it yet another of those alarmist scenarios which has taken on a life of its own, but defies careful and impartial analysis of labour market data?

And is job insecurity the only new cost to descend upon employees? In this chapter we will also investigate the prevalence and distribution of work intensification: the extent to which employees are being forced to work faster and harder than they have been before. Later on in the book, we will return to this issue when we argue that, although the increase in the intensity of work may be more difficult to detect and chart than the change in job security, it provides the greater cause of stress in today's workplace.

Definitions

The question of what constitutes job insecurity is by no means settled. Burgess and Rees and Gregg and Wadsworth have used job tenure – the length of time individuals spend with their employer – as one *objective* indicator.[1] They found little overall change and possibly a slight increase in tenure length for women (probably a consequence of improved maternity leave rights). It is, however, important to differentiate between job stability and job insecurity, as the two may not be correlated.[2] With growing

unemployment and a decline in job opportunities, individuals may reasonably cling to what they have, rather than risk the growing uncertainty of
the external labour market. Others, who may well be able to progress to
better positions in other organisations, stick with their downsizing organisations to collect their severance payments. So, perversely, prolonged tenure
may actually indicate increased job *in*security if employees adopt defensive
labour market strategies.

Another way in which some researchers have attempted to compare
levels of job insecurity over time or between countries is by looking at the
proportion of employees on non-permanent contracts, such as fixed-term,
temporary, casual or agency contracts. Clearly, there is some face validity
to this approach, and surveys have shown that employees on such contracts tend to report markedly lower levels of job security. But, for our
purposes, the rates of non-permanent contracts are too weakly related
to aggregate levels of job insecurity to be a useful measure. For instance,
comparisons of non-permanent workers in OECD countries show enormous
variation; at the two extremes, 36 per cent of Spanish employees are on
temporary contracts, compared to only 2 per cent in the USA.[3] The main
explanation for this is that in the USA, 'permanent' workers are so poorly
protected from dismissal that there is little advantage to an employer in
putting them on temporary contracts. By contrast, Spanish workers enjoy
such strong protection from redundancy and unfair dismissal that employers are very strongly motivated to reduce their commitment to their
employees. In fact, one could even claim that a Spanish temporary worker
enjoys better protection than a US permanent employee!

So, for the purposes of this book, we define job insecurity as the subjective feelings about the risk of job loss, as expressed by the employees
themselves. Several existing surveys have used different formulations to
measure security. Some ask employees to simply rate their level of job
insecurity on a scale from 'very insecure' to 'very secure'. Some ask employees to assess the risk of becoming unemployed in the next twelve
months. Some are less direct, asking employees how satisfied they are with
a number of separate aspects of their jobs, including job insecurity as one
of those aspects. And, finally, some surveys have used multi-item measures
to explore different aspects of job insecurity.

Of course, one could argue that employees are far from perfect in
assessing their own risk of unemployment. They may, for instance, exaggerate the risk because they have been scared by media reports of job
insecurity. Or, in an act of denial, they may underestimate the risk so as
to protect themselves from anxiety, like ostriches burying their heads in
the sand. An economist may view the reliance on potentially inaccurate
self-report data as a flaw in our research. However, we regard employees'
self-reports as being the most important source of data. In this research,
we are not so much interested in how many employees lose their jobs in a
given time-period, or in the effect of redundancy and unemployment on

the individual. Rather, we are interested in the feelings and concerns of the employees. After all, it is their *perception of* the risks associated with their job, not the risk *per se*, which may stress employees and change their motivation and morale. Put another way, an employee who worries continuously about losing her job may suffer real psychological problems, at great cost to her and her family, even if she never actually loses her job. Likewise, employees who perceive that their job is at risk may seek employment elsewhere as a consequence of this perception (thereby adding to the statistics on 'voluntary' turnover!). And, at the aggregate level, trade unions may feel disempowered when their members feel under threat, thus pay rises may be muted. All these effects are from 'mere' perceptions of job insecurity; that is why we see self-report measures not as the second-best but as the *key* indicators of job insecurity.

And the range of these insecurities is broad. To borrow the typology developed by Guy Standing,[4] it includes:

- Employment insecurity – when the employer can dismiss or lay off workers, or put them on short time without great difficulty or costs.
- Job insecurity – when the employer can shift workers from one job to another at will or where the content of the job can be altered or reduced.
- Work insecurity – where the working environment is unregulated, polluted or dangerous in some way, so that the ability to continue to work is at risk.
- Income insecurity – when earnings are unstable, or when transfer payments are contingency-based not guaranteed.
- Working-time insecurity – when the employer can impose fragmented, shortened or irregular hours without great difficulty or costs.
- Representation insecurity – when the employer can impose change in the labour process and refuse to negotiate with effective trade unions and other institutions protecting workers' collective interests.
- Skill reproduction insecurity – when opportunities to gain and retain skills through access to education and training is impeded.
- Labour market insecurity – represented by labour surplus conditions, so that the probability of securing employment is low, with workers readily available wherever jobs arise.

Although, the usefulness of these distinctions has never been tested empirically, they do remind us of the complexity of the phenomenon we are studying. Most of the previous research in the job insecurity field has focused primarily or exclusively on what Standing calls 'employment security', rather than Standing's more specialised definition of 'job insecurity'. Later on in this chapter we will return to these issues and argue that when employees report feeling insecure, they are addressing wider concerns than the simple fear of involuntary severance from their employer.

Job insecurity in the UK labour market 1966–97

The best estimates we have of recent changes in job insecurity in the UK are derived from a survey of 4,000 workers in six UK locations in 1986 conducted by the Social Change and Economic Life Initiative (SCELI), and a representative survey of 2,500 employed and self-employed respondents conducted in April 1997 (the Skills Survey).[5] The two surveys both asked the same questions about job security. The main question asked of all respondents was 'Do you think that there is any chance of you losing your job and becoming unemployed in the next twelve months?' If they answered in the affirmative, they were then asked 'How would you rate the likelihood of this happening?' on a five-point scale ranging from 'very likely' to 'very unlikely'. In the 1986 survey, 20 per cent of respondents reported that they thought that there was some possibility of losing their jobs; in the 1997 survey this had increased, but only very slightly, to 22.9 per cent. Taking into account their scores on the 5-point likelihood scale reduced even this very small difference between the two time-periods.

At first we were rather surprised by these findings, given all the media interest in and policy debates on job insecurity. But, when we re-analysed the data from other studies, we became increasingly convinced that the UK in the 1980s and 1990s had indeed witnessed little *overall* change in job security. Take, for example, the time-series data on job insecurity provided by the General and Municipal Boilermakers (GMB). A large trade union representing skilled manual workers, the GMB has commissioned regular surveys showing the relative importance ascribed by their members to different features of their jobs. These surveys show that, in 1997, 56 per cent of their members selected job security as one of their six most important features, compared to 48 per cent in 1995. The union cites these figures as evidence of a sizeable increase in job insecurity. However, if we take the time-series as a whole, the fluctuations in the figures look like no more than sampling errors. Apart from the 1995 figure, the other five surveys between 1985 and 1997 all obtain percentages between 52 per cent and 56 per cent, and show no pattern over time.[6]

We also re-examined the data used by the Organisation for Economic Cooperation and Development in their 1998 *Economic Outlook*.[7] In this report, the OECD claims that perceived job insecurity rose rapidly in the UK from the mid-1980s to the mid-1990s. The claim is inconsistent with the trends indicated by the Skills, SCELI and GMB surveys but a close inspection of the two datasets on which the OECD base their report reveals serious weaknesses in both.

The first of these datasets was taken from the British Household Panel Survey (BHPS), which was used by the OECD in order to analyse changes in the seven-point item on satisfaction with job security. The BHPS figures show a marked increase in those who were not 'totally satisfied' with their job security, from 61.7 per cent in wave 1 (1991) to between 75.8 per cent and 78.2 per cent in the subsequent three waves (1992–4). However, a closer examination of this data shows that there are other sizeable changes between wave 1 and all the subsequent waves in the series. For instance, there is also a mirrored change at the other end of the 'satisfaction with job security' scale, with fewer respondents being 'totally dissatisfied' with their job security. Furthermore an inspection of the six other scales measuring job satisfaction (e.g. satisfaction with pay, hours and management) reveals that each scale shows exactly the same trend away from the two endpoints of the scale (1 and 7) between 1991 and 1992.

Discussions with those involved in the fieldwork revealed a simple explanation for this curious pattern. While the wording of the job satisfaction items in the questionnaire had remained constant, the showcard was changed. In 1991 only the extremes and the midpoint of the seven-point scale were labelled (i.e. 'totally satisfied', 'neither satisfied nor dissatisfied', 'totally dissatisfied'), while the other points were just numbers on the scale. This caused bunching around the three labelled points. In subsequent waves, all seven points on the response scale were labelled on the showcard, thus reducing the bunching.[8] The OECD's method of analysis – simply looking at the percentages who scored on the extreme of the scale – was highly sensitive to this change. A summary measure that takes all scores into account (i.e. the mean or average score) shows only very slight, non-monotonic and non-significant changes over the period 1991–5.

The other dataset used by the OECD was supppplied by International Survey Research (ISR) Ltd. At first glance this seems to be a valuable large sample dataset, measuring job insecurity using the same measures, in several European countries, at several points in time. The OECD analysis of this data shows that all European countries had experienced a drop in job security over the period 1985–95, but that the UK was the most extreme case, with a massive drop of 22 percentage points in those responding favourably to a question about employment security. However, closer scrutiny of ISR's data suggests that it might be of too poor a quality for use in such a way. ISR is a commercial organisation offering personnel and consultancy services. Companies can buy into their annual surveys and have ISR take a census of their total workforce. For their money, companies receive a description of their own workforce, benchmarked against the total dataset of tens of thousands of cases, supplied by the dozens of other companies who also bought into the survey within the previous three years. While the data might thus be very useful for employer benchmarking purposes, it makes no attempt to provide a representative or stable sample for comparison, either between countries or over time.

Disaggregated analyses: winners and losers

A disaggregated analysis of the changes between the 1986 SCELI survey and the 1997 Skills Survey showed that, while the workforce *as a whole* experienced little change in job security, there were more substantial changes for some groups of workers (in both directions). Workers in higher-paid occupations, those employed in construction or financial services, those who had been in their current jobs for over ten years and the self-employed were significantly more insecure in 1997; those in the manufacturing industry and in sales occupations were more secure in 1997 than in 1986. But the biggest change was experienced by those in professional occupations, who went from being the most secure workers in 1986 to the most insecure in 1997.

An additional item ('How easy would it be to get another job as good as your current one?') was included in both surveys to elicit respondents' perceptions not just about their current job security but about their 'employability'. Again there was little *overall* change between the two time periods (if anything there was slightly more optimism in 1997 than in 1986) but there was considerable variability between different segments of the labour market. In 1986, those in higher-paid occupations were more optimistic about their chances of getting another job than those in lower-paid occupations; this had reversed in 1997. Those employed in finance and construction also felt less secure about obtaining employment in the external labour market, whereas those in manufacturing, and those who had only been in their current job for a year or less, were both more optimistic in 1997.[9]

Earlier changes: 1966 to 1986

The lack of better time-series data does not permit much in the way of survey evidence before 1986; but an analysis of retrospective data permits some understanding of the changes that may have occurred in the period between the 1960s and the 1980s. This can be achieved by examining the work histories supplied by the 6,111 persons in the 1986 SCELI survey (who were asked for details of every single job that they had held since they left full-time education). For those who were towards the upper end of the twenty to sixty age range, this gives data going back as far as the 1940s. Included in the description of each recorded job was the respondent's rating of the security of the job, on a four-point scale from 'very secure' to 'very insecure'.

There are two main problems that affect the reliability of such data. First, there is some concern that people's memories of jobs in the past show considerable errors and biases in recall. Second, as one goes further back into the past, the sample of job holders becomes younger, as the older incumbents would have been aged over sixty in 1986. To ameliorate these problems, the recall period for these analyses was limited to twenty years, going back as far as 1966, and only jobs held by those who were aged forty or under at the time were included in the analysis. Figure 3.1 shows very clearly the pattern of responding over this twenty-year period,

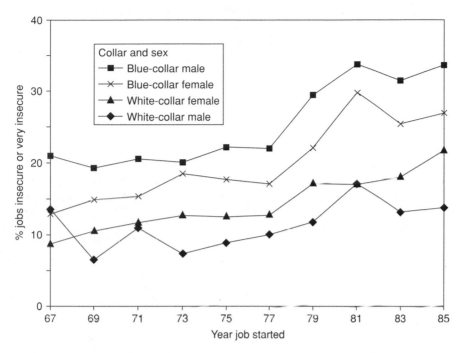

Figure 3.1 Job insecurity, 1967–86

Source: SCELI (1986), Burchell (1999)

broken down by gender and class. Several features of the data stand out clearly. First, white-collar employees have, for all of this period, enjoyed much higher levels of job security than blue-collar workers. Second, this class difference has been much more marked for men than for women. And, third, there was a gradual upward trend in job insecurity, most pronounced for blue-collar workers in the late 1970s and early 1980s. This coincides with the oil shocks and the late 1970s/early 1980s recession that saw increased unemployment (especially among manual workers) and job losses (particularly in the manufacturing sector). Similar analyses can be done for the period 1946–66. Although the data is less reliable for this period, it shows a similar pattern.

Taken together, the data suggests the following chronology with regard to job insecurity in the UK over the past thirty years:

* Over the post-war boom years, job insecurity remained low and stable, but throughout this time the proportion of male blue-collar workers feeling insecure was, at all times, approximately twice as high as the proportion of male white-collar workers. The difference between white- and blue-collar females was less pronounced.

- During the period from approximately 1977 to 1981, there was a considerable increase in job insecurity for all groups, but especially blue-collar workers, widening the class differentials.
- Between the mid-1980s and mid-1990s there was little aggregate change, but a very significant redistribution of insecurity between more and less advantaged workers. The most marked changes were that the professionals and workers in the financial services, previously the most secure occupations and sectors, were now the least secure.

As for the future, it is difficult to predict whether job insecurity will increase. On the one hand, some changes to UK employment law, such as the 1999 Employment Bill, should extend the coverage of employment protection legislation. Alternatively, one could argue that job insecurity is strongly linked to levels of unemployment, which may have been in a trough in the mid- to late 1990s. If this is the case, it is likely that increases in job insecurity will, once again, ratchet up to new and higher levels, if or when we head into another recession.

Job insecurity in the USA in the late 1990s

Although the USA's official unemployment rate is lower than most of its European competitors, the ISR figures (used by the OECD) suggest that, by the end of the 1990s, job insecurity in the USA was considerably higher than the European average. On an index of job insecurity based upon employees' responses to four questions in 1996 (e.g. 'I am frequently worried about the future of my company' and 'How satisfied are you with your job security?') the twenty-one countries included in the OECD's statistics scored an average of forty-four; but the USA was well above this with a score of fifty-two. There were only three other countries with marginally higher scores: Japan, the UK and France (see Table 3.1).

However, because the representativeness of the employees interviewed in each country in the ISR survey is (as described above) somewhat questionable, we have compared the percentage of workers answering 'Yes' to the statement 'You have a secure job' in the 1996 European Survey of Working Conditions. Overall, the agreement between the two sets of data is reasonable.[10] In fact, the only country which is clearly off the regression line is the UK, highest of the EU counties on the ISR measure, but close to average according to the Working Conditions data.[11] We have assumed, therefore, that the ISR statistics can be accepted as a rough indication of the relative position of the USA with respect to the job insecurities experienced by its workforce. We cannot attribute the cause of the US's relatively high level of job insecurity to any one cause, but we suspect that the much weaker legal regulation of the labour market (consistent with the principle of 'employment at will') may be a significant factor.

Table 3.1 International comparisons of job (in)security

Country	Employment insecurity, ISR measure, 1996	Job security, European Working Conditions Survey, 1996
Australia	36	
Austria	35	75.9
Belgium	45	73.4
Canada	45	
Denmark	38	82.7
Finland	47	67.6
France	53	61.1
Germany	45	59.5
Greece	38	65.8
Ireland	43	72.3
Italy	44	74.2
Japan	56	
Luxembourg		84.9
Mexico	38	
Netherlands	38	80.3
Norway	31	
Portugal	45	63.0
Spain	46	73.8
Sweden	47	63.8
Switzerland	42	
UK	54	73.3
USA	52	
Average	44 (unweighted)	70.0 (weighted)

Changes in the level of job insecurity in the USA

The USA is better provided with statistics on job insecurity than most other industrialised countries because the same questions about job insecurity have been asked in the US General Social Survey (GSS) on thirteen occasions between 1977 and 1996. With average sample sizes of around 10,000 this gives a useful series of snapshots of the US workforce over the past two decades. In their analysis of this data, Aaronson and Sullivan found little evidence to suggest that there has been an *aggregate* rise in job insecurity over the past two decades, despite the sharp increase in the attention that job insecurity has received in both the media and learned journals.[12] But the GSS does point to a significant *re-distribution* of job insecurity. As a general rule, until the 1970s, job insecurity was associated with other forms of labour market disadvantage, such as being a blue-collar worker, being from an ethnic minority, or being a non-graduate. By the mid-1990s this polarisation had either been reduced or had completely disappeared. This pattern of change in the USA thus bears a remarkable similarity to that which occurred in the UK.

The consequences of this redistribution in job security, for either country, have not been fully explored. To some extent, egalitarians might welcome the fact that job insecurity is no longer the preserve of the poor, having been spread more equally across the workforce. But serious problems may also emerge now that many of the old professional jobs, once thought of as jobs for life, are made available on the same casual basis as other posts. Such problems include reduced psychological well-being and its impact not just on individuals, but on their families and on the wider community. Moreover, what is particularly worrying about the figures reported for both the UK and the USA, is that job insecurity has remained high throughout the 1990s despite a considerable (and sustained) reduction in the unemployment figures. What this suggests is that job insecurity is not a passing phenomenon linked to cyclical changes in unemployment but a widespread condition which has stabilised at higher levels than in the three decades immediately following the Second World War.

Broadening the scope of insecurity

We can all appreciate that feelings of insecurity emerge when employees are faced with the prospect of lay-offs or redundancies. But, as Greenhalgh and Rosenblatt have shown, the prospect of dismissal is not the only thing that can trigger feelings of insecurity.[13] On the contrary, the loss or erosion of other employment conditions can also trigger feelings of job insecurity. Hence, in today's labour market, many employees are worried not only because they might lose their jobs *per se* but because they are threatened with the loss of valued job features. In other words, they are scared of losing promotion opportunities, of losing control over the pace of work, of losing their ability to complete the entire job, and of losing their customary pay rise (see Figure 3.2). In some cases, the loss of valued job features simply leads to a reduction in the quality of working life, in others it also involves economic losses, and in some instances the employee might be forced to quit the job itself if the changes render the job untenable.

In Chapter 4 we will discuss many of the anxieties associated with the loss of valued job features. But the first thing to note about this fear is its emotional quality. For example, when we asked our respondents to calculate the objective probability of being dismissed from their jobs, most of our respondents thought it highly unlikely this would happen to them within the next twelve months. But even among those who responded that the likelihood of losing their job was 'unlikely' or 'very unlikely', there was a sizeable minority who still did *not* describe their job as 'secure' or 'very secure: 40 per cent of those who said that it was 'unlikely' that they would lose their jobs still described their jobs as 'very insecure', 'insecure' or 'neither secure nor insecure', as did 11 per cent of those who described the likelihood of losing their jobs as 'very unlikely'. This clearly demonstrates that non-specific feelings of insecurity are far more pervasive than

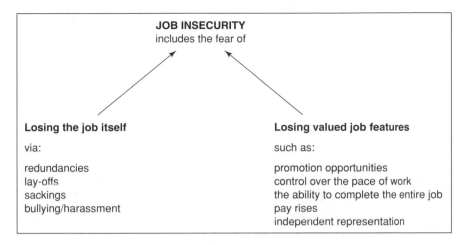

Figure 3.2 The sources of job insecurity

feelings of impending involuntary job loss, and probably include several other features in Standing's 8-point classification of job loss besides 'employment security'.

Moreover, the extent to which people worry about losing their jobs depends not only on their perception of the *likelihood* of job loss but also on their anxieties about the *consequences* of such an event. For example, the data collected from our respondents suggests that, other things being equal, mid-career employees with small children and large mortgages feel more insecure than their older or younger colleagues, not because they overestimate the probability of redundancy but because they are more worried about the impact such an event would have upon their lives. Using this division between the likelihood and the consequences of job loss, Figure 3.3 disaggregates the primary determinants of job insecurity into factors that are principally dependent on what an employee does and who they work for, and those that are not.

Work intensification

Although this project started with a particular focus on the growth in job insecurity, the interviews and early analyses of the data quickly brought us to realise that there were other, perhaps more important, changes affecting the UK workplace. Take, for example, the rising stress levels triggered by the intensification of work. In recent years, a lot has been written about the long and extended hours worked by the labour force in both the UK and the USA (especially when these hours are compared with those of their European counterparts). But while the spread of the 'long hours' culture is an important phenomenon in its own right, work *intensification*,

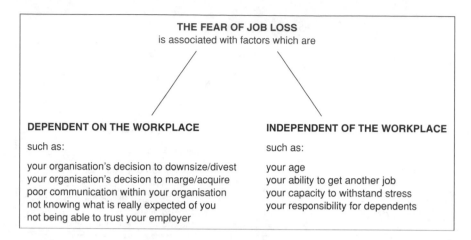

Figure 3.3 Factors associated with fear of job loss

i.e. the effort that employees put into their jobs during the time that they are working, has received less attention. And yet, as shown by the data presented later on in this book, the intensification of work may be a greater problem – in terms of stress, psychological health and family tension – than the lengthening of the working week or the prevalence of job insecurity.

In a recent review of the literature on work intensification, Green suggests a number of ways in which effort might be measured. Apart from self-report, the other possibilities he considers are by quantifiable proxy (for instance, industrial accidents), case studies, productivity and a measure called 'Percentage Utilisation of Labour' based on work study.[14] But he suggests that none of these measures is reliable or valid enough to be useful. There are too many other variables, apart from effort, which influence them. For instance, industrial accidents are also strongly influenced by health and safety regulation and enforcement whilst productivity is a function of skill, managerial efficiency and reliability of machinery, as well as effort.

This leaves self-report measures as the only reliable indicator of work intensification. The questions on which these measures are based are typically couched in one of two forms. First, respondents can be asked how their effort, or pace of work, has changed over the past, say, five years. This was the question we asked in the JIWIS survey, the responses to which are shown in Figure 3.4. Taking these responses at face value, the results are quite remarkable. In both cases, over 60 per cent of respondents reported an intensification of their work, compared to only 4 and 5 per cent respectively who reported a reduction in effort. Other surveys have also found very high levels of reported work intensification. For instance, in 1986 the SCELI survey asked questions about increased effort and pace of work in the past five years, and 55.6 per cent and 38.1 per cent of the 3,000 employees reported increases respectively, compared to only 8.1 per

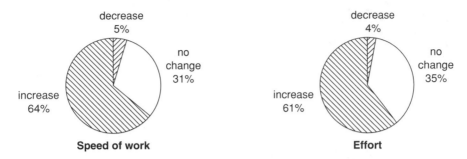

Figure 3.4 The percentage of employees experiencing an increase in the speed
of work and the effort they put into their jobs (over the past 5 years)

Source: Job Insecurity and Work Intensification Survey

cent and 7.8 per cent who reported decreases. And a 1999 UK survey of
the members of the Institute of Management revealed that a massive 69
per cent of the respondents reported experiencing an increase in workload in the past twelve months.[15]

But the results of these surveys are open to challenge. The net increases
may, at least in part, be attributable to either life-cycle effects (i.e. employees having to work harder as they get promoted into positions of greater
responsibility), or to distortions in recall (respondents might be viewing the
past through rose-tinted spectacles). Luckily, there now exists a repeated
cross-sectional measure, which overcomes this problem. The European
Working Conditions Surveys (EWCS) in 1991 and 1995/6 asked 1,000
respondents in each of the European Union countries how much of the
time in their jobs they had to work at speed or to tight deadlines. They responded on a seven-point scale from 'all of the time' to 'never' on both
these indicators. One could argue that, as 'tight deadlines' and 'working
at speed' are somewhat subjective constructs, it is not valid to compare
workers from very different cultures. For example, national stereotypes
would predict that Spanish workers used to a longer, more 'relaxed',
working day may have very different normative templates to their German
counterparts accustomed to shorter, more 'intense' schedules. But, when
we examine the time-series data within each country, we can more safely
chart the relative changes in work intensification between countries.

Figure 3.5 does this, showing, on the horizontal and vertical dimensions
respectively, the changes in the proportion of workers in each country
working at speed and to tight deadlines most or all of the time. As we can
see, the general trend in all European countries has been up, but the rate
of change varies considerably between countries. Some, such as Greece
and Luxembourg, seem to have experienced little or no change. But one
country stands out as having experienced work intensification more than
any other – the UK. This suggests that, indeed, our JIWIS data are grounded

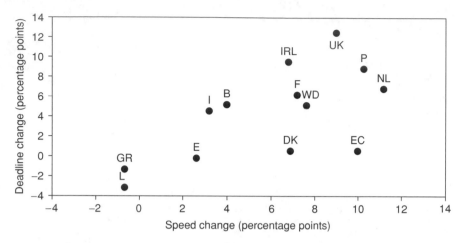

Figure 3.5 Change in percentage of respondents working at speed and to tight
deadlines all or almost all of the time 1991–6

Source: European Working Conditions Surveys

in reality when the employees report that their jobs require more effort
and speed than before.

At the time of taking this book to press, the third wave of the European Working Conditions Survey has just become available. A preliminary
comparison of the 1995/6 and the 2000 data shows that there has been
a further increase in the intensification of work, but a much smaller
increase than in the previous five-year period. The UK data is virtually
unchanged, and some countries have displayed a decrease (especially Portugal and Austria). The greatest increases in intensification took place in
Belgium, Italy, France, Luxembourg and Sweden.[16]

The distribution of job intensification

As with comparisons between countries, it is difficult (if not impossible) to
make direct comparisons of effort between very different jobs. How could
we possibly compare ('objectively') the effort expended by, say, a busy
labourer on a building site and a busy midwife? The former uses his
muscles more, and expends more calories each hour, but the latter might
feel more 'drained' by her work and feel that the job is more relentless.
But can we explore the ways in which the effort required of different
occupations has changed over time?

In the SCELI data, where employees were invited to compare their
effort at the time of the survey in 1986 with their jobs in 1981, there was a
clear social class effect; 64 per cent of professional and intermediate white-
collar workers reported having to increase effort, compared to only 45 per
cent of semi-skilled manual workers and 39 per cent of 'unskilled' manual

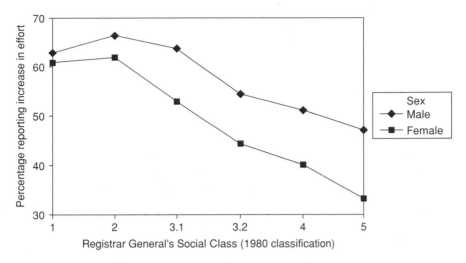

Figure 3.6 Changes in effort between 1981 and 1986, by sex and social class

Source: SCELI (1986)

Notes
1 Professional occupations
2 Managerial and technical occupations
3 Skilled occupations
   (i) Non-manual
   (ii) Manual
4 Partly skilled occupations
5 Unskilled occupations

workers. And as shown in Figure 3.6, this effect was more marked among female workers; female manual workers reported the lowest levels of work intensification. This greatest intensification for the most skilled workers is consistent with the findings of the Institute of Management survey; it only surveyed managers, but found higher levels of reported intensification than other surveys.

Preliminary analysis of the 1995/6 and 2000 European Working Conditions Surveys suggests that the greatest intensification has occurred for professionals, craft workers and elementary occupations, while 'legislators, officials and senior managers' and clerks have recently experienced a reduction in the intensity of work. And, in absolute terms, 'plant and machinery operators and assemblers' and craft workers were working most intensively, both in 1995/6 and 2000.

Reasons for the intensification of work

Like many changes in the labour market, there has probably been more than one force driving the increase in work effort in the UK. It could be the reduction in trade union powers; strict demarcations between workers were one (albeit crude) way in which employees could guard against relentless work. It could be that management are now much better trained and highly skilled at managing the flow of work; previously one heard of employees having to spend much of their working day waiting for plant, materials or supervisors to arrive. Green's analyses of the 1991 and 1995/6 EWCS suggests that computer use might be another predictor of work intensification.[17] Or perhaps jobs are more rewarding now than in the past, and so employees are more self-motivated than they used to be. However, in the eyes of the JIWIS employees, the clear culprits were increased competition and shareholder influence in the private sector, and reduced Treasury funding in the public sector, leading to downsizing, but with an expectation that the reduced number of employees would still achieve the same quantity of work.

But why, you might ask, are we so interested in the speed and intensity of work? If, as Ronald Reagan stated, 'hard work never killed anyone',[18] shouldn't we welcome work intensification as a sign of increased efficiency and competitive advantage? To the contrary, the evidence presented in the following chapters suggests that the intensification of work poses a worrying challenge to health, work–family balance and employee motivation in the twenty-first century.

4 Disappearing pathways and the struggle for a fair day's pay

Maria Hudson

In Chapter 3, we emphasised that the workplace changes triggered by the drive towards flexibility have threatened many of the 'job features' which are strongly valued by employees, including *job security*, control over the *pace and flow of work*, and the enjoyment of *reasonable working hours*. But as we shall see, other features of the archetypal 'good job' have also been threatened by the flexible reorganisation of work. We begin this chapter with a brief description of the de-layering of occupational hierarchies, as manifest in the UK and US labour markets during the 1980s and 1990s. Drawing on the findings of the JIWIS, we then move to a more detailed exploration of its impact on people's promotion and career prospects. We also examine the growing disparity in earnings and the extent to which people feel that they are no longer being paid 'a fair day's wage for a fair day's work'.

Broken ladders

In the early post-war period, white-collar workers in the US and Britain had good reason to feel positive about their career prospects as large-scale business corporations and state-owned institutions expanded. However, by the 1970s the picture had begun to change. Some commentators argued that the third industrial revolution of new technologies heralded a collapse of work.[1] Since the late 1970s, we have frequently been reminded of the way in which senior management have been able to secure cost reductions and productivity gains through cuts in clerical work and middle management.[2] We read articles about 'the whittling away of middle management' and the 'declining role of managers' in 'the corporation of the future'. Instead of 'rising through the ranks', we are advised to build a 'portfolio career' and concentrate on our 'employability'. Competitiveness, it seems, is everyone's responsibility.[3] Employers and employees should work 'in partnership' to develop a 'career resilient', self-reliant, flexible, multi-functioning workforce.[4]

Case studies of US firms undertaken between 1970 and 1992 suggest that the de-layering of occupational hierarchies which took place during this period has made it harder for employees to 'work their way up' an organisation.[5] According to the urban planner, Thierry Noyelle, this 'devolution' of internal labour markets has been driven by the corporate search for flexibility and cost savings together with the advent of information technologies which lead to:

> a kind of universalisation or homogenisation of skills demanded across a wide range of industries, allowing for greater externalisation of training for many middle-level workers. Many occupations have now become more generic and less firm specific than they once were and computer-oriented algorithmic logic has replaced many firm-specific idiosyncratic practices. All of this amounts to a pronounced shift away from on the job training which further undermines the raison d'être of the old internal labour market.[6]

Noyelle's observations are supported by the research conducted by Maury Gittleman and David Howell and by Manuel Castells. Looking at census data from 1979, 1983 and 1988, Gittleman and Howell discovered a rapid growth in both low-wage (contingent) service jobs and in the demand for professional and technical workers. In other words, the US job structure had become 'more bifurcated', with a decline in 'middle-class' jobs and a redistribution of employment 'towards the upper and lower ends of the job quality spectrum'.[7] And when he looked at the employment figures for the 1990s, Castells also identified 'a simultaneous increase of the upper and lower levels of the occupational structure'. Using the estimates published by the Bureau of Labor Statistics for the period 1992–2005, he found that the shares of employment for professionals and for service workers are expected to increase by 1.8 and 1.5 percentage points respectively. Since these two groups together account for about half of total job growth, 'they tend to concentrate jobs at both ends of the occupational ladder: 6.2 million new professional workers, and 6.5 million new service workers whose earnings in 1992 were about 40 per cent below the average for all occupational groups'.[8]

In Britain, over the past thirty years, we have seen a similar reduction in the prospects of upward mobility within careers. At the beginning of the post-war era, large parts of the professional and semi-professional workforce still maintained 'apprentice-type' entry systems. As Jonathan Gershuny puts it: 'dentists and lawyers, as well as social workers and engineering technicians and nurses, could enter these occupations directly, without tertiary level qualifications, and often without completed secondary education'. But over the next three decades the drive towards professionalisation (which emphasised formal educational qualifications) led to a rapid increase in 'career immobility'.[9] Using data drawn from the 1986 Social Change and Economic Life Initiative (SCELI), Gershuny compared the career paths of people fifteen years after they first entered the workforce. As shown in

Table 4.1 The percentage of men who started their working lives in an occupational category that they were still in fifteen years later

	Entry cohort 1941–50	Entry cohort 1951–60	Entry cohort 1961–70
Professional	0.11	0.13	0.37
Semi-professional	0.09	0.09	0.50
Skilled manual	0.08	0.31	0.41
Unskilled manual	0.15	0.22	0.43

Source: Gershuny (1993, Table 6.4)

Table 4.1, among men whose working life first started in the 1940s, only one in ten of the professionals had started out in this category, the rest had worked their way up. By contrast, a third of the professionals whose working life began during the 1960s had always been professionals. And, as it became harder to work one's way into a professional or semi-professional occupation, 'upward mobility from the manual occupations into these higher status occupations was severely curtailed'.[10]

Lovering described internal labour markets in the Britain of the late 1980s as being in decline in both large manufacturing companies and the public sector. Employers were moving from broad and long promotion ladders to more segmented and 'truncated' internal labour markets.[11] Internal labour markets were also in decline in the service industries. Examples included banks, building societies and insurance companies. While there were signs that new internal labour markets were emerging the indications were that 'they would not be comparable in length or breadth to those which were manifestly disappearing within large manufacturing companies and the public sector'. As Britain moved through the late 1980s and into the 1990s, the growing emphasis on formal educational qualifications and the de-layering of occupational hierarchies reduced, still further, the opportunities for intra-organisational career progression.[12]

In the US insurance industry, research by Scott *et al.* shows that the flattening of organisational hierarchies has led to a slowing of career progression, more sideways job moves, fewer promotion opportunities and rising intra-company pay inequality. Batt's study of the telecommunications sector suggests that internal labour markets have been devalued by managerial and supervisory job cuts, more lateral job moves and the broadening of managerial roles. And MacDuffie's study of the automotive industry indicates that, over the last two decades, in addition to downsizing their corporate workforce, the big three manufacturers have sought to reduce vertical layers of white-collar staff and increase horizontal, cross-functional, activity.[13] For some commentators, the breaking of traditional career ladders undermines the whole notion of career 'success' as synonymous with upward mobility in organisation hierarchies.[14]

Disappearing pathways

The evidence from the JIWIS survey is consistent with the trends described above. Indeed, a striking feature of the JIWIS survey was the diverse range of organisations in which the de-layering of management grades and reorganisation of hierarchies had occurred. For example, if we look at the financial services industry, we find that both of the organisations in this sector had implemented substantial de-layering programmes. In the foreign-owned company, 'section heads' had been replaced by 'team leaders' and 190 management roles had been eliminated (with the exception of jobs labelled as 'higher value'). The British-owned company had also eliminated many job titles, as a reduction in its managerial population accompanied the closure of area offices and the devolution of managerial responsibilities to its branches.

De-layering was also a feature of other private service sector organisations. In the independent food retailer, managerial hierarchies had been flattened by the elimination of both senior and middle management positions; and those who retained their jobs had been encouraged to participate in a 'multi-functioning managers' initiative. Elsewhere, occupational grades and titles had been reduced in the independent retailer of travel services and the components manufacturer had taken out four layers of management. Reductions in the number of management levels had also occurred in both the building materials and food and drinks manufacturers. And, in three out of four of the manufacturing organisations, de-layering had been accompanied by the introduction of team working and team leaders.[15] Meanwhile, in the large utilities company, an eradication of job titles was taking place across the workforce, with employees recurrently re-applying for (and re-competing for) their reorganised jobs.

Nor were these processes restricted to the commercial sector. In fact, the de-layering of middle management had been one of the principle objectives of the voluntary early retirement scheme implemented by the government agency. And, as the number of middle-level 'supervisory' grades was reduced, there was a redistribution of control and authority: upwards to senior managers and downwards to line managers. Elsewhere, one of the providers of educational services had reduced the number of senior managers by 25 per cent and slashed the number of middle managers by more than 90 per cent (from thirty-four to two). The public corporation supplying communication services had also de-layered management grades as part of a countrywide restructuring of its workforce.

Across the organisations that participated in the JIWIS, the result of these changes was an erosion of conventional promotion opportunities, particularly when the organisation was slimming down the overall size of its workforce. As shown in Figure 4.1, despite the large number of employees reporting an increase in their job skills and variety of tasks, more than a quarter of employees reported that their promotion prospects had

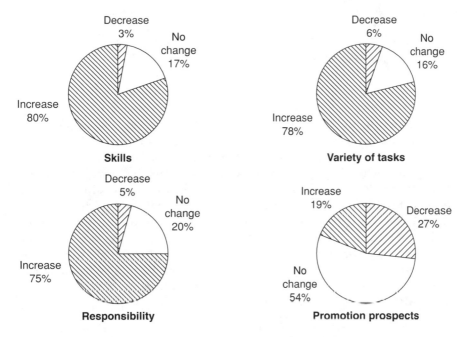

Figure 4.1 The percentage of employees experiencing a change in their jobs
with respect to skills, variety of tasks, responsibility and promotion
(over the past 5 years)

decreased over the past five years. Altogether, 39 per cent of respondents
were dissatisfied with their promotion prospects and 41 per cent said that,
given the chance, they would like to change their position within their
organisation. The following quotations help to illustrate this theme.

> Because of the responsibility that I carry now, I would probably be
> in for a supervisor's job in another workplace. But here they have
> eradicated this job role.
>
> (Mechanical/electrical repairer, utilities)

> Three out of six operational managers went in the redundancy exercise
> . . . in the past there were one or two jobs in the company that 15 to 20
> operational managers could apply for. Now they have to move compa-
> nies to progress further, or make a sideways move as I have just done.
>
> (Operational manager, transport sector)

The large government agency serves as a particularly good illustration
of the tensions generated by the decline in promotion opportunities. The
senior management told us that there had been a heavy investment in
skills, training and development and that one of the key functions of this
investment was to tell people 'that they are responsible for their own

career development'. But, as you may recall, this organisation had also implemented a programme of voluntary early retirement, rather than re-dundancy, geared to making stark reductions in the middle management workforce and several of the less senior managers described how access to middle management (team leader) posts had been severely constrained.

One manager noted that she had good staff to whom 'nothing could be offered' whilst another said that he was unable to make permanent ap-pointments to middle management positions because the organisation was using temporary contracts to cover vacancies at this level. In fact, one of the managers we interviewed had been on a 'temporary' promotion for four years. While happy in his present post he felt the organisation was trying to force people to transfer to other work locations with the inten-tion of forcing them to resign. And another manager confirmed that, despite the changes which had already taken place, the organisation was still perceived as 'top heavy' and that 'the only way to get rid of people is through an early retirement scheme . . . or hope that people will resign'. Further down the hierarchy, several people below the middle management level reported their jobs had been downgraded because of cost pressures, as illustrated in the following quotations:

> because so much of the work is done on the computer they've down-graded the jobs and that's happened all the way down. The process is completely changed. But it's not just new technology, it's also cutbacks which have resulted in downgrading. The job I am doing now was at a higher grade when I started.
>
>   (White-collar worker, government agency)

> I was downgraded . . . because of lack of funds.
>
>   (White-collar worker, government agency)

Elsewhere in the JIWIS we encountered other employees who also felt that their career prospects were being threatened by workforce restructur-ing. Perceived barriers to promotion included access to training and pat-terns of working-time. For example, in the large independent utilities company, tanker drivers linked their lack of promotion prospects to the growing emphasis on 'measurable' rather than 'tacit' skills. Their stories neatly illustrate the way in which changes in the working environment, other than de-layering, may influence perceptions of promotion prospects (even if those prospects had previously been very limited). Redundancies and work restructuring in the organisation had required them to undergo 'personal qualities training', where their knowledge was tested as part of the process of re-applying for jobs. One of the tanker drivers felt he couldn't apply for other jobs in the organisation as he was excluded from personal qualities training. Another driver felt that he needed to do evening classes to secure promotion, but also felt unable to do so because of the long hours he was working.

But, if the restructuring of employment hierarchies has eliminated many of the traditional routes to upward mobility, it has also opened up (a few) new possibilities for promotion. Take the independent food retailer, for example. On the one hand, we spoke to a store manager who told us that while he had worked his way up from being a trolley boy to a store manager, this pathway had disappeared as managers were now all graduate and A-level intakes. On the other hand, when the company introduced its 'multi-functioning managers' initiative, it developed some new 'unconventional' career paths. For instance, by encouraging the 'cross-training' of managers, it had allowed for greater mobility between the engineering side of the business and store management: a development which was welcomed by several of the interviewees we spoke to.

Other organisations in the JIWIS revealed the same pattern: a large group of employees for whom the reorganisation of occupational hierarchies was experienced as a threat to their prospects for career progress *and* a small group for whom it opened up new employment opportunities. Some examples of the latter can be found in the following quotations drawn from three of the organisations where de-layering had occurred, accompanied by the introduction of new working methods and technologies:

[describing promotion from clerk typist to admin assistant] I filled a vacant position in another department when there wasn't enough work in my previous department due to downsizing. Typing jobs have disappeared due to computers for word processing . . .
(White-collar worker, components manufacturer)

I have moved up the ladder. Team leaders were created as a result of the [organisational] changes, which involved country-wide restructuring in which the section heads' job title disappeared. It involved both restructuring and redundancies.
(White-collar worker, large financial services company)

[when the company was taken over] there was a marked change towards team-working and engineers started to be involved in the management process. The culture has changed. We went from multi-level to just a few levels. That's when I applied for this team leader job.
(Engineer/team leader, food and drinks manufacturer)

Nonetheless, even among these 'upwardly mobile' employees, the shifting nature of job contents and job ladders meant that promotion could often be experienced as a curse rather than a blessing. For example, one newly promoted manager and 'team leader' in the financial services sector found that the shift away from technical to managerial work an unhappy and debilitating experience. He, and indeed several of his colleagues, wanted to leave the organisation feeling tired of the pressure, relentless introduction of new initiatives and low morale. And, in some cases, the negative associations attached to the role of 'team leader' were even stronger. Take, for example, the craftsman from the food and drinks manufacturer who turned down the offer of a 'promotion' because:

> They are aiming to make my team a leaderless team. My job has really expanded. I have taken on a lot more responsibility. If I was going to be promoted it would have to be out of engineering. I applied for a job as a production technologist last year but didn't have the experience; but [was] offered a chance as a trainee team-leader instead. I turned this down because I prefer being an engineer rather than managing people.
>
> (Engineer, food and drinks manufacturer)

More generally, we came across a variety of people who did not want promotion because of the extra responsibility that it would involve and others who felt that promotion meant extra workload rather than extra responsibility. A number of women and mothers working part-time did not want promotion because the additional responsibility might encroach on their family lives (and promotion structures were in any case geared to full-time labour market participation).

Hence, while many of the employees we spoke to suggested that the competition for career progression had become more intense – and that employee frustrations had grown because of this – the implications for each individual varied according to the importance they attached to promotion: what it 'meant' to them, how keen they were to stay with their present employer and how confident they were of their ability to secure a better job with a different employer. In other words, the importance attached to securing promotion, or having a readily identifiable and *accessible* career path, was dependent on each person's specific work orientation. In their working lives, and at different stages of those lives, individuals may place a high or low priority on promotion as a life goal. In some cases, promotion may not be welcomed because the potential losses (in terms of increased stress and responsibility) may outweigh the gains (in terms of personal development and greater income). Or, to take another example, an employee whose skills are not readily 'transferable' from one organisation to another, might resent the loss of internal promotion opportunities more keenly than their more mobile counterparts.

Threatened by inequality

When employees describe what makes a job 'good' or 'bad' they mention job security, good working hours, control over the pace and flow of work, and the opportunity for career progression. But they also emphasise the importance of doing 'a fair day's work for a fair day's pay'. And yet, over the past twenty years, the growth in wage inequality – which has taken place across the OECD – has made it increasingly difficult for many workers to sustain the belief that their labours have been adequately and *justly* rewarded.

In their review of US earnings levels, Frank Levy and Richard Murnane describe the period between the onset of the Great Depression and the early 1950s as a 'golden age', a '20-year period in which inequality declined sharply'. And although this trend slowed down in the 1960s and 1970s it was not until the 1980s that wage inequality began to rise again.[16] And yet the widening of earnings disparities which took place during the 1980s was large enough to wipe out all the gains made in the previous four decades. The hourly earnings of a full-time worker in the ninetieth percentile of the US earnings distribution[17] relative to a worker in the tenth percentile grew by 20 per cent for men and 25 per cent for women between 1979 and 1989, leaving the US with an overall wage dispersion[18] greater than at any time since 1940.[19] And as the country moved into the 1990s wage disparities continued to grow. Using data drawn from the Current Population Survey (CPS), Bernstein and Mishel show that wage inequality grew steadily through 1986, flattened from 1986 to 1990 but rose sharply again from 1993 to 1996.[20] As shown in Figure 4.2, when they compared the annualised percentage change in the Gini coefficients[21] over the business cycles covered by their analysis, 1979–89 and 1989–96, the rate of increase during the 1990s was even larger than that during the 1980s.

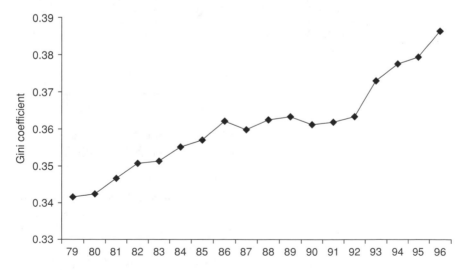

Figure 4.2 Trends in income inequality in the US, all workers, 1979–96

Source: Bernstein and Mishel (1997, Table 4; the coefficient is calculated on the basis of hourly wages)

Table 4.2 International changes in wage inequality (male workers)

	Annualised change	90/10 ratio	
		Late 1970s and early 1980s	Mid-1990s
US	7.3	3.18	4.35
Ireland	6.7	4.07	4.54
Britain	5.4	2.45	3.31
Canada	2.4	3.46	3.77
Italy	2.2	2.29	2.64
Australia	1.3	2.74	2.94
Japan	1.2	2.59	2.77
Sweden	0.7	2.11	2.20
Finland	0.6	2.44	2.53
Germany	(1.3)	2.38	2.25

Source: Machin (1999, Table 11.3)

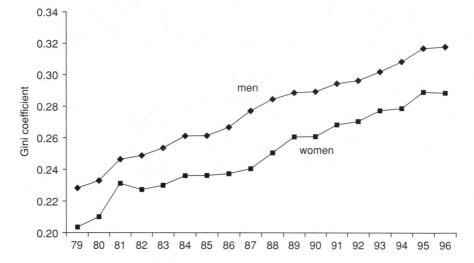

Figure 4.3 Trends in income inequality in the UK, by sex, 1979–96

Source: Machin (1999, Table 11.1; the coefficient is calculated on the basis of hourly wages)

As shown in Table 4.2, the US was not the only 'advanced' country to have experienced a growth in earnings inequality during the 1980s. Here in Britain, the data from the New Earnings Survey shows a rapid rise in earnings inequality between 1979 and 1989, with the Gini coefficient for male hourly wages rising by 26 per cent during this decade (Figure 4.3). And wage inequality continued to rise during the 1990s (albeit at a slower pace than in the 1980s) reaching levels higher than at any time since the nineteenth century.[22]

In the mid-1980s, when this trend towards inequality was starting to become apparent, Alfie Kohn published a book entitled *No Contest: The Case Against Competition*; this cut across the grain of the neo-liberal ideology which dominated the closing decades of the twentieth century. He wryly noted that 'at one end of the spectrum there are countries that thrive without any competition at all. At the other end is the United States.' Speaking as an American, he observed how:

> Our economic system is predicated on competition, while our school-ing, from the earliest grades, trains us not only to triumph over others but to regard them as obstacles to our own success. Not only do we get carried away with competitive activities, but we turn almost everything else into a contest. Our collective creativity seems to be tied up in devising new ways to produce winners and losers . . . No corner of our lives is too trivial – or too important – to be exempted from the compulsion to rank ourselves against one another . . . Competition is a deeply ingrained, profoundly enduring, part of our lives, and it is time to look more closely at what it does to us.[23]

Drawing on an wide range of disciplines, including sociology and social-psychology,[24] Kohn argued that although competition has tremendous productive potential it can also be highly *destructive* if it undermines the social cohesion of the communities in which we live and work. Citing the work of Paul Wachtel,[25] Kohn suggested that the *obsessional* pursuit of competition:

> entails significant costs to our health and safety, makes our working lives unhappy (for all we might gain in quality of working life as consumers, we lose as producers), fails to bring about greater equity, and actually represents a desperate and futile attempt to compensate for psychological and social deficiencies.[26]

From Kohn's perspective competition can be good for people if it brings them together and strengthens their *esprit de corps*, but not when it opens up sharp divisions of income and wealth. But at the time he published these claims, few sociologists (and even fewer economists) realised just how strong the relationship was between inequality and ill-health. Indeed it was not until the mid-1990s that many of us began to take note of the growing body of evidence showing that 'life expectancy in different coun-tries is dramatically improved where income differences are smaller and societies are more socially cohesive'.[27] As summarised in the work of Richard Wilkinson, all the epidemiological evidence suggests that among the advanced (OECD) countries, 'economic growth and further improvements in living standards have little effect on health'. These countries have al-ready moved beyond a crucial stage in economic development when living standards 'reached a threshold level adequate to ensure basic material standards for all'.[28] In these societies, what really affects people's health is no longer the *absolute* differences in material standards but the extent of *relative* deprivation. The US, for example, has a gross GDP per capita which is more than twice as high as that of Greece but life expectancy is higher in Greece.[29] As Wilkinson points out, when an American suffers from relative deprivation they suffer relative to members of their own society. They do not suffer relative to Greeks. A poor New Yorker does not feel better for knowing that she has more 'per capita income' than a middle-class Athenian. What really hurts is the pain of being deprived in comparison to our *fellow citizens*:

> There is no doubt that it is less nice to live in a home where some of the decoration is damaged by damp. Similarly, a poor diet is less palatable than a good one. But taken out of their social context, these material disadvantages in themselves count for rather little compared to the low self-esteem, insecurity, depression and anxiety which relative deprivation so often engenders. Pyscho-social factors can dominate one's consciousness and drain life of its value. What really damages the all-important subjective quality of life is having to live in circumstances which, by comparison with others, appear as a statement of one's personal failure and inferiority.[30]

Another oft-cited illustration of the link between health and equality can be found in Wilkinson's account of the rapid decline in civilian mortality rates which took place in Britain during the two world wars. As shown in Figure 4.4, in the decades which include the two world wars, civilian life expectancy increased twice as fast as the average rate of improvement during the rest of the century. How was this possible at a time when living standards had ceased to rise, when housing standards had deteriorated (especially as a result of bombing during the Second World War) and medical services were diverted from civilian use to meet the needs of wounded soldiers? The most likely explanation for this seeming paradox can be found in the dramatic narrowing of income differences which took place during this period and 'the sense of camaraderie, of people pulling together'.[31] As described by Amartya Sen, the First World War saw 'a remarkable development in social attitudes about "sharing" and in public policies aimed at achieving that sharing'. Likewise during the Second World War, which saw the development of 'unusually supportive' social arrangements related to 'the psychology of sharing in beleaguered Britain'.[32]

What makes the link between health and income distributions particularly intriguing is the suggestion that an increase in income inequality exposes all social groups (not just the poor) to feelings of relative deprivation. As described in the work of Oliver James, increased inequality,

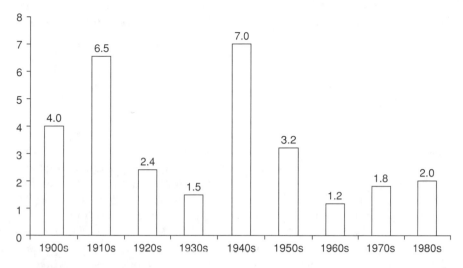

Figure 4.4 Increases in life expectancy in England and Wales each decade, 1901–91 (additional years life expectancy at birth)

Source: Sen (1999)

underpinned by an ideology of competitiveness, raises the stakes for almost everybody, creating a winner-takes-all society marked by high levels of angst. In his book entitled *Britain on the Couch: Why We're Unhappier than We Were in the 1950s Despite Being Richer,* James claims that more and more people 'feel like losers' despite the fact that the country as a whole (and most of those in the middle and upper classes) is richer than ever before. He points out that the most comprehensive study[33] of changes in depression rates reveals that, across the developed world, 25-year-olds born after the Second World War were much more likely to have suffered from a 'major depression'[34] during their lifetime than those born during the pre-war decades. Although people of 'low status' in society were most at risk, the growth in depression rates affected *all* social classes. As James put it, in a country marked by growing inequalities, even the rich and powerful can feel subordinate and inferior as the social environment becomes 'focused on winners-losers, superior-inferior, social comparison, shame and humiliation avoidance'.[35] In this context, we all 'experience death by a thousand social comparisons'.[36]

A question of justice

We have examined the link between health and social inequality and we know that the distribution of wages and income was rising in most of the OECD countries during the 1980s and 1990s. But is there a difference between certain 'kinds' of inequality? Do some inequalities hurt more than others? The evidence from the JIWIS survey suggests that it is not so much inequality *per se* which triggers feelings of resentment and depression but the kind of inequality which is perceived as *unjust* or *unmerited*.

We know from work done in the fields of industrial relations and personnel management just how important it is that people perceive pay differentials as 'legitimate'.[37] The usual pattern by which these differentials become legitimised can be described as follows: organisational pay relativities and 'rates for the job' become norms; and these norms then become embedded in custom and practice and in notions of what constitutes a 'fair day's work for a fair day's pay'. And it is precisely because reward and effort levels are 'socially located and socially determined' that the sudden changing of pay differentials can have such damaging consequences, particularly if they are perceived to be unfair. As Brown *et al.* emphasise, a 'particularly demanding management skill is achieving an acceptable level of stability when changing circumstances alter what is acceptable'.[38] Bad management of payment systems can lead to perceptions of unfair treatment, thereby contributing to the demotivation and demoralisation of a workforce. It is a question of both procedural and distributional justice.

It is this emphasis on legitimacy – on the importance of receiving a fair day's pay for a fair day's work – which characterised the way in which our respondents talked about the pay differentials within their organisations and industries. Alongside experiencing an increase in the pace of work, work intensification, many employees felt that they were being inadequately rewarded for their labours. As illustrated in Figure 4.1 (the pie charts presented earlier), 79 per cent of employees said that their job skills had increased in the last five years and 78 per cent reported an increase in the variety of tasks. On the other hand, 56 per cent of the employees felt they were getting paid less than they deserved. But when we asked employees to explain why their pay was 'less than they deserved' only 24 per cent of the explanations explicitly referred to interpersonal comparisons. Instead, most of the respondents who felt unhappy with their pay said they did so because of their 'responsibility and accountability', the intensity of their workload, the length of their working hours and the effort they put into their jobs (Table 4.3). They were challenging the legitimacy of pay norms in the context of changing job content, functions and intensity. In other words, they felt that they were not getting a fair day's pay for a fair day's work – their contribution was not being adequately recognised. A further indication of the frustration of a sizeable minority was that of the 167 respondents who felt that they were paid somewhat less or much less than they deserved, 44 per cent were dissatisfied or completely dissatisfied with their promotion prospects, while only 28 per cent were satisfied or completely satisfied.

The following quotes illustrate some of the reasons why people, in a broad range of occupations, questioned the legitimacy of their wages and salaries:

Table 4.3 Reasons why employees think their pay is less than they deserve (% of *total* responses)

In comparison to other people	24
In view of my responsibilities and accountability	18
In light of my workload	14
In relation to my education and skills	12
When you consider the hours I work	7
Relative to the effort I put in	5

Because the job I'm doing is about half the job of the next one up.
(Clerical officer, financial services sector)

Because I am doing a managerial and a clinical practitioner's job. Restructuring has wiped out middle management jobs.
(Health professional)

Because of the tasks and responsibilities involved – you get more put on you all the time.
(Manual worker, private construction company)

Because of the kind of work that I'm doing, I'm entitled to more – this is linked to multi-skilling.
(Manual worker, building materials manufacturer)

The work rate has increased. Stress levels have increased. Responsibility has increased. The money has not increased to meet job demands.
(Manual worker, building materials manufacturer)

Because over the last five or six years with [this organisation] we've taken on a lot more work, a lot of devolved work. And we've stayed at the same grade and with the same pay.
(White-collar worker, government agency)

Because I work very hard, I am totally stressed out.
(Clerical officer, financial services sector)

Because they have given us all these extra jobs. The MD takes home £280,000 a year. This is not fair, he does nothing.
(Clerical officer, large utilities company)

In summary, many employees questioned the 'distributional justice' of their working conditions. They felt that they had been the losers in an environment which required them to take on more responsibilities without a commensurate increase in financial reward.[39]

5 Job insecurity and work intensification

The effects on health and well-being

Ines Wichert

As we saw in Chapters 3 and 4, many countries (and Britain in particular) have witnessed a sharp increase in job insecurity and work intensification over the last twenty years. But what are the costs of these developments? A large body of international research now exists which documents the effects of both work pressure and job insecurity on the individual's psychological health and well-being. We will review this evidence, including the findings from our own study, and examine what makes the experience of job insecurity and work intensification so stressful. We will also look at a number of factors which seem to moderate people's reactions to these phenomena.

In this chapter we are primarily concerned with the effects of job insecurity and work intensification on *psychological well-being*, which Van Vuuren *et al.* define as an umbrella term for a number of emotional and cognitive states, including a person's mental health, happiness, work and life satisfaction.[1] Signs of decreased psychological well-being can include increased levels of anxiety and depression, a sense of uselessness, lack of self-confidence, and dissatisfaction with oneself and one's environment.[2] In studies of job insecurity and work intensification, psychological well-being is measured with a wide range of self-report scales and indicators. Examples include the General Health Questionnaire (GHQ), the SCL-90-R (a global measure of health), life satisfaction measures, *general* anxiety and depression measures, as well as more specific measures such as job satisfaction and *work-related* depression and anxiety.

The majority of research in this area is conducted in a stressor-stress-strain framework, where job insecurity and work intensification are conceptualised as the *stressor*, or source of stress, which can lead to the experience of *stress*, which in turn can lead to psychological, behavioural or physiological *strains*. Within this framework, the emphasis is on the *psychological* nature of stress, a term which Lazarus and Folkman define as: 'a particular relationship between the person and the environment that is appraised by the person as taxing or exceeding his or her resources and endangering his or her well-being'.[3] This psychological reading of stress has now gained widespread acceptance.[4]

Job insecurity and psychological health

Most studies of the relationship between insecurity and psychological health are of a cross-sectional nature and show that increased levels of job insecurity are related to decreased levels of psychological well-being. For example, in a sample of 201 employees from two US manufacturing companies, Kuhnert *et al.* found that perceptions of insecurity were positively related to increased levels of depression, anxiety, obsessive-compulsiveness and anger-hostility, as well as to increased difficulties in interpersonal relationships and increased somatic complaints such as headaches, aches and pains, numbness and weakness.[5] Negative effects of job insecurity have also been found with respect to job dissatisfaction in a sample of US MBA students, various psychosomatic complaints in an Israeli and a Dutch sample, depression in a sample of 187 black gold miners in South Africa, and sleep disturbances in a sample of Swedish shipyard workers.[6] But these studies are all based on different occupational groups and are not representative of the working population as a whole.

A more representative sample is available through the British Household Panel Study (BHPS). The BHPS is a longitudinal survey of 5,000 randomly selected British households, in which all adult members in each household were interviewed about various aspects of their working lives over five 'waves' of data collection (between 1990 and 1995). In an analysis of the BHPS data, Burchell reports that for each of the five data collection waves, there was a highly significant, positive relationship between satisfaction with job security and psychological well-being, as assessed by the GHQ.[7] And this relationship was still present even when demographic variables and other aspects of job satisfaction had been controlled for. However, it was found that the relationship between satisfaction with job security and psychological well-being was weaker for women in part-time employment, and that respondents with higher levels of education were more susceptible to the effects of job insecurity. This means that when respondents with higher levels of education felt secure, they had better health than those with lower levels of education, but when they felt insecure their reported health was worse.

Another study based on a large data set is Burchell's analysis of the Social Change and Economic Life Initiative (SCELI) dataset which addressed a wide range of labour-market experiences.[8] Burchell found that, across the sample, perceived job insecurity had a direct effect on GHQ scores. Interestingly, when the sample was broken down into five subgroups on the basis of labour-market experience, the two most advantaged and secure groups had the best psychological well-being, while respondents termed 'labour market descenders', who were characterised by their lack of perceived job security, had the worst GHQ scores. In fact, their GHQ scores were not significantly different to the GHQ scores of the unemployed respondents in the sample.

Further insights into the relationship between job insecurity and psychological well-being can be gained from the study conducted by Amick *et al.* Using questionnaire responses from 33,689 female nurses in the US, the study found that the negative (health) effects of intense work pressures were exacerbated by job insecurity.[9] This means that work pressures were more likely to damage the respondents' health if they were also feeling highly insecure. Hence, not only is job insecurity *per se* a significant source of stress, it also exaggerates the stressful effects of excessive work pressures. We will talk more about the effects of high workloads in the second part of this chapter.

The principal measure of psychological well-being which we used in our own (JIWIS) study was the 12-item General Health Questionnaire (GHQ-12), a measure of mild symptoms of anxiety and depression.[10] It is widely used in organisational psychology, having been shown, in a variety of studies, to be a valid method of detecting harmful levels of stress and a good predictor, not only of a wide range of physical illnesses, but also of rates of premature mortality. We also used Warr's Work-related Well-being Scale to assess positive and negative 'affect at work'.[11] Finally, we included a measure on hours of sleep, as other studies have shown a link between stress and sleep problems. For the purposes of the analyses in this chapter, job insecurity was measured with a 6-item scale[12] which had a high Cronbach's alpha (α) value of 0.89, suggesting that the items do indeed form a valid unidimensional scale. Work intensification was assessed with a 3-item scale which also had a high Cronbach α value of 0.78. Table 5.1 lists the items in both these scales alongside the questions used in the GHQ-12 and in the Warr scale of positive and negative 'affect'.

When we applied these scales to the data contained in the JIWIS survey, we found that job insecurity was significantly correlated with GHQ as well as with both negative and positive affect at work (see Table 5.2 in the following section). This was not unexpected; as we have already seen in this chapter, similar results have been found in numerous other studies of job insecurity, using both cross-sectional as well as longitudinal methods and a wide variety of outcome measures such as levels of depression, anxiety, sleep disturbances, negative mood and job dissatisfaction.

The problem with cross-sectional evidence is that the causal direction of a relationship cannot be established unequivocally. While it is generally accepted that increased levels of job insecurity lead to decreased levels of psychological well-being, it is plausible to argue that decreased psychological well-being might lead to an increased subjective perception of job insecurity. The affected employee might fear that her decreased health status could make her the next on the list for redundancy. There are, however, a growing number of longitudinal studies which support the findings from the cross-sectional studies mentioned earlier. One of these studies, the Whitehall II study, is of particular interest because it constitutes a 'natural experiment' in that baseline data were collected in a

Table 5.1 Overview of independent, moderator and dependent variables used in the JIWI study

Stressor/Independent variables	Moderator variables	Outcome/Dependent variables
1. Job insecurity • I am confident that I will continue to have a job with my present employer • In my opinion I will keep my job in the near future • In my opinion I will be employed for a long time in my present job • I believe that my career is secure • How certain are you that you will NOT be laid off from your job some time in the future? • How certain are you about your job security with your organisation?	**1. Social support** • Emotional support from supervisor • Emotional support from other people at work • Instrumental support from supervisor • Instrumental support from other people at work • Appraisal support from supervisor • Appraisal support from other people at work • Informational support from supervisor • Informational support from other people at work	**1. GHQ** 'Have you recently . . .' • Been able to concentrate on whatever you are doing? • Lost much sleep over worry? • Felt that you were playing a useful part in things? • Felt capable of making decisions about things? • Felt constantly under strain? • Felt you couldn't overcome your difficulties? • Been able to enjoy your normal day-to-day activities
2. Work intensification • How much pressure do you feel from managers and supervisors? • How much pressure do you feel from work-mates and colleagues? • How much pressure do you feel from the sheer quantity of work?		• Been able to face up to problems? • Been feeling unhappy or depressed? • Been losing confidence in yourself? • Been thinking of yourself as a worthless person? • Been feeling reasonably happy, all things considered? **2. Positive affect at work** 'How much of the time has your work made you feel the following' •Cheerful, •Enthusiastic, •Contented, •Relaxed, •Calm, •Optimistic **3. Negative affect at work** 'How much of the time has your work made you feel the following' •Tense, •Miserable, •Worried, •Depressed, •Uneasy, •Gloomy

period of job security, and repeat data were gathered when one department had come under threat as a result of privatisation plans.[13] In this study, Ferrie *et al.* investigated the effects of job insecurity on London-based civil servants. The initial screening showed that the employees in the departments which were to be privatised (unknown to the employees) reported better health overall than those in the other departments. However, once the privatisation plans and the threat to jobs had been announced, the affected employees reported an overall deterioration in health compared to the employees who were not affected by the privatisation plans. This deterioration in health was significant with respect to self-rated general health, the number of symptoms experienced over the previous two weeks and the number of health problems reported over the past year.

Longitudinal studies serve not only to confirm cross-sectional evidence, but also to investigate the effects of chronic job insecurity, where job insecurity is experienced over a prolonged period of time, sometimes over a number of years. It could be argued that harmful stress is most likely where there has been a sudden and unexpected reduction in job security, and that employees might adjust to persistent insecure work without any negative consequences for health and well-being. An alternative view, however, suggested by current models of stress, would be that persistently high levels of insecurity are more likely to result in illness as the individual's capacity to cope with the stressor becomes exhausted over time.[14] The empirical evidence indicates that the latter is the case: prolonged experience of job insecurity leads to increasingly impaired psychological well-being. For example, Heaney *et al.* examined the effects of job insecurity in a sample of 207, mainly male, automobile manufacturing workers in the US and found that chronic job insecurity was predictive of changes in job satisfaction and physical symptoms over time, over and above the effects of job insecurity at any one time.[15] Likewise, Burchell, using BHPS data, found that the well-being of those in insecure work continued to decline throughout the period of insecurity, a finding which is generally not reproduced among the unemployed for whom deterioration tended to cease after a period of about six months.[16]

These findings from both cross-sectional and longitudinal studies are a powerful demonstration that, under certain circumstances, being in employment can be as stressful, if not more stressful, as being unemployed.[17] To quote from Ferrie *et al.*: 'the increasing levels of job insecurity, created by changes in the nature of employment relationships, may lead to greater ill-health in the general population, beyond the direct effects of unemployment'.[18]

Work intensification and psychological health

Different terms, all measuring essentially the same construct of 'having too much work to do' can be found in the occupational stress literature since the 1960s: 'work overload', 'high job demands' and 'role overload' are the most frequently used terms. For example, Winnubst *et al.* define work overload as 'the degree to which employees, in the course of their job, have to deal with too high work demands, which force them to make use of reserve capacities'.[19] The literature also makes a distinction between the *qualitative* and *quantitative* aspects of a person's workload. The former relates to the difficulty and complexity of their work, whereas the latter refers to the amount of work they have to do.[20] Overloading on both these dimensions is associated with stress;[21] but in this chapter we are primarily concerned with the effects of quantitative work overload: having too much to do, in too little time, at too high a pace, with too few resources.

A demanding job can be seen as challenging and can often increase job satisfaction. But studies from around the world show that when jobs become too demanding, leading to pressure and work overload, they exert a detrimental effect on our psychological health and well-being. As Warr reports in his review of the literature, high workloads have been found to be negatively associated with job satisfaction and positively associated with job-related anxiety, exhaustion and work-related depression. The literature also reveals an association between high job demands and general, context-free, measures of well-being such as decreased life satisfaction, increased general distress, high levels of somatic complaints such as upset stomach and sleep difficulties, increased neurotic symptoms, higher incidence of recent minor neurosis (anxiety, depression, obsessionality and hysteria), raised levels of anxiety and context-free exhaustion and depression.[22]

Other studies confirm the findings cited in Warr's review. Hardy *et al.* examined fatigue and fatigability in 1,906 male and 5,703 female NHS staff. They assessed a number of stressors including 'work demands' – which was conceptualised as the extent to which individuals have the time and resources to carry out their job – and found that high work demands and 'role conflict' were the only two stressors (out of ten different stressors assessed) which significantly predicted high levels of fatigue. They also found that high work demands were sufficient to explain occupational and gender differences in fatigue.[23] Similar results were obtained by De Jonge and Schaufeli in their study of 1,437 nurses and nurses' aides for whom job demands were significantly related to job-related anxiety and job-related depression.[24] Work overload was also associated with both increased psychological distress and decreased job satisfaction in a sample of 104 Australian public sector employees;[25] with distress as assessed by the SCL-90-R (a frequency of symptoms measure) in a sample of 300 American dual-earner couples;[26] with emotional exhaustion in a sample of 156 Dutch nurses[27] and with the total number of symptoms reported in a sample of blue-collar, non-managerial workers in a large manufacturing plant in the US.[28]

Table 5.2 Spearman's rho correlations between work intensification/job insecurity and psychological well-being measures

		GHQ[1]	Negative[2] affect at work	Positive[3] affect at work	Hours of[4] sleep
Job insecurity[5]	Correlation	.117*	.271**	−.284**	−.098
	Sig. (2-tailed)	.045	.000	.000	.098
Work intensification[6]	Correlation	.375**	.410**	−.239**	−.149**
	Sig. (2-tailed)	.000	.000	.000	.007

Notes
1 Low GHQ scores indicate good psychological well-being
2 Low Negative Affect at Work scores indicate bad psychological well-being at work
3 Low Positive Affect at Work scores indicate good psychological well-being at work
4 Low Hours of Sleep score indicate low hours of sleep
5 Low Job Insecurity scores indicate low job insecurity
6 Low Work Intensification scores indicate high pressure

Nor are the costs of work overload confined to those in low-waged occupations. On the contrary, Warr's review shows that high workloads, extreme time pressure and deadlines are often mentioned by those in managerial and professional occupations.[29] And, in a recent survey of 819 managers for the Institute of Management, Wheatley reports that 42 per cent of respondents strongly agreed or agreed that they sometimes feel unable to cope with their workloads and that 40 per cent strongly agreed or agreed that they struggle to meet work goals and targets.[30]

In our own (JIWIS) survey, we discovered a strong relationship between work intensification and the three outcome measures: GHQ-12, positive affect at work and negative affect at work. Indeed, work intensification showed an even stronger link to our psychological outcome measures than job insecurity (see Table 5.2). We also found that pressure at work was associated with fewer hours of sleep which, in turn, is often associated with poor psychosomatic or psychological well-being. Once again, these findings are consistent with the literature as well as with many of the statements of respondents in our open-ended interviews, such as this comment from a finance manager with a staff of five:

> I think the stress at the moment is the fact that every day we go into work in the morning, and when we finish work at night, I always tend to draw up a list of what to do tomorrow, jobs which if 50 per cent get done you've achieved something.

New analyses of data from the European Survey on Working Conditions (ESWC) suggest that the physical health of employees is suffering too. The survey, of 1,000 employees in each of the EU countries, asked respondents whether their work affected their health. Analyses of the

Table 5.3 Proportion of sample experiencing work-related complaints, by speed of work and tightness of deadlines (bold indicates doubling of rate)

	Working at very high speed		Working to tight deadlines	
	all or almost all of time	25% of time or less	all or almost all of time	25% of time or less
Nature of problem caused by work				
Ear problems	9.5	4.9	9.4	5.0
Eye problems	12.6	6.8	12.6	6.8
Skin problems	**8.7**	**4.2**	8.1	4.6
Backache	40.0	22.9	36.8	24.6
Headaches	**21.3**	**9.6**	19.0	11.0
Stomach ache	**7.3**	**3.1**	**6.9**	**3.2**
Muscular pains in arms or legs	**27.2**	**13.5**	23.4	15.5
Respiratory difficulties	5.6	3.1	5.2	3.6
Stress	**41.2**	**20.5**	39.8	21.6
Overall fatigue	28.4	14.3	23.4	16.9
Sleeping problems	**10.0**	**4.9**	**10.1**	**5.0**
Allergies	5.1	3.0	5.1	3.1
Heart disease	1.7	0.9	**1.9**	**0.8**
Anxiety	**10.4**	**5.1**	9.9	5.3
Irritability	15.4	7.8	**15.8**	**7.8**
Personal problems	**5.1**	**2.2**	4.7	2.4
Others (spontaneously)	1.5	1.3	1.5	1.4
None	31.1	51.6	34.6	49.5

Source: European Survey on Working Conditions

different patterns of health-related illnesses for those who work at speed 'all of the time' or 'almost all of the time', compared with those who only have to work at speed about a quarter of their time or less, showed that pressure to work at speed increased employees' susceptibility to every single illness recorded, from backaches to heart problems. As shown in Table 5.3, many illnesses and complaints were more than twice as common among those working at continuous high speed, including headaches, stomach aches, muscular pains in limbs, skin problems, stress, fatigue, insomnia, anxiety and personal problems. Similarly, those working to tight deadlines all or most of the time were more than twice as likely to experience stomach aches, insomnia, heart disease and irritability compared to those working to deadlines less than 25 per cent of the time.

Other studies point to the *long-term* health effects of work intensification. Warr cites several studies on work overload which reported *chronic* associations between high workloads and hypertension, gastric complaints and nervous trouble, headaches and slight nervous disturbances, increased consumption of tranquillisers and sleeping tablets and increased risk of coronary heart disease.[31] Rystedt and Johansson examined the effects of subjective workload in a longitudinal sample of fifty-two full-time Swedish bus drivers[32] and found that changes in workload between time 1 and time 2 had a significant impact on psychosomatic complaints at time 2 after controlling for psychosomatic complaints at time 1. In their analysis of the Whitehall II Study, Stansfeld *et al.* also report a longitudinal association between high job demands and increased risk of psychiatric disorder.[33]

The research reviewed in this chapter shows a fairly consistent pattern of results, pointing to the detrimental impact of the experiences of both job insecurity and work intensification on psychological well-being. But it must also be acknowledged that some of this research suffers from methodological weakness and that, in many cases, the studies report only modest statistical correlations. Moreover, a small number of studies provide conflicting evidence in that they show either no link[34] or a positive link[35] between the two sources of stress and psychological well-being. What this suggests is that further research is needed, and that there is a particular requirement for more detailed and disaggregated analysis.

What makes job insecurity and work intensification so stressful?

One of the defining characteristics of job insecurity is the experience of uncertainty and ambiguity.[36] Lazarus and Folkman talk about the stressfulness of 'event uncertainty' (i.e. uncertainty as to the likelihood of an event occurring) and argue that high levels of such uncertainty can have paralysing effects on the coping process.[37] Warr supports this position by pointing out that predictability is important for the coping process, since it allows for the nature and timing of potentially noxious events to be anticipated.[38] Ambiguity, or the lack of situational clarity, can decrease a person's feelings of control and increase feelings of helplessness. Employees who experience job insecurity do not know what to cope with, since they do not know what to expect. The lack of control over the situation does not give the worker the chance to combat the experience of job insecurity.[39] Reduced ability to plan and control one's life in the face of job insecurity may also add to the stressfulness of the experience.[40] In their study of Swedish shipyard workers, Joelson and Wahlquist found that, due to the prolonged uncertainty, the anticipatory phase (the period of insecurity) prior to job loss was perceived to be the most strenuous part of the unemployment process:

> It is a period of agony of varying strength. Rumours about possible decisions and actions are circulating. Reliable information is not available. You have to decide whether you should try to look for another job or not. Sometimes you have too little to do. You hover between hope and despair.[41]

Dekker and Schaufeli point out that certainty about one's job situation, even if it is the unpleasant certainty of having been made redundant, is less detrimental to workers' psychological well-being than a situation of prolonged job insecurity.[42] In other words, anticipation of, or concern about, future job loss may be as traumatic as unemployment itself. Event *uncertainty* may be a greater source of anxiety and tension than the event itself.[43] An additional factor identified by Jacobson is that, in contrast to unemployment, job insecurity is of minimal social visibility.[44] This means that, unless there is strong evidence of imminent job loss, the affected employee is expected to continue working 'as usual'. The insecure worker may therefore have no special status and no opportunities to express dissatisfaction or seek help, which makes the experience of insecurity all the more stressful. Furthermore, a threat to the continuation of one's job means a threat to important 'identity-forming factors' such as the provision of regular activities and the structuring of the day into working and rest periods, contact and interaction with people at work and the definition of personal status.[45] Finally, in times of economic instability and insecure employment, poor working conditions are more likely to be tolerated due to the lack of alternative jobs. And the persistence of these conditions (e.g. exposure to long hours, arduous conditions and poor quality work) adds to the stress experienced in insecure employment.[46]

If the pressures caused by job insecurity are of a 'compound' nature, the same is true of the stress caused by work intensification. As described by Winnubst *et al.*, when employees find themselves in a situation of work overload, they have to fall back on their reserve capacities, a manoeuvre which eventually leads to exhaustion and decreased performance.[47] In other words, it is not so much the short-term exposure to work overload that causes a problem but rather chronic overload, where a person has to deal with too much work over an extended period of time.[48] Winnubst *et al.* also outline another important aspect of the stressfulness of work intensification: the lack of control. When a person can no longer meet the goals set out for him or her then a loss of control over task performance ensues. This may bring on stress reactions and, ultimately, a complete breakdown of task performance. Lazarus and Folkman suggest that work overload also distorts people's capacity to appraise the value of their own talents and abilities. Beliefs of personal control can make people feel confident that they can master the challenges posed by their environment, whereas a lack of control increases a person's feeling of vulnerability and threat.[49] As described to us by an account manager in a large utilities company:

> Jobs built up that I felt I had no control over completing and I wasn't being able to – as hard as I worked, and I worked all the hours under the sun – but every day things would be added to my list that would never get done. So I ended up, well, I got stressed . . .

Moderators of reactions to job insecurity and work intensification

Conclusion

We have seen that uncertainty, ambiguity and lack of control are the factors that make job insecurity and work intensification so stressful. All three have received widespread attention in the stress literature and are recognised as impairing adequate coping. But the stress they cause does not affect everybody to the same extent. On the contrary, each of us is subject to a range of personal, social and environmental 'moderators' which influence our resilience and vulnerability, and thus our susceptibility to the adverse effects of job insecurity and work.[50] In considering the role of these moderators, we will look at the influence of demographic factors such as occupational group, gender and age. We will look at personality factors (e.g. a person's confidence and self-esteem) and workplace factors (e.g. the effect of different organisational 'cultures'). And we will also pay particular attention to the moderating role of social support, i.e. the help received from 'significant others'.

Employment grade

For higher-grade employees there is some evidence that work intensification is less stressful than for lower-grade employees.[51] Possible explanations offered for this are the extra resources available to employees in higher grades and the nature of the work being challenging. For job insecurity, on the other hand, being in a high employment grade or in a managerial position does not seem to buffer the detrimental effects on health.[52] On the contrary, there is some evidence that, due to the flattening of organisational structures and the high (salary) costs of retaining employees in higher grades, these employees are sometimes at higher risk from job insecurity.[53]

Gender

Critique

There is some evidence that men and women may react differently to job insecurity. Burchell found that on aggregate, men suffered more from the effects of job insecurity than women and Ferrie *et al.* reported that while deterioration in physical health was larger for men, deterioration in psychological health was larger for women.[54] Other studies have shown that women may take more time off work due to work intensification.[55] But there is also evidence that, in studies of both job insecurity and work intensification, the effects of gender have often been confounded with other job factors such as tenure, employment grade, pay and control at work. In studies on job insecurity,[56] where such factors are taken into account, no gender differences are reported. It is important, therefore, to have large, heterogeneous samples which allow more detailed multivariate exploration of a possible interplay between gender and other job factors.

Age

It is difficult to draw any firm conclusions on the effects of age based on the small number of studies reported here. For job insecurity, there seems to be a tendency for older employees to experience less stress in response to job insecurity.[57] Possible reasons for this are the ability to take early retirement and changes in values, needs and expectations. It has also been argued that older employees might experience more work intensification due to the introduction of new technology and the lack of training for them.[58]

Personality factors

There are mixed research findings for personality factors such as self-esteem,[59] conscientiousness,[60] type A behaviour[61] and optimistic predisposition.[62] However, one moderator which has been found to be very important, for both job insecurity and work intensification, is the individual's sense of control, in terms of both personal control and workplace control.[63] As was pointed out earlier in this chapter, perceptions of control can have a powerful impact upon the individual's self-appraisal and coping mechanisms.

Workplace factors

While the role of workplace factors such as organisational culture and structure have been acknowledged in theoretical treatments of job insecurity and work intensification,[64] very little empirical attention has been paid to these factors. Initial results indicate that such organisational factors might play an important role[65] but we still need more research, especially with regard to the effect of stress intervention efforts. The effect of workplace factors was certainly apparent in the JIWIS dataset. Take, for example, the graph drawn in Figure 5.1 which shows the relationship between the aggregate level of work intensification reported in each of the employers and aggregate stress levels. The correlation between the two variables only accounts for about 23 per cent of the variance (the relationship between aggregate levels of job insecurity and GHQ scores is even weaker). Put another way, even where two firms are experiencing similar levels of insecurity and work intensification, there may be very different levels of stress response among the employees. The cause of this unexplained variance is not clear, but organisational culture and other workplace factors are plausible candidates. While most moderator and stress intervention research focuses on the individual, this data suggests that interventions at the structural level might prove more effective.

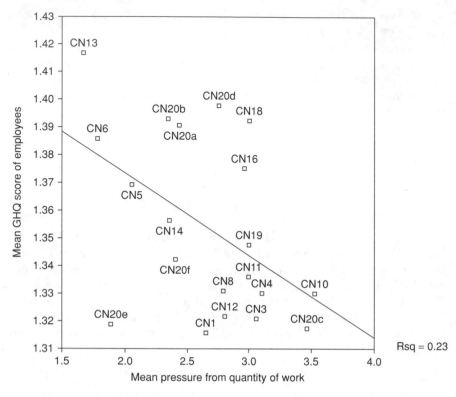

Figure 5.1 Aggregate GHQ scores by pressure from quantity of work

Note
The points on the scatter plot represent the case numbers of each organisation (for details of which see Appendix A). In this graph, case number 20 (the public provider of health services) is disaggregated into the six sites covered by the JIWIS survey (labelled 'a–f').

Social support

While the term 'social support' is widely used in everyday language, and people seem to have an intuitive feeling for what it means, there is no generally accepted definition. For example, House defines social support as 'a flow of emotional concern, instrumental aid, information and/or appraisal (information relevant to self-evaluation) between people',[66] while Thoits states that 'social support usually refers to the functions performed for the individual by significant others such as family members, friends and co-workers'.[67] But, irrespective of their definitional preferences, what unites most researchers in this area is the conviction that social support exerts a positive effect on people's health and well-being in a range of stressful situations and events.[68] House, for example, suggests three ways in which social support may alleviate the impact of work-related stress: first, social support may reduce the importance of the perception that a situation is stressful; second, it may in some way tranquillise the neuroendocrine system so that people are less reactive to perceived stress; third, it may facilitate healthy behaviours, such as exercising or getting sufficient rest.[69]

What makes social support an especially interesting moderator is the fact that, unlike other moderators (e.g. age and gender) it is amenable to change. Thus, interventions in the workplace can aim at increasing the amount of support a person receives from their supervisor and co-workers. But where, and upon whom, should these interventions be targeted? The question lies at the heart of one of the key debates in the social support literature, viz. the extent to which social support exerts a *main effect* rather than a *buffering effect* on the stressor-stress-strain process. A buffering effect is present when the relationship between the job stressor(s) and employee health is weaker in the presence of strong social support than in the presence of weak social support. The buffering hypothesis proposes that support is beneficial for well-being mainly for persons under high levels of stress. In statistical terms, a buffering effect is an interaction effect. The main effect hypothesis, on the other hand, states that social support is beneficial to health and well-being, irrespective of whether a person is under stress or not. In statistical terms, the main effect is an additive effect.

Looking at the relationship between *job insecurity* and psychological well-being, it is difficult to establish an overall trend or pattern with respect to the occurrence of main and/or buffering effects. Dekker and Schaufeli did not find any buffering effects and did not test for main effects in their sample of 105 employees of a large Australian public transport corporation.[70] Armstrong-Stassen in her samples of 200 telecommunications technicians and seventy-four production workers in Canada, found positive main effects for supervisor and co-worker support but did not test for possible buffering effects.[71] In a sample of 102 female nurses in the US, Kaufmann and Beehr found buffering effects for supervisor and co-workers' support, however the direction of all of these buffering effects was opposite to that predicted by the buffering hypothesis.[72] In other words, high support increased rather than decreased the negative effects of job insecurity on the outcome measures. Positive buffering effects of work-based social support in the experience of job insecurity have been reported by Lim, who used mail survey data of MBA graduates in the US.[73] She found that social support from others at work can contribute significantly in buffering individuals against job dissatisfaction and other organisational outcome measures. Similarly, she found that home-based social support was effective in buffering against life dissatisfaction. However, she did not find any buffering effects for home-based support on job dissatisfaction and the organisational outcome measures in the study, and equally, no buffering effects for work-based support on life dissatisfaction. In addition to finding buffering effects, Lim also found main effects for all sources of support and all outcome measures, with the exception of work-based support on non-compliant job behaviour.

The results for the buffering effects of social support in the context of *work intensification* are also mixed. Bromet *et al.*, in their study of female manufacturing workers, for example, found five significant buffering effects for supervisor support, all relating to job demands.[74] However, all these buffering effects were in the opposite direction, in that workers with high supervisor support reported fewer headaches, depression, light-headedness, weakness and multiple symptoms *only* when job demands were low! At moderate or high levels of demands, no differences in these symptoms were observed between women with more or less support. Furthermore, they found two positive buffering effects for friend/relative support and for co-worker support. Winnubst *et al.* analysed data from a longitudinal study of a large sample representative of the Dutch population.[75] They dichotomised their sample into higher and lower occupational groups and found that co-workers' support seemed to reduce the amount of role overload only in the lower occupational group. Another large sample study of the buffering effects of social support was carried out by Wells on a group of 1,809 blue-collar, white male workers in a plastics and chemical plant in the US.[76] Wells tested whether social support could influence the relationship between objective work conditions (as judged by experts in the company) and their subjective perceptions by workers as sources of stress. The results showed that spouse support buffered the effects of interpersonal demands and quantitative workload (both objectively assessed) on perceived work-load. The same was true for friend/relative support, although Wells found no buffering effects for either supervisor or co-worker support.

To summarise, there is strong evidence to show the beneficial *main* effects of social support (i.e. irrespective of levels of stress) but evidence for its *buffering* effect is less consistent. In respect of the latter, the inconsistency of the findings has been attributed to methodological problems, different conceptualisations of the relevant constructs and the use of different outcome measures.[77]

The effect of social support in the JIWIS sample

A number of organisations which participated in our survey were clearly concerned about the health effects of job insecurity and work intensification and had taken measures to reduce stress among their employees, or to assist employees in dealing with stress. As we have already seen, the literature suggests that one of the most promising ways in which stress might be ameliorated is through the provision of social support. We have therefore taken a particular interest in the ways in which the provision of a supportive work environment may be able to break the link between job insecurity and work intensification and stress.

We used four 1-item measures to assess how much support (emotional, instrumental, informational and appraisal support) a person received from two different sources in the workplace: their supervisor and their co-workers. In order to assess the data for possible main or buffering effects we conducted moderated regression analysis as suggested by Cohen and Cohen.[78] Each of the eight potential moderator variables (four types of support from two sources of support) was tested separately for both job insecurity and work intensification on all four outcome measures. Thus, a total of sixty-four (8 × 2 × 4) moderated regression analyses were conducted. This large number of analyses increases the danger of a Type I error (a 'false positive' statistical significance) but it was felt that it was more important at this stage to conduct a detailed exploration of possible main and buffering effects. It has often been suggested that buffering effects depend on the type of stressor, the type and source of support provided, and the outcome measure used. So while such a detailed analysis has problems of interpretation, it was felt that this risk was outweighed by the risk of masking possible buffering effects through combining different measures which might cancel out opposing effects. It can well be imagined that the same type of support provided might have both positive and negative effects depending on whether it is provided by one's supervisor or one's colleague(s).

Our findings suggest that, generally, there was strong and consistent evidence for main effects but only weak and inconsistent evidence for buffering effects. As we pointed out earlier on in this chapter, a main effect, as depicted in Figure 5.3, is an additive effect where high job insecurity and low social support both add up and lead to reduced well being and where low job insecurity levels and high levels of social support add up to produce good well-being. A buffering effect, as depicted in Figure 5.4, is an interaction effect where high social support interacts with high levels of job insecurity to reduce the negative impact of job insecurity on well-being.

The types of social support which had the most direct (*main*) effect on psychological well-being – in the face of both job insecurity and work intensification – were informational support and instrumental support, followed by emotional support. Significant main effects for appraisal support were only found for positive affect at work and also for our sleep measure. All main effects showed that low levels of support lead to lower levels of well-being (see Figure 5.2, for example). A good example of wanting informational support can be seen in this quote from an employee in the financial sector:

> And as far as insecurity is concerned, the thing there would be if there was better communication from the top downwards to tell people exactly what is going on, rather than letting rumours and snippets of information filter out. I think an open communication policy would be the most helpful thing.

The pattern of results was very similar for both the job insecurity and the work intensification measures, indicating that, in this sample, there

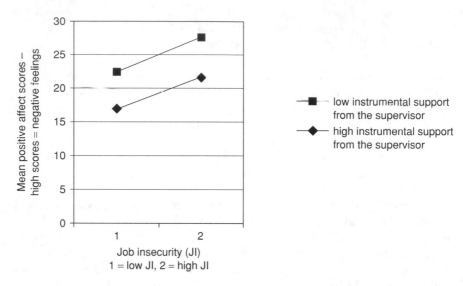

Figure 5.2 'Main effect' of instrumental support on positive affect at work

were no stressor-specific effects. In line with findings already reported in the literature,[79] we also found very few differences between supervisor and co-worker support, although there was a tendency for supervisor support to produce slightly more and slightly stronger main effects. But there was evidence of *outcome-specific* effects in that the strongest and most frequent effects were found for positive affect at work, followed by the GHQ, then negative affect at work; and finally, only a few effects were found for our sleep measure. This is not surprising since it can be expected that work-related stressors and work-based support have a higher impact on work-related well-being than on general well-being and sleep. With regard to work-related well-being, social support in the workplace seems to be more effective in this sample at maintaining positive affect than in reducing negative affect.

As we mentioned earlier, there was very little, and very inconsistent, evidence for buffering effects in our data. In total, we found only four buffering effects, which were all significant at the .05 level. Both emotional support and informational support from the supervisor buffered the adverse effects of job insecurity on GHQ scores (see Figure 5.3). We also found evidence for two negative buffering effects, where high levels of support led to an increase, rather than a decrease, in the level of stress experienced. Both these negative buffering effects were found for appraisal support from co-workers in the experience of job insecurity: one for negative affect and one for GHQ scores (Figures 5.4 and 5.5). Interestingly, at low levels of job insecurity, high levels of social support seem to have a beneficial effect on psychological health while at high levels of job insecurity, the effects of social support seem to have a negative impact on

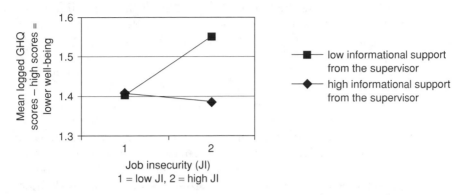

Figure 5.3 Buffering effect of informational support from the supervisor for job insecurity on GHQ scores

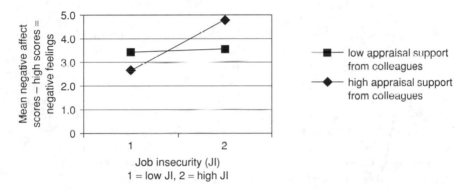

Figure 5.4 Buffering effect of appraisal support from colleagues for job insecurity on negative affect at work

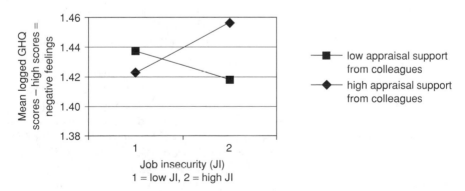

Figure 5.5 Buffering effect of appraisal support from colleagues for job insecurity on GHQ scores

psychological well-being. The four buffering effects which we found therefore constitute 5.25 per cent of sixty-four possible buffering effects, which, at a 0.05 significance level, is just above chance level – a disappointing result, given the liberal tests used.

Let us briefly compare the results presented here with the results from the two-way analyses of variance which we published in earlier reports on the JIWI study.[80] Both sets of results showed evidence of positive buffering effects for emotional and informational support, although the positive buffering effects of instrumental support which we found in our previous analyses of variance (ANOVAs) was not found when we switched to moderated regression analysis. Inconsistencies exist, however, when we look at the stressor-specific outcomes. For the ANOVAs, it was mainly work intensification items which produced the buffering effects, whereas for the moderated regression analyses it was mostly the job insecurity scale which showed evidence of buffering effects.[81]

Overall then we can say that the evidence for buffering effects in our sample was very weak, especially given the very liberal tests conducted to assess for possible buffering effects.[82] But while there is not much evidence in our study for a buffering effect of social support, we found very consistent and encouraging evidence for main effects, particularly for positive affect at work and GHQ scores. And while a lot of emphasis has been put on the buffering qualities of social support, the main effects of social support must not be discarded as a disappointing finding. For if buffering effects are the object of stress *intervention*, main effects are the objects of stress *prevention*. For, as Cutrona points out, a person who receives support in non-crisis times will be strengthened by this support which will enable the person to cope better when confronted with a crisis.[83]

Summary and discussion

As we have seen throughout this chapter, there is consistent, international evidence for the detrimental effects of the experience of both job insecurity and work intensification on psychological health and well-being. The findings from our JIWIS survey add to this body of evidence and, more particularly, they highlight the adverse consequences of *chronic* exposure to job insecurity and work intensification. While some advocate that it is only the change from secure to insecure and from challenging to overtaxing workloads that is stressful, the research evidence suggests that this is not the case: we do not 'get used to' job insecurity and work intensification.

In this chapter, we have also examined some of the factors which moderate the stressful effects of insecurity and work overload. And we have looked, in particular, at the role of social support. The results of our statistical analysis suggest that social support from supervisors and co-workers can have a significant *main* effect upon people's health and well-being. But our attempts to understand the buffering effects of social support were hampered by the problems we encountered vis-à-vis the use of different stressor, support and outcome measures and the use of different statistical methods in quantitative data. Nevertheless, we will continue our focus on the role of social support in stress prevention again in Chapter 8, where we will go beyond the quantitative statistics and draw heavily on our qualitative data. In doing so, we hope to obtain a better understanding of the underlying principles of support and to discover the crucial ingredients and conditions which, if at all, give social support its buffering or preventative qualities. For, only if we understand these underlying principles, can we start to think about effective stress intervention programmes. And with the overwhelming evidence of the detrimental effects of job insecurity and work intensification, finding effective stress intervention strategies has, surely, to be one of the main aims of future research.

6 The intensification of everyday life

Jane Nolan

I find it more difficult to leave work now, because it does tend to impinge on your home life because people phone you up at home and ask you different questions. There's always something that has to be sorted out that you can't always do everything in working hours.

> (HGV driver for an independent utilities company,
> 44-year-old married man with two children)

I think it's just the fact that I don't spend enough time with my son that worries me because I am so tired when I get home from work. Running a house and everything else.

> (Team leader in an insurance company,
> 35-year-old married woman with one child)

In this book, many different levels of analysis have been applied to the terms 'flexibility', 'insecurity' and 'intensification'. At a national level, we have argued that firms are driven principally by the competitive and funding pressures they face in a global market. At an organisational level, senior managers respond to these pressures by introducing flexible contracts, multi-skilling and, if necessary, redundancy programmes. At the level of the group, there is some evidence that an erosion of trust and a 'look after number one' morality has developed. And, at the level of the individual, we have shown that psychological well-being can often be undermined by an accumulation of workplace pressures.

Yet, as the quotations above demonstrate, the participants in the JIWIS survey often articulated their experiences of these stresses and strains within the context of their broader emotional life. To borrow an economic metaphor, their civic and emotional 'investments' came to the fore. In this chapter, I shall explore the ways in which flexibility, intensification and insecurity have influenced the personal, as well as the public, relationships of our participants. To begin with, I will discuss ways in which social theorists have tried to conceptualise the links between labour market flexibility and family life. I will then present empirical data from the JIWIS survey, revealing the extent to which job insecurity and work intensification generates feelings of tension within people's homes and households. This will be followed by an examination of some of the factors which can moderate or exacerbate this process, e.g. the gender of the respondent and their responsibility for young children. I will conclude with a brief reminder of the dilemmas faced by managers when attempting to foster organisational cultures that are genuinely supportive of their employees' family (and social) lives.

Labour market flexibility and families

As they enter the twenty-first century, the mandarins of social and political theory look back on an era in which the structures of family and community life were radically transformed under the influence of cultural and economic change. They point, for example, to the increase in divorce rates which accelerated rapidly during the 1960s and 1970s and continued to increase (albeit at a slower rate) during the 1980s and 1990s (Table 6.1). They also note the growth in lone-parent families (Figure 6.1). By way of example, Ulrich Beck, in his influential thesis on the 'Risk Society', claims that such trends can be explained partly because:

Table 6.1 Number of divorces per 100 marriages in developed countries

						% increase	
	1960	*1970*	*1980*	*1990*	*1997*	*1960–80*	*1980–97*
Austria	13.7	19.6	28.7	36.0	43.5	109	52
Denmark	18.6	26.2	51.4	43.6	37.3	176	−27
Finland	11.1	14.8	32.2	52.6	57.6	190	79
France	9.4	9.9	24.3	36.9	40.7	159	67
Germany[1]	9.4	17.2	26.6	29.6	40.9[a]	183	54
Greece	4.2	5.2	10.7	10.2	15.6	155	46
Japan	8.0	9.2	18.3	21.9	26.0[a]	129	42
Netherlands	6.4	8.3	28.5	29.7	39.7	345	39
Norway	10.1	11.7	29.8	46.4	41.8	195	40
Sweden	17.9	29.9	52.9	47.8	65.0	196	23
Switzerland	11.2	13.7	30.5	28.3	43.7	172	43
UK	6.6	13.4	38.2	44.1	51.9	479	36
USA	25.8	32.8	49.7	48.3	49.1[a]	93	−1

Source: Eurostat (New Cronos, NDIVIND divorce indicators)

Notes
The rates shown reflect the number of divorce decrees issued each year (as a percentage of the number of marriages taking place in that year).
1 Federal Republic of Germany (excluding ex-GDR)
a 1989

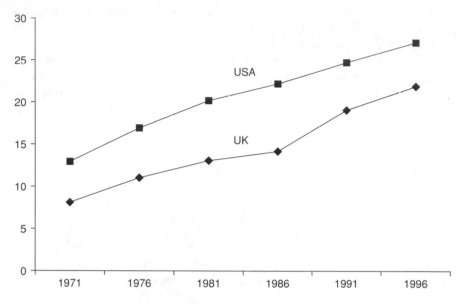

Figure 6.1 Families headed by lone parents as a percentage of all families with
dependent children

> If thought through to its conclusion, the basic figure of fully developed
> modernity is the single person. In the requirements of the market,
> the requirements of family, marriage, parenthood, or partnership are
> ignored. Those who demand mobility in the labour market in this
> sense, without regard to private interests, are pursuing the dissolution
> of the family – precisely in their capacity as apostles of the market.[1]

Although such commentaries offer us one perspective on the transformation in our family commitments, they give us no indication of the extent to
which this change is the result of labour market restructuring as opposed
to other factors such as the rise in female labour force participation, the
decline in religiosity, the increase in residential mobility, or the impact of
individualistic forms of entertainment such as watching television or surfing
the Internet. In the colourful language of Robert Putnam, the mysterious
'unravelling' of our families and communities poses a 'classic brainteaser, with
a corpus delicti, a crime scene strewn with clues, and many potential suspects'.[2]

The controversies generated by attempts to solve this 'brainteaser' are
well illustrated by the debates surrounding the impact of women's increasing participation in the labour market. According to one school of thought,
their involvement in paid labour reduces their economic dependence upon
men which, in turn, reduces their willingness to stay in unrewarding marriages (or cohabiting partnerships).[3] It was a claim endorsed by Anthony
Giddens when he wrote his book on the transformation of intimacy and
when he defended the notion that:

The changing position of women is happening partly for economic reasons – the increasing involvement of women in the labour force – but also for a complex of other reasons too. It is directly related to democracy as well as to the impact of women's movements. Even in more traditional countries around the world, women are less and less prepared to put up with being treated as subordinates within the family and elsewhere.[4]

Others, however, take a more pessimistic stance, seeing women's labour market participation as indicative of a more general shift, and decline, in values. For example, the American sociologist, David Popenoe, an outspoken critic of what he calls the 'me-generation', claims that:

> People are less willing to invest time, money and energy in family life, turning instead to investments in themselves . . . The past few decades have witnessed, for the first time in American history, the rise of adult-only communities, the massive voting down of local funds for education, and a growth in the attitude of 'no-children allowed'.[5]

Interestingly, empirical researchers are more sceptical of both the extreme 'optimist/pessimist' positions claiming that such generalisations often fail to take account of the differentiation and polarisation of women's involvement in the labour market. They point out that, in the UK for example, much of the increase in women's economic activity during the 1980s and 1990s was among mothers of school age children. Typically their employment is concentrated in low-paid 'complementary wage' jobs. So, although a small, elite group of educated women have made inroads into well-paid professional work, they are the exception rather than the rule.[6] In other words, most mothers still remain at least partially dependent upon either their partners/husbands or the state.[7] Recent research also suggests that, for many British women, their entry into the paid labour market is less of a *voluntary prelude* to a more independent life than a *forced reaction* to the declining wages of their husbands/partners.[8] It is certainly plausible to argue that economic independence for some privileged groups of married women may have reduced their willingness to stay in unrewarding marriages. However, the correlation between divorce rates and female labour participation[9] might have little to do with their newfound ability to 'escape' from such long-term commitment. It may simply be a reflection of the added pressures imposed upon relationships when *both* parties have to contend with the demands of 'work' and 'home'.

It is this 'intensification' in everyday living that we hope to explore further in the rest of this chapter. In particular, we want to explore how much the pressures generated by job insecurity and workplace stress impact on family life. If we were to believe the work of Robert Putnam, the answer would be 'not a lot'. When discussing the explanations for the

USA's rising divorce rate, Putnam dismisses the 'spillover' effects of work-place stress[10] and suggests, in a similar vein to Popenoe, that the principal cause of marital 'disengagement' lies in the 'cultural revolt against authority' associated with the 'baby boom' generation:

> Boomers were slow to marry and quick to divorce. Both marriage and parenthood became choices, not obligations. Although 96 per cent of boomers were raised in a religious tradition, 58 per cent abandoned that tradition, and only about one in three apostates have returned . . . Throughout their lives they have expressed more libertarian attitudes than their elders and less respect for authority, religion and patriotism [and] they are less trusting, less participatory, more self-centred, and more materialistic.[11]

And, when accounting for the decline in people's 'civic engagements' (i.e. their participation in voluntary associations) he is equally dismissive of the role played by work-related factors such as time pressures and financial anxiety.

> [Although] pressures of *time* and *money*, including the special pressures on two-career families, contributed measurably to the diminution of social and community involvement, my best guess is that no more than 10 per cent of the total decline is attributable to that set of factors.[12]

However, the work of other theorists, such as Richard Sennett and Ulrich Beck, suggests that Putnam may be using too restrictive a model of the link between our work/financial pressures and our family/community involvements. For example, when Sennett looks at the 'personal consequences of work in the new capitalism', he emphasises that the work intensity and flexibility promoted by the new economy exert both a *direct* and an *indirect* effect upon our families and communities. The direct effect is the result of Putnam's 'pressures of time and money' but the indirect effect stems from something much more 'corrosive' – the fact that flexible labour markets threaten to undermine those 'qualities of character which bind human beings to one another and furnishes each with a sense of sustainable self'. Indeed, when he speaks about the corrosive effects of the modern economy, Sennett makes it quite clear that he is not talking about the 'all too familiar conflict between work time and time for family' but about the conflict between the *ethics* of the new workplace and the ethics associated with conventional models of 'the family' and the local community.[13] In other words, the 'value shift' that Putnam cites as the principal cause of marital and civic disengagement is seen, not as a *sui generis* phenomena, but as the by-product of the same forces that are associated with stressful and insecure work environments.

Drawing on in-depth interviews with a cross-section of US workers, Sennett claims that the orientation towards 'flexibility' and the 'hunger for change' which helps people to flourish in the 'network' economy exert 'dysfunctional' effects upon our 'personal character', particularly in relation to our family life.[14] Citing the case of Rico (the manager of a small consulting firm) and his wife Jeannette (an accountant), Sennett observes that Rico's deepest worry was that he could not offer the substance of his work life as an example to his children of how they should conduct themselves ethically because the qualities that made him successful at work were not the qualities of good character.

> Behaviour which earns success or even just survival at work gives Rico little to offer in the way of a parental role model. In fact, for this modern couple, the problem is just the reverse: how can they protect family relations from succumbing to the short-term behaviour, the meeting mind-set, and above all the weakness of loyalty and commitment which mark the modern workplace?[15]

Similar claims are advanced in Beck's discussion of the *individualisation* promoted by the growth of flexible, decentralised and 'risk-fraught' patterns of employment. The working environment created as a result of this change is one in which the individual must learn, 'on pain of permanent disadvantage', to conceive of himself or herself as the centre of action, as 'the planning office with respect to his/her own biography, abilities, orientations, relationships and so on'.[16] And it is this gradual transformation in our characters, our *mentalities*, which he considers to be among the most worrying features of the new economy:

> To the extent that the individualised mode of existence succeeds, the danger grows that it might become an insurmountable obstacle to the kind of relationship (marriage, family) which is still basically desired . . . The negation of social ties that takes effect in the logic of the market begins in its most advanced stage to dissolve the prerequisites necessary for lasting companionship.[17]

In other words, according to Beck and Sennett, the stability of our families and communities is threatened not just by the immediate 'pressures' of insecurity and workplace stress but by the slow erosion of the character traits and normative orientations which are necessary for the establishment of strong and stable relationships.

The limitations of the individualisation thesis

Suffice to say, then, that the relationship between work and family is a hot topic for our public intellectuals. Whether it be broad-brush assessments

Table 6.2 Responses to the question: 'Why is a secure job important to you?'

Response	Women	Men	Significance of chi-square
Needs financial security, e.g. mortgage, bills to pay	97	66	0.314
Has family responsibilities and children to support	24	38	0.001*
Needs clarity and predictability	26	35	0.014*
Generally dislikes stress and pressure	22	20	0.201
Is the main breadwinner in the family	13	2	0.017*
Finds it difficult to work well when feeling insecure	10	5	0.427
Losing the job would undermine self-esteem	11	3	0.092
Other members of family are/have been insecurely employed	11	1	0.013*
Enjoys the current job	9	3	0.193
Too old to get another job	3	6	0.150
Insecurity would impact on individual lifestyle	5	4	0.942
Provides personal feeling of independence and empowerment	1	3	0.197
Other (less than 4 per category)	3	9	
Total (some respondents gave more than one reason)	235	195	

Note: * indicates that the difference between men and women is statistically significant

of the rights and wrongs of women's employment, or commentary on the rising tide of individualistic values, the debates are dense and wide-ranging. To be fair, it is not feasible to unpack all these arguments fully in this one chapter, nevertheless, what we think we *can* say is that the sermons and scoldings issued by social theorists appear somewhat exaggerated in the light of the interviews we conducted for the JIWIS survey. Indeed, the employees we spoke to bore little relationship to the 'egotistic' individuals described by Popenoe, Putnam and Beck or the emotionally 'drifting' parents depicted by Sennett.[18] When we invited people to tell us, in their own words, *why* job security was important to them, the typical response made reference to the needs, particularly the financial needs, of their families and dependants (Table 6.2). For most of the respondents, their prime concern was *not* the success of their personal 'biographies'[19] (what Beck refers to as the 'self-reflexive' obsession with an individual 'career' or 'performance') but, quite simply, their ability to maintain the financial outlays upon which other people (e.g. their partners and children) depended. It was the weight of their *interpersonal* responsibilities – to settle the bills and meet the mortgage payments – that came to the fore whenever they thought about the prospect of job loss.

There were no significant differences between women and men in the importance they attached to job security,[20] but there were interesting, and significant, differences in the way women and men chose to articulate *why* it was important to them. Men were more likely to refer specifically to their families than women, yet both implicitly referenced the *financial* needs of their families (in terms of paying bills and servicing mortgages). This could indicate the way in which many men continue to perceive their family role principally in terms of 'breadwinning'.

In a sense, this is hardly surprising. However, the *diversity* of modern family forms also emerged as an important theme. The specific phrase, 'being the main breadwinner' was used more often by women than by men. But, within this category, ten of the thirteen women were full-time employees and single mothers. The significance of employment to this group was manifestly more pressing than for women with employed partners. Women were also more likely to want a secure job when other members of their families were insecurely employed, highlighting the importance of female employment in providing financial security to families. Indeed, many commentators have noted that women's employment, including part-time jobs, now plays a critical role in keeping families out of poverty.[21] This also, of course, underscores the notion that people do not cope with insecurity by simply adopting individualistic, 'psychological' strategies, but that they make deliberate attempts to develop *family*-level strategies too.

If the 'individualisation' thesis of the social theorists were correct, however, and insecurity was causing people to reflect anxiously on their 'biographies' and mentalities, then we would surely have expected to see *personal* concerns reflected more strongly in people's responses. Although there were some mentions of issues such as self-esteem, independence and empowerment, what is most noticeable about this table is the strong emphasis participants place on the importance of family responsibilities, particularly financial responsibilities, in their need for job security.

We are, therefore, less worried than Sennett and Beck about the *indirect* effects of insecurity and work intensification on people's 'characters' or mentalities, and their motivations for forming long-term relationships. However, we do also think that Putnam and Popenoe have underestimated the *direct* impact of these workplace pressures on our families and communities. In the following sections we show the influence that the strains of the workplace can have on tension in the home.

Insecurity and tension at home

To assess the degree to which the job insecurity felt by the employees in our sample spilled over into their family relationships we asked the following question '*Does job-related stress cause tension within your home/household?*' to which interviewees were asked to respond using a 5-point scale ranging from 'very much' to 'not at all'. We then compared the answers to this question with the various job insecurity measures described in Chapter 5. Not surprisingly, we found that the more insecure people felt at work the

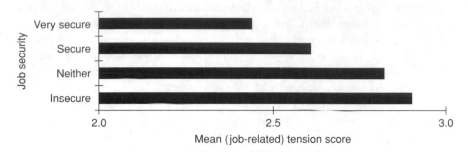

Figure 6.2 Scores for job-related tension in the home when asked: 'How secure
    do you feel with your present employer?' (higher numbers indicate
    greater reported tension)

more likely they were to experience tension in the home, although, as can
be seen from Figure 6.2, the relationship was quite modest.[22]

Given this rather tenuous association, is it possible that contemporary
speculation about insecurity causing family breakdown has been exaggerated?
Maybe. But it's important to consider some of the other workplace pressures our sample face in a little more detail first. In earlier sections of the
report we outlined the substantial restructuring which has taken place in
all our organisations, and of employers' increasing emphasis on multi-
skilling and 'flexibility'. However, while multi-skilling may be good for the
employer, Wheatley suggests that it can often lead to 'work-overload'.[23]
That is, employees find that the new tasks they are expected to perform are
too difficult and cause them confusion, or, alternatively, that they simply
have too much work to do within their contracted hours due to the low
staffing levels in their organisation. In the following section, we find very
clear associations between these other workplace pressures and tension in
family relationships.

Workplace pressures and tension at home

To examine the degree to which workplace pressures spilled over into
people's family lives we asked them the following question: '*How much
pressure do you feel from the following sources: managers, colleagues and sheer
quantity of work?*' to which they were asked to respond using a 5-point scale
running from: 'a great deal of pressure' to 'none at all'. In addition, we
also asked them to rate the adequacy of the staffing levels within the work
area (on a 4-point scale running from: 'more than adequate' to 'very
inadequate'). While we found highly significant associations between tension in the home and all four workplace pressures it was 'sheer quantity
of work' which seemed to have the greatest impact (Figure 6.3). And in
our in-depth interviews, the participants emphasised again and again that
the tiredness and irritability they felt at the end of a working day was a

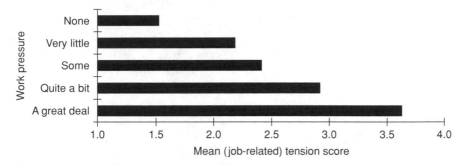

Figure 6.3 Scores for job-related tension in the home when asked: 'How much pressure do you experience from sheer quantity of work?' (higher numbers indicate greater reported tension)

reflection, not so much of job insecurity, but of the physical and mental exhaustion resulting from work overload:

> My manager said last week, 'Don't take your work home with you'. I just thought that was the most stupid thing you could ever say... because you do. I know I'm stressed and I kick it out on the wife, the kids, the cat and just about anything really.
>
> (Manager in a financial services company, 39-year-old married man with two children)

> The big thing is going home at night time and not being able to relax properly because you've got work spinning round in your head and you're thinking 'God, I'll never get it all ready'.
>
> (Lecturer in a college of further education, 34-year-old man with partner)

Other chapters have charted the way that downsizing and restructuring is often accompanied by new management techniques such as team working and 'total quality' management. Although these systems are sold to employees as encouraging cooperation and trust, they are often experienced as a new source of workplace stress. Fewer people do the same work, simultaneously facing increased pressure from peers. A study of the Nissan Corporation found that while the team concept was used by management to convey a new respect for employees (claiming that 'people are our most valued resource'), the employees themselves had a very different perception of events. One worker described the experience as 'eight-hour aerobics. You feel like you've done three days' work at the end of the shift'.[24] A recent survey of 3,000 US employees carried out by the Families and Work Institute in 1993 found that 75 per cent felt used up at the end of the day, and 70 per cent were still tired when they woke up the following day. Essentially, however, work overload and relationship tensions raise crucial issues concerning time pressures.

Families and the time squeeze

British employees now work among the longest and most unsociable hours in Europe.[25] Employees in the USA work, on average, 200 hours a year more than their European counterparts (bar the British). More specifically, in the USA, during the period between 1976 and 1993, there has been a significant increase in the number of people who work over forty-nine hours per week, noticeably among managerial, professional, sales and transportation occupations.[26] Similar patterns have been found in the UK.[27] While some suggest that this style of working is entered into voluntarily,[28] others indicate that working long hours, particularly among middle management grades, can be linked to the increasing job insecurity associated with 'flexible' labour markets.[29] Thus employees may work longer hours than is strictly necessary, in an attempt to be 'visible' in the organisation and to try and reduce their chances of being the next in line for redundancy. Cooper and Williams label this phenomenon 'presenteeism', and have suggested that it is particularly prevalent among managerial employees.[30] Yet others have linked overtime with trends towards multi-skilling. Employees sometimes find that the new tasks they are expected to perform are too difficult and/or they simply have too much work to do within their contracted hours.[31]

Interestingly, in our sample, we found no significant association between job insecurity and overtime as suggested by the 'presenteeism' hypothesis. We did however find strong associations with overtime and workload pressures.[32] The factors which drove people to work consistently over and above their contracted hours were all too often associated with 'work overload', as one participant said:

> So many people are going home with work to do that they haven't really got time to do. I find myself going home feeling physically exhausted, although I've done hardly anything physical.
>
> (Lecturer in a college of further education,
> 34-year-old man with partner)

In a survey of 6,000 British parents, Ferri and Smith showed that when men work more than fifty hours a week their involvement in joint family activities (e.g. family meals and outings) is severely reduced. This study also demonstrated that lack of male involvement in the family can be detrimental to mothers' psychological well-being, and corrosive to family cohesiveness.[33]

However, a telephone survey of British employees carried out by the Institute of Personnel Directors found that those working more than forty-eight hours a week tended to express *more* satisfaction with their relationships at home than those working fewer hours. It is important to note, however, that they were also more likely to see themselves as having *control* over the hours they worked, rather than feeling *obliged* to work longer hours just to keep up with their workloads. They also tended to describe themselves as workaholics. A really basic issue here then, appears to be the extent to which people work long hours at their own personal discretion, rather than being *compelled* to stay at work by heavy workloads. And, of course, although the 'workaholics' in this study may have been happy with their relationships, their families' perceptions of events may have been somewhat different.

Indeed, not all research blames unsupportive, high-pressure workplaces as the cause of difficulty in striking a happy balance between work and home. In her ethnographic study of a large US organisation, Hochschild suggests that professional couples don't really *want* a balance between the two domains. The organisation she studied offered remarkably generous 'family-friendly' programmes, yet her interviews suggested that employees' reluctance to take up the packages available to them was not due to a 'hostile' culture, but was the outcome of the values and preferences of the employees themselves. For them, Hochschild claims, work had become their main source of friendship, fulfilment and fun. It was actually their home life and their families that had become the onerous unrewarding and tedious environment they were trying to escape.[34] Certainly, our in-depth interviews revealed an occasional reticence by some 'workaholics' towards their families:

> Yeah. Yeah. I mean on paper I think, you need to make time for such stuff, but it's usually friends and partners that go first. Work does always seem to take priority.
>
> (Administrator at a college of further education,
> 37-year-old married woman)

> To me, work is on the same par as my family life. I know it might sound a bit strange to you, but my family in the last five years, my family life has suffered because of the type of work I do, the type of person I am.
>
> (Supervisor in a manufacturing company,
> 34-year-old married man with three children)

Further support for this was found in our quantitative survey, where we found a high correlation between levels of tension in the family and working long hours because of a strong *commitment* to work (Figure 6.4).

This, of course, raises an interesting conceptual, and moral, issue. It is conventional wisdom (particularly neo-liberal wisdom) to assume that giving individuals control over their own lives will, necessarily, lead to an improvement in their *quality* of life. Here, however, we have an instance of how personal control of working time (these employees were *not* working overtime because of workload or external pressures, but because of their

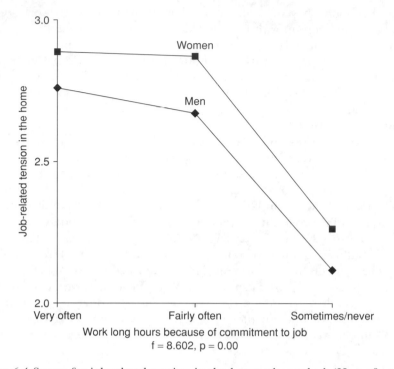

Figure 6.4 Scores for job-related tension in the home when asked: 'How often
do you work longer than you have to because of your commitment
to the job?'

'commitment' to their jobs) was associated with troublesome relationships:
giving these employees 'freedom' to work as they pleased actually turned
out to be *detrimental* to their family life. Could it be the case that, contrary
to current social dicta, in order to live more balanced lives, what people
really need are not more freedoms but more external impositions? (In
this case constraints on working time.)

This is a big question, and one which we hope will stimulate debate.
However, in fairness to JIWIS participants, while some were paying the
emotional price for excessive *personal* commitment to their jobs, for others,
it was *uncontrollable* workplace pressures which impinged on their relationships. We found that *regularly* working beyond basic hours was correlated
with tension at home (Figure 6.5). And, when we asked respondents *why*
their family suffered because of their working hours, 22 per cent claimed
it was because they felt tired and irritable through too much work, 26 per
cent that work overload meant they simply didn't get to see enough of
their partners and children and 24 per cent that it specifically restricted
the social life of their family. To use a hackneyed expression, lack of
'quality time' together seemed an important issue. Some participants felt
that the intrusion of work into their meal time arrangements diminished

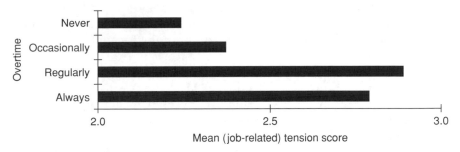

Figure 6.5 Scores for job-related tension in the home when asked 'Do you work longer than your basic working week?' (higher numbers indicate greater reported tension)

the quality of their family interactions. In terms of the quotidian cycle, the demands and conflicts of personal and public life seemed to be at their most 'intense' during the early evening. One man describes how organisational restructuring meant he now often had to work 'an extra hour or two a day'. Although, overall, he was working less than fifty hours a week, the change in working time had a significant impact on his family life.

> Yes, it was the dramatic change that caused the upset. The fact that instead of being able to work normally between let's say 9 and 5 or half past 9 till half past 5, we were then being told that you must work till 6.30 was tough . . . You see, we've been used to me coming in at an agreed time and the meal would be ready and the four of us would sit around the table and have our meal and then all of a sudden, three other people in the household can't eat their meal till about twenty to seven instead of when they choose to eat. So I didn't like what it was doing to me, but I also resented what it was doing to my family.
>
> (Engineer in a utilities company,
> 45-year-old married man with two children)

Many anthropological studies discuss the social significance attached to the act of sharing a meal.[35] Some look at the intricate game of dependence/ subordination between guest and host, or the ways in which gender roles within families and wider society are acted out at meal times. Others even define households as those who eat together.[36] Yet food is also the prototype of the charitable gift, and mealtimes can provide family members with the opportunity to gossip and provide mutual support. In this sense it plays an integral part in the provision of social, particularly emotional, support. Many participants felt the need to discuss personal difficulties at work with their families (72 per cent seeing families as their principal source of emotional support). However, when shopping, cooking, eating and cleaning up takes up the time of tired parents or partners, this supportive function can be undermined. The mealtime, rather than being a time for relaxing and catching up becomes a time of tension. As another participant describes it, his meals were the only occasion when his family came together, but their pace of life was such that the opportunity for mutual exchange was insignificant:

> So you really only see each other at meal times – first thing in the morning, possibly breakfast time when everybody gets up and everybody's crashing about wanting to get out to work anyway, so you don't have conversations then. But we haven't sat down and said let's talk this out or sort the other out for ages. We just don't seem to have time for that sort of thing. Everybody's too busy.
>
> (Part-time lecturer at a college of further education,
> 55-year-old married man with two children)

We shall extend our discussion on the importance of spouse support in the following section, however, our main message thus far is that characteristics associated with 'flexible' labour markets impact on people's lives *beyond* the workplace. In this very general respect, we are in agreement with the theorists. We disagree, however, with regard to the *mechanisms* they propose for the 'spillover' effect. Their claims that job insecurity undermines trust and commitment in both the home and the workplace, or that rampant individualism is tearing families apart could not be grounded in the answers of JIWIS participants. Although there was some evidence that relationships pay the price for high levels of work commitment, the principal concern of most participants was providing *financial* security to their families. And while the pressures they faced from sheer quantity of work *did* seem a source of family tension for a significant proportion of people, the reason for this was quite simple: they were tired and exhausted at the end of their working day. In the following section we explore the ways in which this tiredness created conflicts at home.

Gender differences, spouse support and the presence of children

Occupational psychologists have proposed a number of theoretical models to account for the 'spillover' of negative emotion from one sphere to another. In particular, the *conflict* theory of Greenhaus and Beutell (1985) has proved particularly popular with stress researchers.[37] They suggest that there are three distinct ways in which conflict between work and family could occur. First, the amount of *time* spent at work, by definition, reduces the time and energy available for family. Second, work stressors can preoccupy the individual when they are not at work and this *psychological strain* can undermine family relationships. Third, the *behaviour* considered appropriate in one role may not be appropriate for another. For example the verbal aggression and politicking required in some workplaces may not always be conducive to good quality interactions with either children or partners.

Since women continue to assume the primary responsibility for domestic work and child care, we would assume that work-related stressors would be more strongly linked to work–family conflict for full-time women than full-time men, as their overall burden is greater (this has been shown in numerous other studies).[38] Interestingly, however there were no statistically significant differences between men and women or between full-timers and part-timers on any of the workplace stressors we examined in the previous section: job insecurity, work intensification or working time pressures. There seemed to be no 'battle of the sexes here'; employment strain seemed equally distributed among all groups.

We did, however, find that *parents,* both mothers *and* fathers experienced greater family stress when faced with a high workload (Figures 6.6 and 6.7). This is not, in itself, an earth-shattering finding. However, it takes on more significance when one considers that most social science research has focused on the 'problems' faced by (and, for some, caused by) working *mothers*; fewer have turned their attention to the difficulties experienced (and perhaps caused) by working *fathers.*[39] Comparing Figures 6.6 and 6.7, we notice that while parents under high pressure at work experience greater overall family tension than non-parents, fathers seem

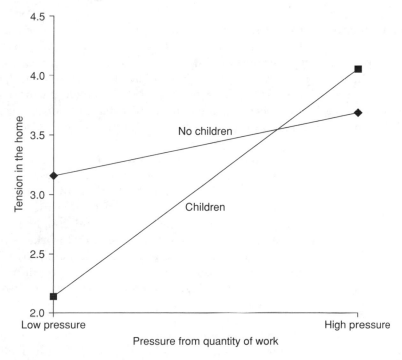

Figure 6.6 Men's scores for job-related tension in the home

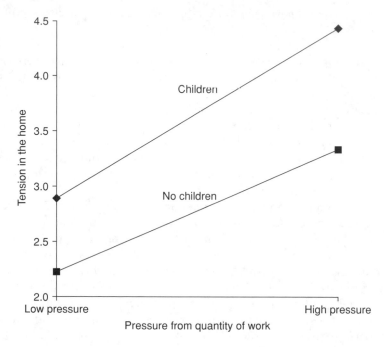

Figure 6.7 Women's scores for job-related tension in the home

to have the most 'extreme' reaction to high pressure at work. The concept of emotional support, and the differences in style between women and men, is very helpful in understanding this particular outcome. Cutrona suggests that, taken as a whole, men tend to have fewer close confidants than women and are more inclined to rely on their female partners for emotional support.[40] However, at the transition to parenthood men can find that their relationship with their wife deteriorates as they cease to be the 'number one' focus of attention.[41]

Thus, in our own survey, it could be that men with children may experience greater family stress when under a heavy workload, not just because having children can be a strain in itself[42] but also because their principal confidant may not have the time or personal resources to offer the needed support. In our qualitative study, the experience of one couple clearly illustrates this process. Mark, 31, is a self-employed manual worker working over fifty hours a week, and Julie, 29, is a full-time homemaker. With two children under the age of five they talked openly about the different pressures they both face in a day and the difficulties they have in providing emotional support for each other:

Mark: For me if I've had arguments with people at work and I come home, often I've got a headache and I'm just feeling very . . . [very tired]

Julie:	Well, I'm usually stressed out by the time he gets home anyway.
Interviewer:	Because of having the kids all day?
Julie:	They are quite demanding, both of them. They are both quite hyperactive. I have to have time to get to sleep. They have been on the go all day. So if he [*Mark*] comes home in a bad mood usually we've both had a bad day.
Mark:	Oh yes. 'Cos they're tired, well, Kevin is. It's his worst time and then I get home, so we're pretty much all stressed out aren't we?

The finding that mothers experience higher family tension when facing pressure from work overload than women *without* children could also be interpreted using the concept of emotional support. As women often *supply* more emotional support to their partners than they *receive*, women in high-pressure jobs may be losing out on two fronts: (1) lack of support from overworked colleagues and supervisors; and (2) a further lack of support from their partners when they arrive home at night. One participant, a 35-year-old woman working in the financial sector epitomises this dilemma. She is the main breadwinner in her household, under great strain as her organisation faces a merger, and lacking support from her husband:

> The last thing he wants to do is talk to me about my work and we've always had that problem about communication about my work. And yet he's said to me – after your meeting [about the merger], phone me, because he wants to know. Now I'm thinking do you want to know because have I got a job, or do you want to know because I'm alright? ... Because he knows that we couldn't live the lifestyle that we've got without my job.

Several studies have shown that spouse support is an important moderator of the impact of job insecurity and work intensification on the family for *both* women and men. However, in dual-earner couples the ability to provide this support can be undermined.[43] We also found that those participants who had a partner who worked full time, and were experiencing a heavy workload, had significantly lower levels of *psychological* well-being than those whose partners worked part time, worked from home or didn't work at all (Figure 6.8). The effect was not moderated by gender, nor did it have a significant effect on family well-being *per se.* Nevertheless, it does indicate the complexity of forces at play in exploring the dynamics of the relation between work and home. And it highlights the potential role of emotional support in mediating the relationship between workplace pressures, psychological well-being and family well-being.

Finally, however, it is also important to question the assumptions of both social theorists and psychological researchers about the *inevitability* of work pressures intruding into family life. Although they *can* have a negative

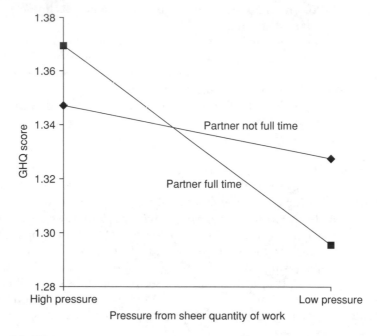

Figure 6.8 GHQ scores and pressure from quantity of work

influence on the family lives of many this needn't apply in every single case. Indeed, 'only' 8 per cent of our sample claimed they were concerned about the very *stability* of their relationships because of job-related stress. Certain people seemed to have access to resources (both personal and economic) which enabled them to resist these stressors to some degree. Some quotes may help to illustrate how a different set of personal values can alter the degree to which stresses and strains are carried over into the home.

> a thing blew up . . . and my manager said to me, 'Oh well, that appears to be your weekend gone'. In other words, 'Take this home and do this, mate'. I took it home but I didn't do it, mate! I wasn't going to prejudice my weekend, which involved going out with the children and watching my boy playing football – that's more important to me.

> We walked across the country, my wife and I. We had this deep and meaningful conversation sitting on our rucksacks in the middle of nowhere one day. Why are we in the rat race? We can live like this! You know. And that was what we've decided to do and plan for the future. So because of that, it won't have an immediate impact on my life if I lose my job.

In other words, we also found some evidence that certain people have a tendency to 'compensate' for bad experiences in one sphere by making special efforts to find enjoyment in the other. This raises another important and, as yet, not fully explored issue about the importance families play in providing emotional security to those coping with job insecurity. Simpson, drawing on Eriksonian psychology, highlights the way in which a personal sense of security – what he calls 'ontological' security – is established through kinship.[44] For him, the role of kin becomes increasingly important at a time when other social and cultural securities are evaporating:

> The sense of security (or insecurity) generated by growing up within this or that arrangement of family and kin is not simply a spatial phenomenon, but one capable of bringing order and predictability over time. During a period when the apparent certainties of public life such as employment, community, environment and economy are subject to turmoil, fragmentation and unpredictability, the ability to locate oneself in an actual past and an imagined future is indeed an esteemed resource.[45]

Unfortunately, however, for the majority of JIWIS participants, as much as they strive to protect the security and stability of that 'esteemed resource', contemporary employment practices serve to undermine it.

The viability of family-friendly policies in the 'intensified organisation'

To conclude, we shall briefly consider how 'stresses' at the organisational level, as well as the individual level, can spill over into families. We found evidence that when organisations and teams are under intense strain to perform then two things seem to happen. First, the informal goodwill of colleagues and supervisors, essential for parents, can be severely undermined. Second, the formal inclination of senior managers to develop 'family-friendly' policies diminishes. Similar patterns have been found by other researchers in both the USA and the UK, and several of the key studies are outlined below.

Drawing on in-depth interviews with 220 managers in the UK, Simpson suggests that, during restructuring, intense rivalry develops between project teams, which can often lead to uncooperative and insular cultures. She found that in this environment female managers feared being perceived as 'lacking commitment' if they gave family reasons for leaving work early or taking extended lunch breaks. Many compensated for this by using other types of 'excuse' to explain absences.[46] However, these sorts of 'macho' cultures do not just make life difficult for mothers. Cooper and Lewis suggest that fathers often have to resort to deception too, using reasons for absence that specifically do *not* mention their parenting commitments.[47]

Indeed, men frequently experience even less support for their parenting role from the workplace than women.[48] A British survey carried out for the Institute of Management found that 45 per cent of male managers claimed that not seeing enough of their children was a major source of stress.[49] Further, in the USA, a study conducted by Galinsky and Bond showed that, of a nationally representative sample, *both* mothers' *and* fathers' well-being was higher in workplaces where both supervisors and colleagues were sympathetic to their caring responsibilities. Unfortunately, this support was often undermined when the organisation was insecure and the workload perceived as high.[50]

This theme also emerged in the JIWIS study. As the following two case studies illustrate parents, particularly mothers, expressed a need for both clearly defined organisational polices and for the informal support of colleagues. However, we also found evidence that providing this support at the level of the organisation can be extremely difficult to achieve during a period of restructuring. Our first case study focuses on an insurance organisation undergoing its second merger in two years. One middle manager, a married mother with a 5-year-old son was hoping to switch from full-time to part-time work. Interestingly, however, she didn't expect her needs to be accommodated by the company she had worked for for eighteen years. For example, when asked about the possibility of switching to a job share, or the usefulness of workplace crèches, she highlights the practical and cultural barriers surrounding the delivery of 'family-friendly' policies in an insecure organisation facing yet another restructuring:

> At the moment the emphasis is literally on let's get the structure, let's get the organisation right. Let's get the right people on board and let's carry on being customer focused. At the end of the day I can understand yeah, quite rightly too, because at the end of the day we're not here to be a playground are we?

Indeed, this ambivalence towards the provision of family-friendly policies was fairly widespread among her colleagues. Each work team in her organisation felt strained and insecure, and their inclination to provide extra support to those with family commitments was diminishing. With staff levels already low, tension had built up between employees with children and those without. Feeling somewhat insecure about her own future, one single woman was becoming ill-disposed to the needs of parents around her:

> We've always got to back down – that is sort of an issue when it comes to holidays and kids are off . . . But they [parents] shouldn't think just because they've got kids that they can have the same time off with their kids. It doesn't always follow . . . But we are supposed to be prepared to back down more, being single.

Some academics and policy advisers try to promote family-friendly, or 'work–life' policies to organisations by highlighting the bottom-line advantages they can provide.[51] However, what our qualitative data suggests is that the implementation of family-friendly working practices is low on the list of management priorities at times of economic uncertainty. As Lewis has commented, the commitment of senior managers to family-friendly policies is often extremely fragile. To use her terminology, they are often introduced simply to 'play around at the margins', rather than to create a genuinely supportive environment for parents.[52] In our second case study, this indifference was quite apparent. The organisation we selected was a college of further education that had experienced a major restructuring in the last eighteen months. The casual cooperation of management on which parents had relied was beginning to dry up under a new management regime. As one part-time lecturer said:

> Up until recently, I think this happened the end of last term, all of us who had children, if it was half-term, we brought them in. It was just automatic. Nobody seemed to mind and we never thought anything about it . . . Well, of course, at the end of last term it was suddenly stopped. We got memos round to say we weren't allowed to bring the children in.

Although the mother of grown-up children and not directly affected by this herself, another female colleague had been more seriously affected. Gillian, a 38-year-old single parent with a 4-year-old daughter, was finding it increasingly difficult to arrange appropriate child care when she had to lecture in evening classes. Her relationship with one of her supervisors was becoming strained by what, she felt, was his apathy towards her situation. This was exacerbated by the fact that he was also her union representative.

> The male manager people would see as quite a selfish character, which I expect he is, I approached him and told him – this has happened twice now at this time of year when the evening class issue comes up – and both times his response was, 'Well, nobody else can do it! And if you don't do it, you put pressure on other people' . . . So instead of saying I'm your union rep, I know I'm your manager but I'm also your union rep, I can see your point, he was still playing very much the role of manager.

The experiences of this participant echo the well-documented accounts of trade union resistance to women in the workplace, and their general antipathy towards the whole 'family-friendly' debate.[53] There is some evidence that trade unions view women's interest in family-friendly policies as 'special pleading', and indicative of women's lower commitment to paid work, and therefore implicitly undermining their right, to such work.[54]

While we can only interpret the particular experiences of Gillian from her 'side', it seems that although her supervisor was trying to 'play fair' and protect other, pressurised, team members, he simultaneously failed in his duty as her union representative. Although the difficulty of combining supervisory roles with union representation is a problem more commonly faced in white-collar unions,[55] this particular episode affected Gillian's ability to trust both her supervisor and her organisation. Shortly after her concerns over evening classes had been raised, she received a crèche link-card in the internal mail providing details of a child care agency. Her reaction was not positive, and she saw the move as a cynical attempt by college management to 'wash their hands' of a potentially complicated equal opportunities issue:

> I thought, 'How insensitive!' . . . I thought that's very cool and I don't like that . . . I just saw it as a way of saying well, we've provided you with a number to sort out your child care, therefore you don't really have an excuse.

The problem was eventually resolved through an *informal* arrangement Gillian made with a female colleague who needed extra hours, highlighting the fragility of *formal* family-friendly workplace practices, and the contradictory roles of supervisors in maintaining employee loyalty and commitment when cost-cutting exercises loom large. Indeed, in our quantitative survey, we found strong associations between job-related tension in the home and two measures of employees' organisational commitment: (1) their levels of satisfaction with supervisor relations and (2) their ability to trust management more generally (Figures 6.9 and 6.10).

Perhaps Richard Sennett is partly right then; there clearly *are* links beween low levels of trust and workplace commitment and higher levels of family tension. We suspect, however, that this has more to do with the everyday stresses, strains and preoccupations employees face in intensified, low-trust organisations, than with the transference of low ethical standards from one domain to another, as Sennett's 'corrosion of character' thesis implies. In the words of one 33-year-old male lecturer:

> Although I work with a good bunch of people, you can't be absolutely certain – especially as a newy – only been here two years – who you can trust and how far you can trust them, which can be problematical. At the end [you] take all those things home and mulling them over yourself [you end up] screwing yourself up.

Clearly, what we can say for sure is that there are some cases when the practicalities of delivering organisational policies which are supportive of people's personal, as well as their public, lives are put under immense strain before, during and after organisational restructuring. When cost-cutting

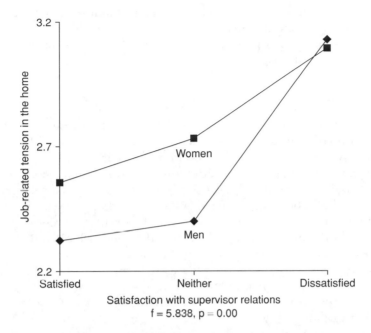

Figure 6.9 Scores for job-related tension in the home when asked: 'How satisfied or dissatisfied are you with your relations with your supervisor or manager?'

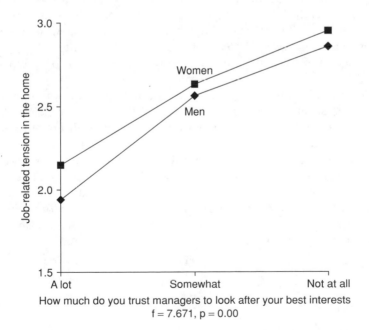

Figure 6.10 Scores for job-related tension in the home when asked: 'How much do you trust managers to look after your best interests?'

pressures bear down on organisations, being 'family-friendly' or 'work–life' friendly is an attitude many may not feel inclined to foster. Likewise, when teams are feeling pressured and insecure, their inclination to offer informal support to parents can wear thin.

Conclusions

We have come a long way. From grand theoretical sweeps on insecurity and individualism to the gritty detail and contradictions faced by participants in trying to balance work and family in their everyday life. Broadly speaking, we are in agreement with the social commentators: experiences in the labour market are linked to experiences in personal relationships. More specifically, however, we feel that Putnam and Popenoe underestimate the importance of both time conflicts and workplace stress in creating difficulties for families. Yet we also feel that the 'culturally altered *mentalities*' and 'reflexive biographies' found in the accounts offered by Beck, Giddens and Sennett are perhaps more extravagant than needs be. The problem that JIWIS participants had to contend with was quite simple: how do you maintain good quality relationships when your job leaves you constantly tired and exhausted?

Furthermore, our study shows that considering the 'work–family' issue as principally a 'woman's problem' can often lead to a distorted view of the dilemmas families face. We have shown how the stresses that *fathers* face at work, as well as mothers, can also be associated with tension in the home. Historically, however, both research and media interest has tended to shy away from this aspect of the debate and to see only women's *employment* or men's *unemployment* as problematic for family life. The pressures fathers face at work, and sometimes bring home, are all too often simply ignored.

More generally, the practicalities of 'reconciling' employment and family have to rest on the willingness of organisations to offer clearly defined family-friendly policies and, more specifically, on actively encouraging the support of managers and colleagues. However, in insecure, intensified organisations, the inclination of both teams and organisations to respond in this way can be severely undermined. Finally, therefore, as far as broader policy issues are concerned, it seems that there is a real dilemma for governments that are concerned to promote the flexibility of their labour markets while simultaneously claiming to be committed to supporting families in their everyday lives.

7 The organisational costs of job insecurity and work intensification

Roy Mankelow

The preceding chapters have described the changing nature of work organisation and the effects which this, along with the insecurity and pressures associated therewith, have brought to bear on employees at all levels of the occupational hierarchy. In Chapter 2, we saw how many of the organisations in our survey had restructured their workforce in order to increase the temporal and functional flexibility of their employees. In the majority of cases, the employers we spoke to claimed that the new organisation of work had enabled them to increase productivity and profitability. Indeed, some of them asserted that without these changes their companies would no longer be in business. But, if, as our findings suggest, the new work environment generates high levels of stress and insecurity, the question arises as to whether these conditions can be sustained over the long term. If job insecurity and work intensification undermine the health and well-being of *employees* (and of their families), do they also damage the health and efficiency of the *organisations* for which they work?

Insecurity and the loss of goodwill

We have already seen that many of the processes by which flexibility has been gained, for example, through downsizing, work intensification, delayering and the erosion of traditional job demarcations, were also associated with feelings of anxiety and stress. We have also demonstrated that the demoralisation and demotivation which accompany such feelings undermine one of the principal sources of flexibility, namely the goodwill of the workforce. The fear must be therefore that if employers exact functional and temporal flexibility at the cost of *attitudinal in*flexibility, or, more importantly, *behavioural in*flexibility, the *net* gain from flexibility will be correspondingly reduced (see Figure 7.1).

In his study of the impact of 'downsizing' and delayering' on US middle management, Charles Hecksher found that many managers continued to show great loyalty to their organisations even after the company had pushed through several rounds of redundancies.[1] So too in our study, a large majority of employees said they felt 'a real sense of belonging' to their

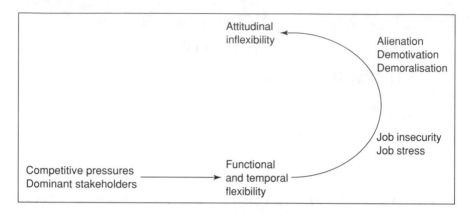

Figure 7.1 The trade-off between temporal and functional flexibility and
attitudinal inflexibility

organisation even where their employers had recently carried out major
programmes of downsizing and restructuring. But if their *organisational*
commitment (i.e. their loyalty to their fellow workers and their customers)
remained strong despite the fear of job loss, the same could not be said of
their trust in senior management.

Indeed, several of the managers we spoke to were quite open about the
'management problems' generated by feelings of job insecurity. One senior
manager noted that workforce resentment was hampering the introduction of multi-skilling. Another admitted that people had woken up to the
fact that increased training made downsizing easier for the employer,
raising the danger that the more valuable workers would decide to 'jump
ship' before they were pushed. But perhaps the most interesting reflection
on the effects of job insecurity was offered by an education service provider who stated that: 'for flexible working practices to be successful the
goodwill of the employees is essential'. And yet, in her organisation, she
felt that the 'psychological contract' between management and staff was
being undermined as a result of the insecurities fostered by the competitive pressures under which they had to operate.

Indeed, the negative relationship between goodwill and insecurity was
clearly illustrated when we asked our respondents whether they agreed or
disagreed with the following statement: 'In this organisation, managers
and employees are on the same side'. As shown in Figure 7.2, those employees who described themselves as feeling very secure with their employer
were much more likely to agree with this statement than their more insecure
counterparts.

Our research also suggested that the loss of goodwill is particularly
acute when employees suspect that managers are exaggerating the 'need
to be competitive' for the sake of short-run profit gains.[2] Take, for example,
the resentment experienced by one of our respondents who described

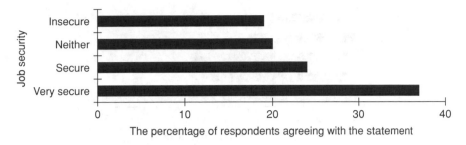

Figure 7.2 The percentage of respondents who agreed with the statement that:
'In this organisation, managers and employees are on the same side'
(by how secure they felt with their employer)

how his company (in the financial services industry) had committed itself
to increasing profits 'year-on-year', frequently resorting to redundancy to
ensure that the target was met. He indicated that although many of his
workmates accepted that redundancy was sometimes necessary to keep a
business afloat, they felt bitterly unhappy when colleagues lost their liveli-
hoods at a time when the company was posting record profit figures.[3]
Indeed, those companies which execute redundancies during periods
of high profitability send out an especially demoralising signal to their
workforce, suggesting that management are more concerned with short-
term cost reductions than with long-term growth and expansion. As described by Ridderstråle and Nordström, employees are all too aware that
'downsizing easily becomes dumbsizing instead of rightsizing' and that
'there is no way of creating new wealth by simply reducing costs and
getting rid of people'.[4]

Insecurity and demotivation

In conventional economic theory, it is often assumed that job security
creates a sense of complacency among workers, and that they might not
feel a necessity to exert themselves at their work to the same extent as
their more insecure counterparts. Those who are insecure, so this argument goes, might feel obliged to put in that little extra effort to help their
employers stay in business, while at the same time making themselves
more valuable to the firm and thus less likely to be chosen as a victim in
any downsizing exercise.[5] But this argument was not endorsed by any of
the managers we spoke to. On the contrary, most of them suggested that
if job insecurity had any effect on the work effort of their employees, the
relationship was a *negative* rather than a positive one. For example, in one
of the colleges of further education, the principal described how the
morale of her staff had suffered as a result of fears of redundancy. In her
opinion, the job insecurity experienced by her employees had reduced
rather than increased productivity and efficiency within the organisation.

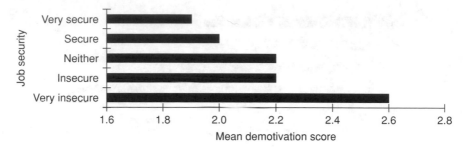

Figure 7.3 Mean demotivation scores by how secure people felt with their employer

Note

The demotivation scores or the X axis are derived from a 5-point response scale: 1 = very motivated, 2 = motivated, 3 = quite motivated, 4 = hardly motivated, 5 = not at all motivated.

Similar views were expressed by the senior manager of a large water company who stated that job insecurity had dealt a double blow to his company's efficiency, first because of its adverse impact on employee motivation levels and, second, because 'Line managers are spending an awful lot of time trying to improve worker morale; holding staff meetings, listening to the fears and worries of the workers and trying to reassure them.' He maintained that if 'worker morale could be improved, then the line managers' time could be more profitably spent in improving the provision of the company's services'.

That the majority of the senior managers we spoke to were deeply concerned at the adverse organisational consequences of job insecurity and poor morale is hardly surprising given the pattern of responses which emerged when we talked to their workers. For, as illustrated in Figure 7.3, the motivation levels of the respondents we interviewed were inversely correlated with their sense of job insecurity. Surveys of the US labor market also reveal the way in which job insecurity tends to lower employees' productivity and work effort.[6] As described by Charles Hecksher, fearful employees do not make the hardest workers. On the contrary, they tend to narrow their sights 'to just get the job done and go home'. 'The reaction to fear is to scatter' with everybody 'protecting their individual flanks'.[7]

But, as we shall see, although managers are keenly aware of the demoralising effects of rationalisation, redundancy and restructuring, their good intentions often disappear under the pressure to attain production and profit targets. The tensions which result are well illustrated in the words of one manager in the financial services industry who told us that he had recently been required to ask his staff to make a special effort to get everything in order in preparation for a prospective merger, i.e. at a time when his staff were already experiencing considerable feelings of insecurity. He said it was very difficult because:

I empathise with their insecurities and I feel less committed. I'm sure they feel less committed, yet I can't show them that I feel less committed. It's not fair on them to see that, and it is actually very difficult to get them to take on more than they're currently doing.

Stress and lost productivity

As we have observed in earlier chapters, although there is a clear association between job insecurity and psychological ill-health, there is an even stronger relationship between pressure at work and poor psychological well-being. Thus, it was hardly surprising that, of the respondents we spoke to, those who described themselves as feeling very pressured at work exhibited the lowest morale and the strongest feelings of alienation (see Figure 7.4). Moreover, as emphasised by the government's Health and Safety Commission (HSC), work stress gives rise not just to demoralisation and disaffection but also to increased rates of absenteeism and other manifestations of work-related illness.[8] Included among the work-related 'stressors' cited by the HSC are: the working environment and working conditions, new technology and other forms of change in the way work is performed, work overload (and underload), lack of control over how the work is done and the pace at which the worker is forced to operate, poor communications and involvement in decision-making, as well as issues such as performance appraisal, job insecurity and organisational style (e.g. whether it is participative or authoritarian).[9] Each of these stressors can act to 'reduce work performance and productivity, increase absenteeism and employee turnover' and, in some instances, they can also 'increase the likelihood of accidents'.[10]

Moreover, during the interviews we conducted for the JIWIS survey, we were reminded that the impact of work stress is not confined to the individual employee.[11] As one financial services worker said to us: 'Once the stress starts and you start getting locked into the routine of arguments and strained relationships and difficulties with the kids and all this sort of stuff it's a very quick downward spiral.'

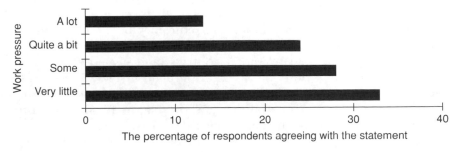

Figure 7.4 The percentage of respondents who agreed with the statement that: 'In this organisation, managers and employees are on the same side' (by how much pressure they felt from the sheer quantity of work)

The same sentiments were also expressed by an employee of a further education college when she described the way in which stress at work 'spills over' into stress at home:

> My sister who is a full-time lecturer in Crawley, she's doing 9 to 9 Monday, Tuesday and Wednesday, teaching, which is absolutely knackering, apart from the fact that you don't get enough to drink, and you get headaches because your kidneys aren't working properly, and that has a knock-on effect in the home because obviously her partner is not very happy. And I do think people should be protected against that sort of thing.

On the subject of excess workload and its impact on home life, we heard many such comments, but perhaps the most poignant of these was the statement made by a manager in the financial services industry when he told us that:

> I think over the last week or so it's begun to hit home really just how much stress you are under . . . As part of the merger we have been asked to make sure our house is in order . . . And as a result they are pushing for productivity, which means that you are being pushed by management, and you are pushing your staff and they are pushing back. And . . . my manager said last week, 'Don't take your work home with you', I just thought that was the most stupid thing you could ever say. Because they have instilled in us as part of the culture to care about our staff. To nurture and bring them on, encourage them, and when you've been doing that for nearly two years, to have all these changes made and try to promote them and see the effect it has on them, and then (for my boss) to say don't bring it home, I think is a really silly comment. Because you do. I know I'm stressed and I kick it out on the wife, the kids, the cat and just about anything really.

Nonetheless, the 'knock-on' effects that are of most concern to senior management are not those which impact upon their employees' family life but those which damage the health and efficiency of the organisations they work for. And recent decades have seen a plethora of studies seeking to estimate the 'true' costs of workplace stress (and suggest ways of controlling these through closer involvement with and by the workforce). In their assessment of the 'costs and benefits' of 'stress prevention', Cooper *et al.* cite a study by Harris purporting to show that, by 1985, US industry was losing as many as 350 million working days per annum as a result of absenteeism. Using estimates supplied by Elkin and Rosch, they then suggest that 54 per cent of these absences 'were in some way stress related'. They also point to evidence suggesting that stress was a 'contributory factor' in 60 per cent to 80 per cent of all accidents at work.[12] Another calculation of the costs imposed by workplace stress has been published by Greenberg *et al.*, estimating the total cost of anxiety disorder in the USA at approximately $42 billion per annum.[13] In Canada, meanwhile, the figures published by the insurance company, Sun Life, show that during the 1990s claims related to stress rose from 10 per cent of total disability claims to more than 30 per cent.[14]

Within the European Union, Cooper *et al.* estimate the death toll from occupational accidents and disease at 8,000 per annum and claim that 'a further 10 million people suffer from some form of work-related accident or disease',[15] the cost of which – in terms of annual compensation payments runs to more than ECU 20 billion (£12 billion). In the UK alone, according to a recent report by the Confederation of British Industry (CBI), sickness absence amounts to some 200 million days per annum, representing 3.7 per cent of total working time, at a total cost to employers of £10.2 billion.[16] The report also notes that, among non-manual workers, workplace stress is now the second highest cause of absence, behind 'minor illnesses' such as the common cold.[17]

Nonetheless, among many of the people who were interviewed for the JIWIS survey, there was a deep frustration at their managers' failure to recognise the inefficiencies created by work-related stress. This frustration is well illustrated in the comments made by an education service provider when she told us that:

> We have somebody off at the moment. A diabetic, but a lot of stress has built up and he is now off for some time. Not only the union but also the management should take that on board and recognise what's happening. It's ignored because I think they don't want to deal with it. But it should be recognised because I can see, again it's back to the selfish attitude of companies, that actually if they are aware of employee welfare and will try to do something about it, they will actually get something back [from the staff] . . . What is happening here is management aren't responding and unions aren't responding and stress is building up and you can see the absenteeism, the result of that. People looking elsewhere. They're all the results of management digging their heads in the sand and not wanting to deal with the issue, which is stress building up.

Frustration at the productivity lost as a result of workplace stress was also evident in the comments made to us by a manager in the utilities sector when he suggested that the best way for any manager to improve the performance of his or her staff would be through:

> taking more account of what I call the human factor, and not trying to put on your employees all of the tasks in the world that you know they're not going to complete. It must be known what a person can do

reasonably within a day, and give them a little bit less than that and then maybe they'll be a bit creative as well. Rather than if you're overloading people, I'm sure that's what causes most of the stress.[18]

Other respondents reminded us that the costs of workplace stress are not restricted to sickness and absenteeism. Excessive work pressures (as with job insecurity) can also damage the goodwill and morale of the workforce. As a lecturer at a college of further education commented:

I'm sure they're fully aware we work excessive hours but at the same time, they're looking to increase those hours and the workloads, so what they say in terms of feeling compassion towards the number of hours that we actually work, doesn't match up with the number of hours they want us to work. So in terms of loyalty towards them, I don't have a great deal of loyalty towards the management team.

Some of the employees we spoke to also stressed the demoralising effect of feeling 'that you cannot make a mistake'. And their comments support the observations of Ridderstråle and Nordström when they argue that the innovative organisation needs to have a high tolerance of mistakes and that the failure to adopt this tolerance as part of the organisational culture inhibits creativity – one of the most valued qualities in any successful business. As one worker in the electrical engineering sector put it:

Things will go wrong in manufacturing, but when you know that your immediate boss is a listener and he's a good administrator who can make his own mind up whether you've done something wrong or the guy on the floor has done something wrong, or you've done right and recognise what is going on, not only do you feel confident, you feel comfortable that I could work in this environment.

Moreover, in addition to the costs imposed by absenteeism, workforce turnover and production difficulties, there are also the insurance and litigation costs generated by the growing number of court cases brought by workers seeking compensation for work-related illness. For example, with much of the UK's employment law now being driven by the European Union, British firms are being progressively required to introduce measures to protect workers from unreasonable exploitation. Meanwhile, the size of court settlements for work-induced stress has grown sharply in the past few years and employees are now more willing to sue their employers, partly because of the growing pressure under which they are working, but also because of the publicity given to the large sums being awarded in compensation.[19]

In July 1996, a senior social worker with Northumberland County Council became the first person to succeed in arguing at the High Court (with the aid of his trade union, Unison) that his employers were liable for the nervous breakdown he had suffered as a result of an impossible workload.[20] He was awarded damages of £175,000. Another well-publicised case was that brought by Beverley Lancaster (who was also supported by Unison) who, in July 1999, won damages of £67,000 from Birmingham City Council, in compensation for the work-related stress which had forced her to change job from senior draughtsperson to housing officer. Six months later, an even more spectacular settlement was achieved by Randy Ingram who accepted a record £203,000 out-of-court settlement for the stress caused by the physical and verbal violence to which he was subjected as an employee of Hereford and Worcester County Council. Other, less publicised claims, were being pursued in other parts of the country. By the end of 1998, the TUC reported that the number of stress-related compensation cases handled by the trade unions[21] had soared to 783 in that one year alone, an increase of 70 per cent over 1997.[22]

For the employers, the problem they now face is that each successful prosecution increases the likelihood that more will follow. When a school teacher won £47,000 in October 1999 because she had been made ill by the excessive amount of work she had to complete, the door was opened to a flood of new cases from a profession that has been increasingly vocal in its protestations about the stresses of their work and, in particular, their ever increasing workload. As Graham Clayton, the senior solicitor of the National Union of Teachers, pointed out, 'a teacher forced into retirement in her mid-30s could expect a settlement of up to £250,000' reflecting the years she would normally have expected to have continued teaching.[23] Indeed, so serious is the risk of large sums of compensation for stress, and other industrial illnesses, that insurance companies are now asking many employers to document the measures they have introduced (or plan to introduce) to alleviate workplace stress. And it is likely that those firms which fail to take appropriate action will, in future, be required to face higher insurance premiums.[24]

Nonetheless, there is no shortage of advice as to the steps necessary to improve the working environment. The employers' associations, such as the CBI and the Institute of Directors have published material discussing health at work, and suggesting some of the actions employers should consider taking in order to reduce levels of stress. Unison has issued guidelines to its branches to tackle the problems of stress in the workplace[25] that, perhaps understandably, highlight the need for management to work in partnership with the trade unions in this area. The Health and Safety Commission produced a discussion document in 1999 in which the outline of a possible draft Approved Code of Practice and Guidance on work-related stress was set out. It remains to be seen what success this initiative will have with employers, and whether a voluntary code of practice will be sufficient to ensure worker protection.

The management response

In light of the costs imposed by stress and insecurity, it is no surprise to find that British managers are keen to boost the morale and motivation of their workforce. But the evidence from the JIWIS survey points to some of the difficulties they have encountered in their attempt to mould their employees into a workforce that can prove itself 'adaptable and proactive in stressful situations'.[26] With the single exception of a small family-owned firm of builders, the senior managers of all the companies visited claimed to have at least one policy specifically designed to motivate their workers. To our surprise however, only three firms mentioned the use of 'performance-related pay' or some other form of financial incentive. In fact the most frequently mentioned motivation policies were those intended to improve *communication* and allow for greater *autonomy* and involvement in decision-making.

Most of the establishments included in our survey carried out regular opinion/employee-attitude surveys, while one organisation arranged a twice yearly 'upward appraisal system' (run by an external agency), in which workers rated line managers on a number of different criteria. Surgeries (sessions where employees could have a one-on-one meeting with a manager) took place at three firms, and one large financial services group had established a complex series of meetings and conferences (attended by senior managers, junior managers and supervisors) intended to involve the workforce in designing new ways of working to help facilitate a planned merger. Another organisation had even set up a joint management–union hotline to help resolve problems on the shopfloor as they arose. The intention behind most of these schemes was to achieve 'motivation through participation' in the hope that such policies would generate *esprit de corps* within the organisation and discourage antagonistic relations between managers and employees.

Nevertheless, although most of the senior managers we spoke to believed their motivation policies had been quite successful, of the 322 employees who were asked to detail or describe the motivation policies used in their firms, no less than 49 per cent claimed that no such policies existed, and another 15 per cent were not aware of any policies – a total of 64 per cent of respondents were thus unaware of any single policy intended to increase their motivation at work. Moreover, of those who *did* point to the motivation policies used by their employers, the policy that received the largest percentage of mentions was that of financial incentives, an issue which in fact ranked very lowly in the senior managers' list of most important motivators.[27] And, when asked how much these policies motivated them, ten people replied 'a great deal', fifty-six said 'quite a bit', thirty-one answered 'only a little bit', eight said 'a very little bit', and ten 'not at all.' If we take the number of employees who believed that their firms did *not* have any motivation policies – and who presumably are not conscious of attempts to motivate them – and add them to the above figures, the policies pursued by the organisations included in our survey will have motivated only a fifth of their employees 'quite a bit' or 'a great deal'.

Of course, the fact that people are unaware of a policy does not mean that they are not influenced by it. And, had such policies not been implemented, it is possible that the motivation levels among our respondents might have been lower. Nevertheless, what these figures *do* suggest is the scale of the difficulty faced by many of our organisations in their attempts to communicate policies effectively to their workers, and to get them to understand what it is they are trying to achieve. Indeed, in some of the establishments we visited, the discrepancy between senior managers' understanding of the success of their motivational policies and the views held by the people to whom these policies applied could hardly have been greater. And in the case of one large financial services company, the extremely poor morale exhibited by the employees we interviewed was in stark contrast to the impression we derived from speaking to their senior managers. Although the latter had made a genuine attempt to communicate with their staff and treat them with consideration, it seems as if the organisation's complex system of communications had failed to generate honest *upward* communication and was better designed to discuss the needs of the job, and to pass the employer's messages down to staff, than to hear what people were really thinking. As one employee put it: 'Communication downwards is working OK, but there isn't enough detail, not enough fact. Communication reaches from top to bottom OK but it doesn't reach from bottom to top at all. That's the main point'.

Other respondents were equally critical of the way communication and participation appear to be designed not for listening to what employees have to say, nor to empower them, but rather to put across a managerial message. Even in the self-managing teams, we were told of many instances where the team leader was a former manager, a situation which risked diminishing the free play of discussion within the team. For example, an employee who was asked: 'To what extent do you have real power in being consulted by higher management on anything that relates to policy?' responded: 'None whatever!' And similar feelings were expressed by one of the team leaders who criticised the company's 'brainstorming' on the grounds that management used them merely to get agreement for their own programmes:

> There are some instances where we have been brought together as a management team – team leaders and management together – with the managers leading the session that is designed to get our input and our suggestions on something to be implemented. But there's a lot of talk about what the issues are and what we need to do, but then there's very little time to actually brainstorm the decision-making and I feel sometimes it's a bit sort of contrived and they're doing it knowing what they want to get out of it, and channelling it in that direction.

Listening to these respondents was a reminder of just how difficult it can be for managers to get their policies across to, and understood by, their workers, or indeed to establish communications that effectively inform them what their staff are actually thinking about the initiatives they implement. But it was also a reminder that the further one looks up the management ladder the more removed from everyday problems on the 'shop-floor' top management can be. And, as described in the following section, the growing disparity between the remuneration of senior managers and 'rank and file' employees is making it even more difficult for British companies to raise the morale and motivation of a workforce still suffering from the debilitating effects of redundancy and other forms of workforce 'restructuring'.

Equity and organisational commitment

In Chapter 4, Maria Hudson noted the way in which feelings of stress and insecurity are triggered not just by *absolute* changes in income and living standards but also by *relative* changes. And she described how the growth in wage inequality, which took place across the OECD during the 1980s and 1990s, had encouraged feelings of depression, shame and humiliation. Drawing on evidence from the JIWIS survey, she also emphasised that 'it is not so much inequality *per se* which triggers feelings of resentment and depression but the kind of inequality which is perceived as *unjust* or *unmerited*'. It is an argument which we endorse but also extend, so as to include the impact of inequity not just on the individual employee but on the organisation for which he or she works.

Our model of the relationship between inequity and organisational efficiency is drawn from the work of Sabine Guerts and her colleagues at the universities of Nijmegen and Utrecht. In their review of the literature on the association between 'inequity in the employment relationship' and 'absenteeism' and 'turnover intention', Guerts *et al.* conclude that 'the results of various studies show that when expectations of reciprocity remain unfulfilled or a violation of one's psychological contract is experienced, employees develop feelings of resentment, grievance, betrayal and mistrust' that, in turn, trigger various 'behavioural withdrawal reactions'. And in their study (of Dutch health-care professionals) the authors also discovered a strong association between perceived inequity and *turnover intention*[28] which was 'fully mediated by poor organisational commitment, which was in turn, partially triggered by feelings of resentment that were associated with perceived inequity'.[29] They also found an even stronger association between inequity and *absenteeism* – an association which held even in the absence of any open expression of resentment (see Figure 7.5).

In light of the negative association between perceptions of inequity and absenteeism/turnover it is worth noting the results taken from the Institute of Management's report on the *Quality of Working Life*. Published in

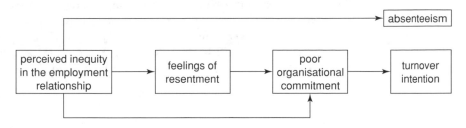

Figure 7.5 Absenteeism, turnover intention and inequity in employment
relationships

Source: Guerts *et al.* (1999, p. 261)

Table 7.1 Net satisfaction with aspects of present job by managerial level

	Chair/CEO/MD	Director	Senior manager	Middle manager	Junior manager
Level of autonomy	80	64	43	25	14
Career opportunities	65	37	9	−5	−13
Recognition for performance	51	30	11	−8	−17
Reward and remuneration	49	40	17	0	−14
Job security	47	30	12	1	3
Training opportunities	39	28	26	18	10

Source: Worrall and Cooper (1999, Table 9.3)

Note: The 'net satisfaction' is the percentage who were 'very satisfied' or 'satisfied' minus
the percentage who were 'dissatisfied' or 'very dissatisfied'.

1999, the report detailed the latest findings from Les Worrall and Cary
Cooper's on-going survey of 'managers' changing experiences'. As shown
in Table 7.1, the results suggested that middle and junior managers were
extremely dissatisfied with what they perceived as an unequal distribution
of rewards – in terms of reward and remuneration, autonomy and job security. Or, as the authors of the report put it, 'there are massive differences
in the perceptions of managers at different levels in the organisational
hierarchy'.[30]

Moreover, if junior and middle managers perceive the employment
relationship is unjust it is most unlikely that other (non-managerial)
workers will be immune to the same feelings of resentment and dissatisfaction. Indeed, as we discovered during the JIWIS survey, the majority of
employees – in managerial and non-managerial positions – believed they
were inadequately rewarded for the effort they put into their work, and
most believed that their employers were failing to take adequate steps to
balance the needs of the organisation with the requirements of workers'
social and family life. During the 1990s, these perceptions of inequity,

coupled with continuing fears about job security, will have made it more difficult for British organisations to raise the morale and motivation of their employees. And if these perceptions are maintained, the work of Guerts *et al.* suggests that the result will be manifested in the persistence of high levels of absenteeism and turnover, and yet higher cost implications for performance and profitability.

Trust and credibility

If managers' efforts to restore the health and organisational commitment of their employees are hindered by perceptions of inequity in the employment relationship, they are also undermined by a lack of trust. For, as described by Peter Makin *et al.*, although trust is hard to gain it is easy to lose: 'Trust takes a long time to establish, but only a single instance of betrayal can destroy it' and 'as trust declines so does the extent to which each group is prepared to be honest and open with the other'[31] – a fact recognised by all the senior managers we spoke to during the course of the JIWIS survey. Indeed, when we asked them to rate the motivational importance of twelve different factors, trust was described as 'very important' more often than any other factor. And not without good reason, considering the pattern of responses displayed in Figure 7.6 which shows that employees who did not trust their management were also much less likely to describe themselves as 'very motivated' or 'motivated'.

Nevertheless, over the past five years many of the organisations we visited have found it extremely hard to keep the trust of their employees. Not least because so many employees suspect that even if the organisation is sincere in its commitment to the welfare of the workforce, the pressures placed upon their managers make it increasingly difficult for them to honour this commitment. As explained by one team-worker employed in a public utilities industry, managers are not 'free agents' – even where they might wish to support their subordinates their own room for manoeuvre is often limited. Describing her line managers she stressed that:

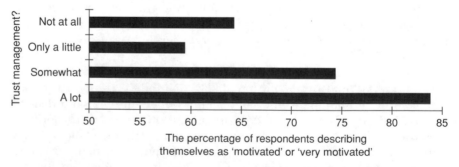

Figure 7.6 Relationship between trust in management and motivation

Source: JIWIS survey

They're in a difficult position because they've got to please two masters . . . They've got to look after the people, specifically a team leader has got to look after her team, but she's also got to serve her manager. So she's getting it from both sides.

The constant pressure for managers to get more work out of the workforce was also recognised by a lecturer at a college of further education when she told us that:

They're fully aware we work excessive hours but at the same time, they're looking to increase those hours, and the workloads, so what they say in terms of feeling compassion towards the number of hours that we actually work, doesn't match up with the number of hours that they want us to work.

Moreover, if employees doubted the ability of their managers to resist the pressure towards work-intensification they treated their organisation's promises about job security with even greater scepticism. Consider, for example, the efforts made by two of the manufacturing companies which had recently been through a series of large-scale redundancies. In an effort to restore worker morale both these companies had introduced comprehensive job security agreements offering guarantees to the workforce against compulsory redundancies for between three and five years. Employees from these companies to whom we spoke were clearly relieved to have these agreements in place; as one employee said when we asked him if there was anything more his employer could do to improve job security for the workforce: 'They've got a five-year no redundancy contract and you can't really ask any more of an employer than this'. Nevertheless, although the job security agreements were welcomed, many of those interviewed were not convinced that, when placed under pressure, their employer would actually stick to the agreement. As illustrated in the words of three respondents (quoted below) there is a big difference between making promises about job security and getting employees actually to believe in these promises:

The agreement is very comprehensive as long as the plant remains secure against closure. But I'm concerned about the selection procedures to be used to decide who goes to the new plant. They may get rid of shop stewards. They have cut jobs so much in the past.

(Manual worker, manufacturing industry)

I don't know really. They should continue with the agreement but when you're dealing with this company you've got to realise that they do cheat. They can turn it to themselves. For example, they're going to spend millions building a new plant even though they could upgrade this one.

(Manual worker, manufacturing industry)

> Now they wrap things up in ribbons – all fluffy and nice. They've had redundancies in the past and the new agreement is all the same package as before, it's just wrapped up in ribbons.
>
> (Manual worker, manufacturing industry)

The employees were not alone in finding job security agreements somewhat lacking in credibility, the same was true of some of the managers we spoke to. In fact, although eleven of the organisations which participated in the survey claimed to have 'a stated policy of deliberately avoiding compulsory redundancies', the responses to our questions make clear that, for those firms that do have them, or have even negotiated agreements on this issue, they are not seen by senior management as legally binding and will be broken if, in their eyes, circumstances warrant such action. Indeed we were made aware of one existing agreement that the management had already decided could not be maintained in view of a forthcoming merger. As a senior manager of the company concerned put it, 'although it is our basic operating philosophy to avoid redundancy, in the event of a merger all bets are off in respect of the undertakings given by the company to the staff on no compulsory redundancies'. Moreover, in this organisation and in the other companies that had offered an explicit commitment to job security, it was made quite clear to the workforce that such commitments would be 'conditional' upon the 'good behaviour' of the workforce, that is, they would be dependent upon the acceptance of flexible hours, shift work, retraining and relocation.

Indeed, the problem of credibility was a theme that emerged in all of the organisations we visited. When we asked employees to explain why they could not trust management to look after their best interests, many of them told us that, although management might have good intentions, they could not keep their promises in the face of the 'external pressures' exerted by competitors and dominant stakeholders (i.e. shareholders/ fundholders) and by the threat of mergers and aggressive takeovers:

> They [managers] do tend to change. It's the demands of other people, i.e. the shareholders, which makes them change their minds and target areas for cuts even after they have promised not to.

> I don't trust them a great deal because external forces are external forces! Even if they wanted to maintain the headcount, the shareholders and economics will finally decide what happens.

> I don't trust them at all because in the last few years we've got this new atmosphere where managers don't care and they're powerless to do anything about it even if they do care.

Conclusion

It is clear that relationships of trust play a vital role in maintaining the flexibility, morale and motivation of employees. And, as Ines Wichert describes in Chapter 8 of this volume, British companies – and their counterparts in Europe and the US – still have plenty to learn about the kinds of employment relationship work which best serve to maintain the health and productivity of their employees. Nevertheless, the findings presented in this chapter should remind us of the limits to which the *individual* organisation can provide a credible, long-term commitment to the health and security of its employees. The intensity of the competitive pressures to which producers are subject means that the single workplace, or even the single firm, is unlikely to provide a secure enough base for creating and maintaining the long-term commitments necessary for establishing and sustaining trust and cooperation. As will be discussed in Chapter 9, we need to foster those institutions which regulate the competitive relationship *between* firms.

In particular, we have in mind the role played by the trade unions; by the regulators of the newly privatised industries, by the Monopolies and Mergers Commission; and by the agencies charged with the implementation of new forms of corporate governance. In the end it will be these institutions, and perhaps new ones yet to be established, which will be charged with the ultimate responsibility for encouraging and enabling each individual employer to make a genuine commitment to the long-term interests of the workforce. The financial consequences in terms of absenteeism, sickness, compensation for industrial illness, staff replacement and training costs are rising continuously, and, with increasing use of industrial tribunals and the introduction of employment protection legislation, those costs are bound to become ever more onerous for those employers who fail to foster genuine partnership with the workers, and who decline to provide conditions and rewards appropriate to a 'partnership' with the workforce.

8   Stress intervention

What can managers do?

Ines Wichert

In the previous three chapters we looked at the costs – to workers, families and employing organisations – of job insecurity and work intensification. In light of these costs, it is not surprising that stress intervention in the workplace has become the subject of a growing number of research reports, some of which have received extensive coverage in the mass media. Much of this research examines the need for organisational health promotion programmes and employee assistance programmes, of which stress management is often an integral part. There is a very wide variety of existing practices and an equally diverse literature on various forms of organisational stress management programmes such as biofeedback, relaxation classes and various cognitive techniques for dealing with stress. Another area of stress intervention which has received a lot of attention is the provision of social support, the impact of which was demonstrated in Chapter 5 where we concluded that:

*   Social support has a beneficial effect on health and well-being for all employees, not just those suffering from job insecurity or work intensification.
*   That support can be effective from either managers or peers.
*   Several different types of support can be useful, including the provision of direct help, of information or of emotional support.

This chapter will build on these findings, and explore in more detail the extent to which the problems outlined in the previous chapters might be alleviated by the presence of more supportive managers and organisational cultures. And, as we examine the benefits and problems associated with the provision of social support, we will draw upon the twenty-six in-depth interviews contained in the JIWIS dataset.

The chapter will be divided into three parts. In the first part we will examine the various pathways through which social support alleviates the impact of work-related stress. In the second part, we will point to some of the problems encountered by managers and supervisors in their attempts to provide this support. In the third part, we will outline a number of steps which employers can take to ensure the success of programmes aimed at tackling the stress caused by overwork and job insecurity.

How does social support alleviate stress?

What gives social support its preventative and buffering qualities? With respect to the *main* (preventative) effects of social support, Shumaker and Brownell state that the enhancement of overall physical and mental health can be reduced to three specific functions:

- *Gratification of affiliative needs* where support can meet people's needs for contact and companionship and thereby mitigate the deleterious effects of isolation and loneliness.
- *Self-identity maintenance and enhancement* where people can evaluate and clarify their belief system by comparing their own opinions, attitudes and beliefs to those of others.
- *Self-esteem enhancement* where supportive exchanges can help to validate a person's sense of his or her own value and adequacy.[1]

These health-sustaining functions are particularly important during times of stress, and their effectiveness before the onset of stress can determine how much strain a person experiences in times of stress. This means that if people continuously receive support which provides them with a sense of security, bolsters their self-esteem and strengthens their self-identity, then they are less likely to be susceptible to stressors than those people who have not received such support.[2]

With respect to the *buffering effect*, social support may be important at two different points in the stressor–stress–strain relationship:

- Social support may intervene between the stressful event and the experience of stress by *reducing or eliminating the stress response*. The stress response might be reduced or eliminated through other people helping a person to *redefine a potentially stressful situation* as less stressful. Research by Shumaker and Brownell indicates that social support can broaden the individual's interpretation of the event and promote its clearer understanding.[3]
- Social support may intervene between the experience of stress and the onset of impaired health and well-being by either *reducing or eliminating the psychological, physiological and behavioural responses* that follow the stress reaction or by directly *influencing the illness behaviours and physiological processes that are triggered by these responses*.[4] Shumaker and Brownell argue that social support can interface at this stage by *broadening the number of coping options*. The resources provided include referrals to appropriate professional service agencies, encouragement to seek assistance, and the provision of information and problem-solving techniques.[5]

If we examine the data from the JIWIS sample, we can identify several types of social support, each of which fulfils one or more of the functions specified above. Take, for example, the emotional support received through the act of talking and being listened to. In our twenty-six in-depth interviews, we asked our respondents to describe what it was about the process of talking with others that made it so helpful in dealing with work-related stress.[6] In response, they said it provided an opportunity:

- to remove the feeling of isolation through sharing one's experience
- to boost a person's confidence and to give them reassurance
- to allow a person to unload their problems and to 'get it off their chest'
- to show interest in a person and their problems
- to exchange information, give advice, make suggestions and help with problem-solving.

And, of these five functions, the most frequently cited was that of 'combating isolation'. To quote from a male manager in a utilities company:

> What causes the worry to get worse in the first place is that you feel isolated. You think that you're the only person that feels that way and that you're the only person that can't cope. And I suppose just the knowledge of talking – just talking to other people, a group of other people and finding that you're all in exactly the same position. Then all of a sudden, probably three-quarters of the stress has gone away. The workload is still there, you've got to deal with that but you're not having a problem because you're thinking Oh, I can't cope and I'm abnormal. All of that's gone because you know that everyone's in the same position.

Not surprisingly, when respondents were asked what they *themselves* had done to help other people at work deal with job insecurity and other forms of workplace stress, 'talking and listening' proved to be the most common form of social support. The emotional character of this support is illustrated in the following quotation from a 'team leader' in the insurance industry:

> Yes, as part of this management team we reciprocate with one another. One of our team leaders who is on a similar level to myself, works in a different sub-office which we now know is closing down and she is very emotional. When we heard the big news she was very upset and I made it a point to go down to the branch and see her and go into a different room with her and sit down and chat.

Three of the twenty-six respondents in our qualitative interviews described in more detail what happens during the process of talking about personal problems. The following quotes illustrate this in the respondents' own words. The first two describe a situation in which they were helping someone else, whilst the third describes the kind of support she herself is looking for:

> how you're feeling, are you alright now, what's been happening, do you want to tell me about it but you don't have to.
>
> (Male team leader in retail bank)

> chat . . . about what she thought and why she felt that way. What she was going to do . . . how things are going. Have you changed your mind about leaving, have you reconsidered your thoughts? Do you think you can stay with the company and do something else?
>
> (Male team leader in insurance company)

> Listening, I think. Just having somebody to talk to, somebody who's interested and cares about what you've got to say, what's happening to you!
>
> (Female lecturer in further education college)

These three examples show that during the process of talking, the support provider seems to encourage the support recipient to unburden and unload. The support provider shows an interest in the person's problems by asking questions about the person's situation. The support provider invites the support recipient to talk and signals that he or she is prepared to listen. It is important to note here that support is offered and not 'enforced': *'Do you want to tell me about it but you don't have to . . .'*. It is easy to see how 'enforced' support can be harmful. A person who intrudes into someone else's life and provides unwanted advice or wants to know all the details of a person's troubles, which that person does not want to share, is likely to have detrimental rather than beneficial effects.

A theme which is closely related to talking and communicating is that of exchanging information. The exchange and provision of information seems to fulfil a particularly important role in the experience of job insecurity. As we saw in Chapter 5, one of the defining characteristics of job insecurity is the experience of uncertainty and ambiguity.[7] And the need for honest and timely information was clearly apparent in the JIWIS sample. When our in-depth interviewees were asked about what could be done in order to alleviate the stress associated with job insecurity, 'better communication' and 'being kept informed' were consistently mentioned. This desire for better communication is reflected in the following quotation (from a male team leader in the banking sector):

And as far as insecurity is concerned, the thing there would be if there was better communication from the top downwards to tell people exactly what is going on, rather than letting rumours and snippets of information filter out. I think an open communication policy would be the most helpful thing there.

So what is it that makes the provision of information on the situation of the organisation so important in times of insecurity? One of the important functions fulfilled by the provision of information is that it allows a person to plan ahead (as illustrated in the quotations below). As described by Warr, predictability is important for the coping process since it allows for the nature and timing of potentially noxious events to be anticipated. By contrast, high levels of uncertainty can have paralysing effects on the coping process.[8]

if there was more open communication . . . the certainty that you know something's going to happen and you can start thinking about it and planning for it.

(Male team leader in a retail bank)

They [the employees] know the information first hand and they're aware, so they can make a decision as and when necessary.

(Male product manager in manufacturing company)

Furthermore, in the analysis of our quantitative data, we found that in situations of both job insecurity and work intensification, good 'communication between you and your immediate supervisor' showed strong positive associations with employees' general health as assessed by the GHQ. But communication was also found to be important in a wider organisational context. Judgements about 'the quality of communication within your organisation' also showed strong positive associations with employees' general health.

It becomes apparent, then, that while information on the situation of the company seems to be particularly important for dealing with job insecurity, information and good communication on a more general level also seem to be important for dealing with work intensification. This might also explain why informational support was one of the types of support which showed the most consistent positive main effects on employees' health and well-being in the analyses of our quantitative data which we reported in Chapter 5. As we saw earlier on in this chapter, and as has already been indicated here, the provision of relevant information might broaden a person's coping resources and therefore reduce the strength of the stress response which follows the stress appraisal, as suggested by Shumaker and Brownell.[9]

Nevertheless, it is important to remember that too much information may not be welcome. A growing literature now exists which documents the detrimental effects of information overload often caused by excessive use of e-mail and memos. This danger of information overload was also mentioned by a few respondents in our in-depth interviews. One respondent said that his manager passed on '*tons of information*' which the respondent felt was far too much. What he wanted was '*brief information . . . just enough to be informed*'.

In addition to clear and timely information, the respondents in our survey also talked at great length about the importance of receiving positive feedback. Our qualitative data showed that the beneficial effects associated with receiving positive feedback were 'a boost to one's self-confidence' and 'keeping up one's motivation levels'. As described by a female lecturer in a regional college, constructive feedback helps people to feel good about themselves:

> I've had a lot of positive feedback, so possibly that for me relieves a lot of the stress which is why maybe I'm less stressed at work than in other situations, because not that you get constant feedback, but I think probably in education every now and again either from another lecturer or student you get very positive comments. It reinforces feelings in yourself that you're not doing a bad job, really. I get them regularly enough to feel quite good . . .

In our in-depth interviews, five of our twenty-six respondents used the word 'appreciation'. Three of these five said that a *lack* of appreciation (from their employers and supervisors) had made them feel let down and demotivated and had decreased their organisational commitment. By contrast, the two respondents who reported that they received appreciation outlined how beneficial it was for them. It made them feel 'happy and secure' – a response that accords with the predictions of Greenberg and Baron, who argue that the recognition of employees' accomplishments is one of the most important ways for people to satisfy their esteem needs.[10]

However, these observations need to be viewed in light of the results which emerged from our quantitative analysis. In the self-completion questionnaire, all the respondents who took part in the JIWIS survey, were asked how much feedback they received on the quality of their performance. When we examined these responses we could find no correlation between psychological well-being and the amount of feedback received. This result suggests to us that there may be a crucial difference between *accurate* feedback and *positive* feedback. In other words, when our in-depth interviewees talked about the positive benefits of feedback, they may have been thinking less about the information derived from performance appraisals than about the emotional support that comes from feeling appreciated (an issue to which we will return at a later point in this chapter).

Talking (and being listened to), timely information and positive feed-back were not the only forms of social support that were valued by our respondents. There was also a desire for practical, 'instrumental', forms of support. For example, when we asked our in-depth interviewees what could be done to help alleviate the stress associated with work overload, the responses made consistent reference to (a) having more people to do the work, (b) having less work to do and having less performance pressure, and finally (c) having more time to do the work. As described by a team leader in a retail bank:

> Stress in general I think could be sorted out a lot by having the right number of people to do the work. That's the main thing . . . Stress appears from when people are trying to do too much with too little.

A connected theme here is the indirect provision of instrumental support by a supervisor through instilling a supportive climate in his or her work team. While a lot of support might already be taking place among co-workers, Greenberg and Baron point out that the reciprocity principle can be used by the manager to instil high degrees of cooperation and support in his or her team:

> The key task in establishing co-operation in organisations, then, seems to be getting it started. Once individuals, groups or units have begun to co-operate, the process may be largely self-sustaining. To encourage co-operation, therefore, managers should do everything possible to get the process under way. After it begins, the obvious benefits of co-operation, plus powerful tendencies toward reciprocity, may be expected to maintain it at high levels.[11]

Time constraints and supervisor stress

Adequate provision of social support through the supervisor requires time and resources on the part of the supervisor. However, as we have already pointed out in Chapter 5, managers have suffered more than any other group from the intensification of their own work. Cost-cutting, along with technology changes, restructuring and the loss of key personnel are the key reasons given by managers for their higher workloads.[12] Indeed, a large literature now exists on the stressfulness of managerial jobs. These trends were also reflected in our data. One problem that repeatedly emerged in both our quantitative data and our qualitative data was that supervisors were far too busy and stressed themselves to be able to provide support. As a male team leader in financial services noted:

> I think, if you talked to a line manager and told him about the stress at work, the initial thought would be the reaction – tell me about it,

because I've got more than you! This sort of attitude. I think it would be a case of yes, I know, because I'm in the same position. If you find out what the answer is tell me! That sort of thing. I don't think there is any support in that direction.

One employee reported that when she approached her line manager to talk about her stresses at work, she ended up listening to her line manager's problems because her line manager was so stressed herself! The next quote from a male team leader in the insurance industry is a good example of a supervisor talking about the stresses of being a supervisor.

I'm definitely more stressed than the people in my team. Anyway . . . because where I feed out information, I'm dealing with the other five or six people on a regular basis asking them about their problems and concerns, and trying to talk to them of what might be and what might not be, knocking down rumours, promoting connection. This sort of thing . . . And because you care about these people, you try and sit down and work a sort of strategy for turning it round to an advantage. That stress that it puts on you just for that is hard to control.

The conflict of roles, the stigma of stress and confidentiality

But it is not only the stressfulness of supervisors' jobs and their lack of time that make their provision of social support for their employees problematic. The conflicting roles which a supervisor has to fulfil also make the provision of social support problematic. It is not only part of a supervisor's job to help her subordinates deal with their problems but also to ensure that production goals and targets are met by her and her team (and very often this is the part of a supervisor's job which is perceived to be the more important function). This can often make it very hard for an employee to talk about matters such as stress at work with their manager.

Respondents in the in-depth interviews were asked what they see as the 'pros and cons of talking to your supervisor about stress at work'. Some respondents perceived talking to a supervisor about stress as having advantages such as raising a supervisor's awareness of problems and giving him or her an opportunity to be supportive, as well as receiving support, understanding and empathy from the supervisor. Most of the time, however, talking to a supervisor about stress was associated with the disadvantage of the supervisor thinking that the person cannot cope or cannot do the job, which in turn was perceived as having negative effects on potential future promotions. A male manager in a utilities company had the following to say:

Right. See they are the people that very often will be able to enhance your career, if they think you've got the capabilities. So if they think you're capable of doing another job, then they might be the person that will make that happen for you. But if they don't think you're capable, which might well be the case if you've talked to them about a mental problem – not a mental problem but being in stress doing this, you know – then they might have the perception that – Oh, I won't ask [him] to do this because last week he got stressed about this and I don't want to put too much pressure on him.

In our in-depth interviews two managers in particular spoke about the stigma that is attached to suffering from stress in the workplace. Both reported that they do not ask for any emotional support from other people at work. The environment in which they work is very competitive. Showing signs of stress in this environment would be interpreted as a sign of weakness and is therefore avoided. One manager was off sick with stress for a couple of days but did not tell anybody about it at work because he was afraid that managers would think that he was not capable of doing his job.

Closely related to the reasons for the above-mentioned reluctance of talking to a supervisor about personal problems such as experiencing stress, are supervisor characteristics such as trust and respect. Respondents stated that they would only approach a supervisor for help if they trusted and respected him or her. A male manager in a utilities company said the following when he was asked whether he thought that it would help if his boss had the time to talk to an employee about problems:

I do, if they were a nice kind of person that you felt you could talk to. My boss currently, I wouldn't tell him anything about my personal life, because I'm sure he'd probably discuss it with other people and I wouldn't trust him. I don't respect the man.

The need for trusting and respecting a supervisor, however, was not only mentioned with respect to talking about personal problems but also about problems related to work itself. Another important prerequisite for deciding whether to approach a supervisor for help is confidentiality, as can also be seen in this last quote.

There seems to be evidence that it is more difficult to talk to one's supervisor about stress in the workplace rather than talking about problems related specifically to the immediate work process. It is often not easy for employees and is often associated with negative consequences for a person's career, due to the dual responsibilities of a supervisor for her team as well as for achieving the goals that have been set out for the team. When people say that they want to talk to a supervisor, this does not necessarily mean that they want to talk about personal problems but rather to clarify a specific query, solve a problem, lay out action plans, etc. Not all talking and listening necessarily needs the emotional, social component as

Kiesler points out.[13] For supervisors to be able to help their subordinates to deal with stress, however, it is necessary for employees to be able to talk to their supervisors about their experiences of work-related stress and to receive sympathetic reactions and helpful actions. In this context trust, respect and belief in confidentiality are also important.

Lack of information and rumours

In the in-depth interviews it became very apparent that respondents felt that information on the situation of the company in insecure times was very important. Many respondents, however, reported that they were not receiving any such information from the organisation which created a lot of rumours, suspicions and uncertainties, which in turn increased the feeling of job insecurity as can be seen in the next quote from a male lecturer in a further education college:

> Rumours. Everybody knows someone else who works in another college and rumours, as in any office, are very, very easily spread and you can find them taking over. Not just yourself but lots of conversations in the staff room. Other people talking about, chatting . . . people stirring each other up with gossip and rumour. And that creates a sort of spiral of insecurity, I suppose . . . I think other things that contribute to that are lack of communication or poor communication from management.

The importance of rumours was recognised in one insurance company and employees were encouraged to approach their line managers with any rumours which they had heard so that those rumours could be either verified or denied. Of course, while it has been shown widely that keeping employees informed in times of insecurity and uncertainty is important, very often in such times information is not available or cannot be divulged. One female line manager in the banking industry pointed out that she believed that the only thing that was going to reduce feelings of job insecurity were answers to all her staff's questions that at this stage she could not answer. But other respondents pointed out that even by outlining what is known and what is not known, rumours could be stopped and thus feelings of job insecurity and the related stresses.

Negative feedback and performance appraisal systems

Feedback on how well a person is doing in his or her job is now often given in the context of employees' half-yearly or yearly performance appraisal. But, in contrast to the beneficial impact of informal positive feedback, our quantitative data showed that performance appraisal systems – a prevalent feature of modern organisations – tend to increase stress and decrease well-being. Only very few respondents in the in-depth interviews reported that their performance appraisals were good and helpful. According to our respondents, the majority of the performance appraisal systems in their workplaces seemed to focus on the negative rather than the positive aspects of a person's performance. A cashier and credit controller in an insurance company reports on his experience of a performance appraisal:

> Yeah. We got on OK but I thought I deserved something different. At that time I used to come in early, work late, really working hard and at the end of it I thought I have put in 110 per cent, there's no way I'm going to walk away with a good! So we were arguing and I said I won't accept it. The thing is, with the new system, if we don't agree you have to carry on until you do agree and it can go on for hours and I was there till 6 o'clock at night and we just didn't agree. Then in the end she goes – I gave her one or two other examples and she said yes, OK, I think you do deserve it. I think the reason she was emotional was that she was leaving that week to go to Birmingham. I think I started crying first because I was really straight with her and I said there's no way I'm going to accept it so in the end she said OK I do deserve it, then she started crying. Had to go through it again with Peter anyway. The system's just not right.

Other problems associated with performance appraisal systems were found in our quantitative data. Being subject to individual performance targets, especially when these targets are unachievable, exerted a negative impact on employees' GHQ scores and was associated with more negative feelings about work. If anything, our data showed that the stressful nature of appraisal systems may be even more acute for insecure employees. Furthermore, official performance appraisals only take place every six to twelve months. So respondents felt that there is a need for informal day-to-day feedback and praise but also constructive criticism and guidance. One respondent reported that she perceived her performance appraisals as good and helpful but that the feedback she received on a daily basis was very negative and unconstructive, which she found very frustrating.

Also, what became evident in the interviews was that performance appraisals were not only a problem for the people receiving them but also for those giving them. Asked what the company could change to make his life better, a team leader in an insurance company had the following to say:

> It would be the appraisal system. I think it's appalling. It's so inconsistent, so subjective. I really don't enjoy it at all. I was talking to a friend the other day and saying there's one particular aspect of my job that I really don't like and apart from that, it's not usually that bad, my job. But my appraisal system I just really don't look forward to doing it at all.

When it comes to alleviating feelings of job insecurity, two respondents pointed out that performance appraisals can both increase and decrease feelings of job insecurity: they felt that performance appraisals give some assurance if a person's results are good and if the person is on target, but that they increase feelings of insecurity if the results are bad and if a person is not on target. The majority of respondents, however, felt that performance appraisals, even when they showed that a person performed to the company's expectations, cannot reduce feelings of job insecurity. One supervisor in the banking sector pointed out that he felt that performance appraisal did not help people in dealing with job insecurity since the local managers who were conducting the assessment did not know either what was 'around the corner'. Similar feelings were voiced by other respondents too who pointed out that a good performance appraisal will not be a guarantee for keeping one's job because, ultimately, the decision on whether further redundancies or restructuring have to take place are determined by outside pressures.

With regard to work intensification, the use of performance appraisal was also mentioned a few times. One finance manager, for example, reported on how he had helped a subordinate deal with his high workload by outlining what was expected of him, which he said had helped the employee to realise that '*it was not as bad as he thought and that he was 70 per cent to the answer*'. One team leader in an insurance company, on the other hand, pointed out that the constant upgrading of targets, set as part of the performance appraisal system, only added to the already existing pressures from work intensification.

Overall, it can be said that performance appraisals, if conducted in a constructive and positive way, and informal feedback are very important to keep up an employee's confidence and motivation when dealing with everyday stresses. However, feedback and performance appraisal are not very important tools in allaying fears of job insecurity. This seems not only to be due to the negative perceptions of performance appraisal systems but also to the feeling that possible job loss is beyond the company's control and therefore also beyond the control of the appraising line manager.

Moreover, while constructive feedback on what is expected of an employee might help to deal with high workloads, increased performance pressures might only add to a person's high workload and stress. In such conditions, feedback (particularly that which takes place within a system of formal appraisal) might be perceived, not as a personal, informal and supportive act, but as bureaucratic, goal-oriented and lacking a personal and supportive touch. This might explain why we found neither main nor buffering effects for feedback support on GHQ scores in our quantitative analysis. Alternatively, it is possible that performance appraisal systems work very well and to employees' satisfaction in some companies in our sample and not at all well in other companies so that the net effect has been cancelled out. But this seems unlikely given that, in our in-depth interviews, few employees had good things to say about their appraisal systems.

Lack of instrumental support and resources

Although having less work to do, and having more time and more people to do the work were constantly mentioned by respondents in our in-depth interviews as ways of alleviating the stress from work overload, supervisors seem to be able to do very little to provide these resources, as a quote from a male team leader in the financial sector illustrates:

> Well, I sort of manage myself and the line managers, if you like, in the position I'm in I can see there's not a lot they can do either because of the downward pressure on them. So it's not something – having said that, I know other people do and it comes on to me, trying to get more resources or more assistance with things. But that doesn't work either, they would only get temporary help and it would go again because the organisation has very tight controls on resources that are available. Managers can only manage what they've got anyway. If I go and ask for an assistant for the next six weeks to do my work, I know what the answer will be! So I'm not going to bother asking.

Wheatley found in her survey that one way in which managers tried to deal with their own high workloads was by delegating some of that workload to their subordinates.[14] Therefore, in order to deal with their own workload, managers often have to burden their subordinates with more work rather than being able to reduce their team's workload. Furthermore, since restructuring processes and redundancies often aim at losing personnel, which increases the workload for the remaining people in the first place, getting more people to do the work is often impossible (as was illustrated well by the previous quote). Immediate supervisors are powerless, since there are just no resources in companies any more which a supervisor can secure for his or her team in order to help them to do the work.

There are also problems with the *indirect* supervisor provision of social support. Although helpful colleagues and a good working climate are important for employees' well-being and motivation, there are barriers to instilling this helpfulness among colleagues, even if Greenberg and Baron point out that the operating principle of reciprocity should make it easy to establish a cooperative working environment.[15] Similar to our findings for seeking support from supervisors, we found that respondents felt that they needed to know someone and be able to trust them in order to talk to them about their problems and approach them for help. In this context respondents mentioned talking about their problems and worries to 'friends at work' rather than just 'mere' colleagues. The provision of emotional support might therefore require a certain degree of friendship and intimacy which can only be found in the workplace when colleagues have become friends. And such friendship and trust, of course, cannot simply be imposed from above. Friendships have to form and depend on interpersonal liking.

Also, like our findings for supervisor support, we found that high workloads, pressure and stress might make the exchange of supportive behaviours less likely. One effect of work intensification which respondents mentioned in the in-depth interviews was that people who are off sick, who have to leave work earlier due to family responsibilities or who are struggling at work are victimised by their team rather than being supported. In extreme cases one respondent mentioned that people even shout at colleagues for 'not pulling their weight'. Therefore, *support provision* is reduced. Equally, the *seeking of support* is also hampered. Respondents reported that they are turning up for work when they are ill because they are reluctant to burden their already overstretched colleagues with even more work. And in the modern, high-pressured workplace, providing support might just be perceived as being too costly since there is no time available to support others without neglecting one's own work:

> You come in when you feel one degree under – it's only when you get to five or six, maybe ten degrees under – whatever that means – that you decide that's enough, I just can't do it. But you know full well that if you don't go in, stuff you miss out on doing is still going to be there when you get back, doubled.
>
> (Male lecturer in further education college)

Possible solutions

We have seen that the provision of social support, especially types of support important in dealing with stress at work, are not always easily provided in the insecure and intensified workplace. Stressed line managers, conflicts between people- and task-management, lack of information and inadequate feedback systems all play a part here. So what can we do in order to facilitate the provision of social support in workplaces which we and others have found to be so important for employees in times of difficulties, constant changes and high pressure at work?

Let's look first at what conditions must be satisfied in order for employees to feel they can safely seek support from a supervisor for problems with work-related stress. To begin with, managers need to make clear that talking about stress will not lead to reprisals. The employees need to feel that they can talk about their problems or experiences of stress without being punished for it by being passed over at the next round of promotions. This is not an easy task, however. Viewing stress as a sign of weakness is still a very prevalent attitude in workplaces, especially in competitive workplaces. While a manager can go some way to instil a culture of stress acceptance in his or her team or department, the overall company culture will still determine this in large part.

However, managers and supervisors 'buying in' to the idea that stress is a weakness can further perpetuate this ill-adaptive attitude. Wheatley, in a recent report on manager stress,[16] points out that managers who accept high levels of stress for themselves and suffer from those, rather than actively trying to reduce them, will set bad examples for their subordinates.

And then there is of course the problem of conflicting supervisor roles: managing people and achieving targets. One way of overcoming this problem to a certain degree might be through the use of employee assistance programmes (EAPs). A lot of workplaces now have EAPs and phone-lines. EAPs are independent companies that offer a range of services to employees, including stress and legal telephone services and access to counselling services. Like all stress-related health services, the take-up of these services may be low due to the stigma associated with mental health services, so organisations will not only have to make these services available but will also have to actively promote them if they are to reach employees suffering with stress-related illnesses.

The fear of non-confidentiality can also be a deterrent. In most cases the human resource department will need to be involved in the referral of an employee to a counsellor, and will want to know something of the diagnosis and outcome, but will not divulge confidential information to the employee's department. Of course, EAPs will only be taken up by employees if they feel that the service provided is confidential. Our own data and other findings suggest that there is a higher level of perceived confidentiality with services provided by organisations outside the company rather than in-house services.

It would be wrong to suggest, however, that any kind of stress-related problem should be dealt with through an EAP. Very often, employees need an *immediate* point of contact to talk about both personal and job-related problems. Alternatively, as suggested by one respondent, a mentor system could be built up where a supervisor from a different team could act as a mentor, so that the process of provision of help and appraising someone for further promotion would be separated. But, while a stress counsellor and a mentor can deal with the symptoms of stress, they cannot usually deal with the source of stress. In some circumstances counsellors are able to make recommendations for changes to organisational practices where they are seen to be a cause of the stress, but this is a very indirect and roundabout route for organisational change.

Talking to a trade union representative might also be a possible avenue for an employee to follow. Many trade unions have their own policies on stress and now see tackling stress in the workplace, and representing their members who are subject to unacceptable levels of stress, as among their most important roles. However, the weakened bargaining position of trade unions and the lower levels of membership mean that this option is not open to all employees. And, as we have seen in Chapter 4, in some organisations, there can be similar problems of confidentiality and trust with trade unions as with management – indeed in some white-collar situations an employee's manager is also their trade union representative!

But encouraging employees to seek support and to talk to someone about stress and personal problems is not enough in itself. During the process of talking, a number of rules have to be followed. Making time to talk to employees is not always easy for supervisors since their own workloads are very often even higher than those of their subordinates. However, once a manager has agreed to talk to an employee about a problem, then this is, as Austin points out, an implicit promise to listen actively and not only to go 'through the motions'.[17] Seyper *et al.* found that the better a person is as a listener, the more likely he or she is to rise rapidly up the organisational hierarchy.[18] Although there is good evidence that good listening skills are important aspects of good management, a lot of managers seem to be unaware of what others think about their listening skills. Brownell found that managers overestimated the quality of their listening skills.[19] While they rated their listening skills as good or very good, their employees did not agree. Brownell also discovered that those rated as good listeners by their employees were those who had previously been trained in listening skills, which suggests that such training in listening and spotting and dealing with stress might be a good investment in managers.

The literature on leadership and effective management does recognise the importance of manager training. Such manager training is not only advocated for listening skills but also for skills referred to as *initiating structure* and *consideration*. The initiating structure skills are mainly concerned with production and getting a job done. Supervisors high on this dimension engage in actions such as organising work, inducing subordinates to follow rules, setting goals, and making leader and subordinate roles explicit. Consideration, on the other hand, is primarily concerned with establishing good relations with their subordinates and being liked by them. Supervisors high on this dimension engage in actions such as doing favours for subordinates, explaining things to them, and ensuring their welfare. Since the two dimensions seem to be largely independent,[20] a manager can score high on both dimensions, which has been shown to be the most beneficial management pattern.[21] This may not always be easily achieved, however, as Greenberg and Baron point out. Managers high on concern for other people might be reluctant to act in a directive manner toward subordinates and often shy away from presenting them with negative feedback.[22] And if leaders score high on concern for production then employees may soon conclude that no one cares about them or their welfare. However, Blake and Mouton have developed a way of training managers ('grid training') to score high on both these dimensions.[23]

In addition to encouraging employees to seek help for work-related stress and to provide appropriate social support through listening, talking, giving advice and setting out goals, managers need to take an active stance on stress management in their teams. They need to learn how to monitor stress levels and intervene before the first symptoms of stressed team members appear. Cox in his report for the Health and Safety Executive talks about the need for 'timely reaction' which refers to recognising and dealing with problems as they arise.[24] In the UK employers now have a duty of care regarding work-related stress in exactly the same way that they are responsible for safety from hazardous chemicals in the workplace. And if employers' sense of moral obligation for their employees' well-being is not enough, the considerable settlement figures in recent legal cases involving stress at work have started to focus employers' minds on stress prevention too. Employers need to show that they have in place adequate procedures, both to detect stress in the workplace and to deal with it before it becomes more serious. The importance of monitoring systems in this early detection have been emphasised by the Health and Safety Commission.[25] Many organisations now monitor several indicators of stress (such as absenteeism and sickness) so that differences between departments or changes over time can be detected and, if necessary, acted upon.

Conclusion

As has become apparent in this chapter, a radical rethink is necessary as to how workplaces are structured and what values and attitudes are adopted. Supervisors and managers suffer from ever-increasing levels of work-intensification and stress. They are targeted for redundancy in efforts to create a flatter organisational structure and the surviving managers have to deal with increased workloads both in terms of managing bigger teams and having increased task responsibilities. And by putting too much strain on supervisors, a vital part of their jobs – people management – can no longer be performed adequately. And this means that a vital source of support for an also ever-increasingly stretched and stressed workforce is taken away.

Susceptibility to stress must not be seen as a personal weakness. While people might differ in their susceptibility to stress, and general stress intervention programmes such as relaxation classes and cognitive restructuring might help here, it cannot be dismissed as the individual's responsibility to deal with ever-increasing levels of stress in the workplace. As Lazarus and Folkman point out, 'better adaptation might come about through changing the social or organisational structure'.[26]

The current form of people management – both the 'managing' of managers and the 'managing' of the workforce – will not be sustainable over a longer period if work intensification continues. We need a radical rethink at senior management and employment policy level and an endorsement of a new culture that accepts stress as something that is real, that needs to be monitored and managed systemically, and that must not be ignored and written off as a sign of personal weakness. And, as with other efforts to change the workplace, endorsement by senior management both through clear communications and also through setting good examples is vital.

9 What can governments do?

Frank Wilkinson and David Ladipo

Confronted with the pressures and insecurities experienced by today's labour force, what, if anything, should our governments be doing? Should they embrace the philosophy of *laissez-faire* and put their faith in the auto-corrective powers of the free market or should they strengthen the laws and institutions that regulate the markets for labour and capital? The *laissez-faire* response is certainly the most popular, particularly among British and American politicians. But, as this chapter will illustrate, the experience of some of the world's most competitive economies suggests that the regulatory protection of social rights is of vital importance not just to the health of the individual worker but to the effective operation of the economy as a whole.

Laissez-faire

At the heart of free market economics lies the theoretical proposition that the economy is largely self-regulating because the market evaluates the effectiveness of institutions and selects out those with efficiency-retarding tendencies. In the words of Adam Smith:

> The natural effort of every individual to better his own condition, when suffered to exert itself with freedom and security, is so powerful a principle, that it is alone, and without any assistance, not only capable of carrying on the society to wealth and prosperity, but of surmounting a hundred impertinent obstructions with which the folly of human laws too often incumbers its operations.[1]

For Smith and his successors, the 'unencumbered' operation of the market does not require the complete *absence* of regulation. On the contrary, they acknowledge that, for markets to work effectively, certain regulations need to be enforced in order to prevent collective and individual monopolies operating in restraint of trade.[2] Indeed, most neo-liberals still pay lip service to Smith's description of 'monopoly' as an 'enemy to good management'. But they also insist that the urge to regulate must be tempered by the recognition that, in the final analysis, the market provides the best opportunity for individuals and society. For, whilst the market concentrates economic power, it also yields important benefits for society in the form of technical progress and economic growth. What is good for business is also good for society, and although some business practices may require checking, progress would be retarded if market opportunities were unduly restricted. Moreover, in some cases, a degree of monopoly power might help to stimulate, rather than restrict, the emergence of efficient forms of organisation.

The argument is well expressed in the work of Friedrich Hayek and his followers, for whom market success and growth are the results of entrepreneurial ability in discovering new profit opportunities in a world of uncertainty.[3] The belief that monopoly profits are necessary to encourage innovators to develop new products and processes can also be found in the reassurances issued by the disciples of Joseph Schumpeter that, although large size may be the reward of success, big firms can only survive by generating enough operational and dynamic efficiency to keep their feet in the market-driven 'gale of creative destruction'.[4] Such are the claims that have helped to justify the concentration of economic power that has accompanied the rapid capitalisation of the UK's economy. For, according to this Schumpterian perspective, the stock market serves as the best mechanism for *corporate control*, providing the means by which shareholders can punish inefficient and malfeasant managers and reward the successful and reliable.

The managerial pursuit of shareholder value may put at risk the interests of other *stakeholders*[5] (e.g. employees, suppliers, customers and communities) if it leads to a worsening of the terms and conditions of employment; to downsizings, plant closures and environmental pollution; or to the neglect of long-term investment in the interest of meeting shareholder demands for more and higher share dividends. Nevertheless, the advocates of corporate liberalism[6] argue that any restrictions on the market mechanism aimed at widening the objectives of the corporation to include the interests of stakeholders (other than shareholders) would blunt the efficiency generating capabilities of the market.[7] As we saw in Chapter 1, these arguments have had a marked influence on the formulation of the UK's corporate governance policy; and, until quite recently, they underpinned the refusal of the British government to legislate in favour of a greater prioritisation of (non-shareholder) stakeholders' interests.[8]

But the *laissez-faire* agenda extends beyond the freedom of the capital market to encompass the deregulation of the labour market on the grounds that statutory and union-imposed labour standards lead to lower profits, reduced investment and slower productivity gains. Thus, it is argued that any attempt by trade unions to raise the price (or govern the supply) of labour would, most likely, trigger a cut in output and employment, the effect of which would only *increase* the workload and job insecurity of the country's labour force. For in the neo-liberal catechism, the freedom of workers to sell, and of capitalists to buy, labour in the market ensures that the nominal wage is equal to the value of the marginal product of labour, beyond which point it is no longer profitable for firms to hire more workers. Left to itself, the market will establish equitable pay and conditions of work, in the sense that they will reflect the quality and quantity of the labour input of individuals. Moreover, provided the labour market is working 'freely', everyone can find work so long as they are prepared to invest in the necessary skills and accept the real wage the market offers for their capabilities. And, if the government or trade unions try to interfere with this mechanism – whether through restrictions on the ability of employers to dismiss their workers 'at will', maximum limits on working time, health and safety legislation or minimum wage laws – they will undermine the productivity and 'competitiveness' of the economy upon which rests the health and security of the nation's workforce.

Over the years, the popularity of this argument has waxed and waned. It lost some of its attraction in the wake of the Great Depression and the ascendancy of Keynesian economics. Indeed, from the Second World War until the mid-1970s, the wide consensus in advanced industrial countries was that an effective and equitable floor of employment rights was both socially and economically beneficial. Decent standards of pay and working conditions were regarded as having a central part to play in reducing exploitation and poverty and encouraging the more effective use of labour. But, with the inflationary crisis of the 1970s, these views changed as neo-liberalism established its hold over economic theory and public policy. Profligate governments, excessively powerful trade unions, state intervention in the labour market and over-generous welfare benefits were, once again, held responsible for high inflation, growing unemployment and declining productivity growth. And as we begin the third millennium, the heirs of William Temple and Bernard Mandeville can be found insisting that joblessness is the result not of unemployment but of *unemployability* and that the main weight of short-term job creation should rest on 'welfare-to-work' programmes (participation in which is to be 'encouraged' through the removal of out-of-work benefits).[9]

Yet how can the state deregulate the markets for capital and labour without jeopardising the trust, goodwill and cooperation of the workforce? It is a question that has dogged the neo-liberals ever since the 1930s, when the negative effects of an unrestricted ('scientific') managerial prerogative were first revealed by the Hawthorne Experiment and other social psychological investigations into work organisation. By stressing the extent to which worker performance could be enhanced by improving *human relations*,[10] these studies turned the role of the personnel department into an increasingly important managerial tool targeted at the diseconomies of traditional work organisation.[11] The emerging belief in the productive power of collective, rather than divided, labour was further strengthened by research conducted during the 1940s, such as the war-time experiments in the Tavistock Institute, that were targeted at the rehabilitation of servicemen suffering psychological disorders.[12] After the war, the industrial application of these ideas was promoted by an international network of research institutes including the Norwegian Industrial Democracy Project, which explored the benefits of improved worker/management relations and developed participatory 'socio-technical systems' which it diffused to other countries.[13]

In turn, these developments encouraged the adoption of Human Resource Management (HRM) as a replacement for traditional industrial relations functions designed around conflict management.[14] Ideally, HRM's purpose is to foster pre-emptive rather than reactive approaches to operational efficiency, quality control and process development. It requires shifting accountability for decision-making towards the shop floor, where production teams share responsibility for identifying and solving problems in the production process as they arise; the aim being to 'maximise organisational integration, employee commitment, flexibility and the quality of work'.[15]

But has HRM really solved the neo-liberals' dilemma? Has the balm of 'empowerment' and 'involvement' assuaged the feelings of anger, distrust and powerlessness engendered by the decline in independent representation and the unrestricted operation of 'market forces'? As we saw in Chapter 2, the evidence from the JIWIS survey suggests that employees have welcomed the opportunities for greater involvement and decision-making that have accompanied the introduction of HRM policies. But our research also points to a widespread distrust of management and the perception that pay levels have failed to compensate adequately for the extra responsibility, accountability, workload, working hours and effort that workers are now expected to bear. Likewise, although our research demonstrates the extent to which supportive managers can moderate their employees' feelings of stress and insecurity, it also makes clear how difficult it is for managers to perform this function when they themselves are anxious and overworked.

These observations point to the enduring tension between liberal capitalism, where markets and managerial power are largely unrestricted, and cooperative, high-performance work systems. Caught between the demands of customers (for more for less) and of shareholders (for higher returns), the new forms of work organisation become new forms of exploitation, made more sophisticated by worker involvement in the process. This is particularly true of Britain and the US where, unlike their counterparts in other parts of the world, employers have not engaged in any radical reform of their work systems, preferring to incorporate degrees of worker involvement and other HRM practices into existing managerial structures. Consequently, little has been done to change 'the fundamental nature of the production system or threaten the basic organisation or power structure of the firms'.[16] Instead, what has been happening is that, in both the public and private sectors, power has become increasingly concentrated in the hands of top management at the same time as managerial de-layering and work reorganisation has increasingly decentralised responsibility to the shopfloor. Thus, while the former strives to collective effort, the latter de-collectivises and individualises risk. Take, for example, the following statement made to us by one of the senior managers we interviewed:

> The executive has set out . . . to offer genuine job security, because it believes a happy staff gives better service and keeps clients happy, which in turn brings customer loyalty and higher rewards for all – company, management, shareholders and employees. If this is achieved, staff bask in the reflected glory of the company.

Soon after this statement was made, the company announced a merger involving the projected loss of hundreds of jobs. There is no doubt that after the dust of the merger settles, the manager (if he survived) could attempt to rebuild the morale of the workforce; but, in the meantime, the announcement had made a mockery of his commitment to 'genuine job security'. The important point here is that largely *unconditional* demands are being made of workers by their employers whilst the commitments to job security, and the other promises by employers to their employees, are *conditional.* Under such arrangements, workers are required to be totally committed to organisational objectives, yet readily disposable.

To some extent, the conditionality of employer promises is a reflection of economic uncertainties that are largely unavoidable.[17] On the other hand, the experience of the JIWIS organisations suggests that it is also a product of organisational uncertainties (driven by corporate restructuring and by merger and takeover activity undertaken in the pursuit of shareholder value) that are institutionally driven and therefore *can* be avoided. But, as we saw in Chapter 7, although senior management were aware of the 'negative feedback' generated by broken promises, they were also conscious that, *in the short run*, the organisational costs of distrust and insecurity would not appear on their balance sheets. Because they can externalise the costs of their actions (onto families and communities), firms that intensify the pressures on their workforce know they can obtain short-run advantages over their competitors. And, in an economy where managers are driven by the fear of hostile takeovers, the temptation for others to emulate their actions becomes especially hard to resist. The consequence of this is a form of Gresham's Law, as bad labour practices drive out good.

Nor is it easy for the *individual* firm to escape this law. As suggested to us by many of the employees who took part in the JIWIS survey, although management might have good intentions, they cannot be trusted to keep their promises in the face of the pressures exerted by 'the market'. The scepticism of these workers reminds us that the kinds of investment necessary for building and maintaining relationships of trust typically extend beyond the capacities of the individual employer. For if the 'software' of trust is developed by a learning process which takes place *within* firms, the 'hardware' of trust – upon which depends the credibility of the employers' promises – can be established only by investment in the institutions that regulate the competitive relationship *between* firms.[18]

Protective regulation

In contrast to the neo-liberals' faith in the healing properties of the *self-regulating* market, we believe that the most effective way to reduce the stress and insecurity felt by so many workers is to invest in the laws and institutions that regulate and restrict the market economy. As such, our arguments are in line with the writings, not of Smith and Hayek, but of Keynes and Polanyi, for whom 'the alleged commodity "labour power" cannot be shoved about, used indiscriminately, or even left unused, without affecting also the human individual who happens to be the bearer of this peculiar commodity'.[19] For, like theirs, our reading of the history of Western capitalism shows, time and again, that the statutory protection of social rights is essential to the health and well-being of workers and their families. Of course, we recognise that systems of regulation 'must respond to a variety of diverse local conditions' and that 'solutions which work well in one context may not be readily supplanted into others'.[20] Nonetheless, although the specifics may vary from one country to another, we believe that policy makers need to be reminded, now more than ever before, of the protective force of their regulatory powers.

One of the obvious forms of protective regulation is that which restricts the ability of employers to 'fire at will'. But, in Britain, the trend over the past twenty years has worked in the opposite direction and international comparisons show that British employers now find it easier to terminate employment contracts than any of their European counterparts.[21] Other countries have a wide variety of hurdles that employers must cross before making employees redundant, including longer periods of notice, more serious consultations with employee representatives, higher severance payments and penalties for unfair dismissal, stronger rights to reinstatement, shorter periods of minimum tenure to gain eligibility for protection, the granting of permissions from local authorities and the drawing up of social plans. Given the social and efficiency costs of job insecurity, there is an obvious argument to be made that British workers need to be better protected from the threat of unfair or avoidable dismissal, and we welcome the attempt to bring British regulation more into line with that of our European partners. Indeed, such regulation may become increasingly necessary if, as our findings suggest, redundancy is no longer a last resort in the face of economic downturns, but a tool which is increasingly being used, *at any point in the economic cycle*, by managers who are constantly searching for cost savings.

Another important way in which labour market regulation can enhance security is through the provision of comprehensive safety nets via a welfare state that protects the victims who fall out of employment. Yet the continued high levels of unemployment over the past quarter-century have been accompanied by a shift in government policy away from offering protection from economic uncertainty to one of coercing the unemployed into work. This change in the perceived role of transfer payments has no doubt added to the sum of uncertainty, as the low levels of replacement income offered by the welfare state compound the cost of job loss.

But if we value the structures which protect workers from the costs associated with redundancy, we must also bear in mind that insecurity is not limited to worries about job loss; it involves more general concerns about the intensification of work pressures and the loss of valued job features. As we saw in Chapter 4, the percentage of respondents in our survey who were working 'excessive hours' mirrors that of the British labour force as a whole. Given the worrying increase in the number of hours worked by British employees over the last fifteen years we welcome the EU working time directive[22] and hope that it will protect some of the employees whom we interviewed. Yet we should not overestimate the magnitude of any likely benefit. Less than a fifth of the full-time employees in our survey worked longer than forty-eight hours per week, and some of those who did were forced to because of their low wages. In the absence of tougher minimum wage legislation, a reduction in their hours might actually increase their economic hardship.

Moreover, a combined effort to regulate working time and raise minimum wages would still do little to reduce the pressures felt by those who are working part-time (or are unable to work extra hours) yet still felt under extreme stress from work overload. Hence the need to consider other ways of reducing work pressures besides setting maximum limits on the number of hours that people work. For instance, policies aimed at the development of *family-friendly* working patterns could extend employees' access to overtime, shift work, flexi-time and periods of leave, for a variety of family-related reasons. For, as shown by Purcell *et al.*,[23] many jobs based on forms of flexible working hours are beneficial to employees with heavy domestic commitments.

Health and safety legislation constitutes another important form of protective regulation. However, despite increased recognition that stress at work is a 'health and safety' issue and should be regulated as such, the legal remedies available where British employers act in breach of these duties are still severely constrained. While, in theory, an employee may sue an employer for breach of contract, in practice, the only course of action open to an employee seeking redress is to resign from his or her employment and claim constructive unfair dismissal. In doing so, the employee must countenance all the implications of job loss and the difficulties of re-entering the labour market. Moreover, although we welcome the legal decisions that have recently expanded the employers' duty of care towards their employees,[24] we are also conscious that, unlike hazardous substances or dangerous machines, many of the stressors experienced by workers are neither easily identified nor limited to particular industries or occupations.[25]

Trade unions and staff associations can help to enforce the statutory protections against unfair dismissal and hazardous working conditions. But, as we saw in Chapter 1, the last two decades have seen a dramatic drop in trade union density, from 50 per cent in 1980 to 30 per cent in 1997, affecting all workers in the British labour market regardless of their union affiliation. Two decades ago, 70 per cent of British workers had their basic terms and conditions of employment (such as pay, hours and holidays) determined by collective agreements negotiated between employers' and employees' representatives. By 1997, following a widespread dismantling of the institutions and structures which supported collective bargaining, the figure had fallen to 36 per cent. Nevertheless, many of the employees who took part in our research still felt a clear need for trade union protection; they felt frustrated because decisions were so often made over their heads and they suspected their employers were not doing everything they could to maintain employment, look after their welfare and develop family-friendly practices. They wanted both *effective* voice and *independent* representation.

Whilst recognising the importance of their role in *protecting* employees from employers, we are conscious that trade unions can also play a valuable role in *partnership* with management. As they did in several of the JIWIS organisations, they can assist in the construction and sustenance of job security agreements. More importantly, they can help to enforce industry-wide labour standards and prevent ruthless employers from driving out good practice. Indeed, their role in this respect is needed now more than ever before. At a time when managers are under increasing pressure from their competitors and from their dominant stakeholders, there is an urgent need for organisations and institutions that prevent them over-exploiting their most valuable resource – the health and well-being of their workforce.

But if policy makers are genuinely concerned about the quality of our working and family lives, they must look to the regulation, not just of the labour market, but of the capital market. Indeed, one of the recurring themes in our case studies was of senior management looking over their shoulders to protect themselves from hostile takeovers whilst simultaneously seeking to make opportunistic gains through mergers and acquisitions. Thus, even when managers were unhappy with the pressures being brought to bear on their workforces, they often felt powerless to make real decisions over the internal running of 'their' companies because of the external forces controlling their capital. Indeed, the past twenty years have seen a decisive shift in the balance of power away from employers exercising internal control towards forces controlling companies from outside. In sharp contrast to the German and Japanese systems, British institutional shareholders are not bound into company strategies through a range of social and legal commitments. On the contrary, with a company law system that is principally aimed at the maximisation of shareholder value: 'every day that dawns there is a market in individual company shares which allows shareholders an escape route should they choose to use it'.[26]

What is at issue, therefore, is the balance of power between dominant stakeholders and employees. For if 'market solutions involve some but not others', in the decision-making process, this is particularly clear with respect to merger policy where *let the market decide* means that 'the shareholders of the company make the decision, without any input from workers, consumers or government'.[27] And, with the public sector being squeezed by the Treasury (in the name of value for money for taxpayers), many of Britain's non-commercial organisations are also finding themselves under intense pressure from their 'dominant stakeholders'. In the short term, this drive to reduce costs and/or increase profits has intensified work and may well have increased 'efficiency' but, as argued below, the forces that are currently driving British industry may have worrying implications for the country's long-term growth rates.

Productive regulation

The doctrines of neo-liberalism suggest that many of the regulations intended to protect the health and well-being of workers are self-defeating because they damage the ultimate guarantor of economic security, namely the productivity and competitiveness of the employers for whom they work. But the argument, despite its current popularity, is hard to maintain when one considers the vital role played by government regulation in *stimulating*, rather than hindering, the technological development and dynamic efficiency of countries such as Sweden, Germany, Japan, Denmark and the Netherlands.

Within these countries, the productive value of government regulation has been particularly noticeable during periods of rapid change in technology or consumer demand; especially when these changes have threatened a reduction in the number of firms and/or the level of employment.[28] The uncertainty generated during such periods can lead to a cycle of destructive competition whereby individual firms are driven to intensify the pressures on their workforce in order to gain short-run (but critical) advantages over their competitors. Breaking such a cycle to secure an orderly recovery, replace obsolete technology or restructure industry may well require *competition-limiting* cooperation, such as price-fixing, order-sharing and equipment scrapping. In Japan, for example, the consolidation of ownership and the creation of 'crisis cartels' have been effective means to these objectives[29]. In addition, the protection of labour standards by industry-wide wage agreements has helped prevent the erosion of skilled labour and, by taking wages and other employment conditions out of competition, worked to stabilise the product markets.

The evolution of the Swedish labour market provides another example of the kind of regulatory system that helps to foster high-trust and high-performance work systems. Early settlement between capital and labour at the national level established the rights of managers to manage, the rights of unions to organise and represent their members, and the rights of employees to share in the benefits of technical change. During the late 1920s, the political wing of the Swedish labour movement responded to high levels of unemployment generated as a result of industrial restructuring by accepting the state's responsibility for joblessness; a commitment which laid the foundations for the country's welfare state. In subsequent decades, the government also accepted responsibility for the high rate of job displacement resulting from rapid technical change and developed active labour market policies combining high quality training, job creation and measures to encourage labour mobility. Then, in the 1960s, as the country was struggling to contend with the disruptive effects of rapid economic progress and growing shopfloor opposition to Taylorist work organisation, the Swedish government enacted a series of measures designed to limit managerial prerogative.

These measures included the outlawing of unfair dismissal, protection of the physical and psychological health of employees, and the establishment of rights to paid leave for education. New legislation also introduced co-determination, which gave unions the right to negotiate local agreements for the joint control of hiring and firing, work assignment and disciplinary matters. Supported by these policies, Swedish unions combine strong representation, a commitment to technical progress and wage solidarity in such a way that poor firm performance cannot be compensated for by low pay. Indeed, the involvement by unions and their members in the introduction of technological innovations, the promotion of environmental improvements and the reorganisation of work, has contributed significantly to the development of socio-technical systems in which job satisfaction, responsibility and learning constitute an integral part of the social relations of production.[30] In turn, these developments have met with the support of employers who recognise their beneficial effect on competitiveness.[31]

What the Swedish example demonstrates is that there are points beyond which firm- and industry-level measures cannot go, and that, in such cases, what is required are procedural, behavioural and performance standards designed to encourage the development of new industries, new forms of work organisation, training and retraining, and industrial and occupational flexibility. These broader objectives must then be supported by policies aimed at securing full employment and environmental protection, and by regulations on trade and capital flows aimed at preventing unfair competition, disruptive price fluctuations and global uncertainty. And, increasingly, these questions need to be addressed at the international level where, as yet, the democratic interests of the vast majority of populations are not sufficiently well represented.

The revolution in information technology provides another example of the way in which statutory regulations affect the trajectory of technical development and hence the dynamic efficiency of productive systems. For instance, in Britain and the USA, the form taken by the deregulation of telecommunications has allowed telecommunications companies to deploy new technology in ways that eliminate labour. It has also enabled them to segment product and labour markets to their distributional advantage and to extend these processes internationally through the construction of global networks.[32] The primary benefits of the new technology therefore, have accrued to the management and shareholders of the telecommunication companies (and their large business customers who have access to alternative providers) rather than to the residential and small business customers (whose markets continue to be effectively monopolised). For the latter, 'customer service' is routed through automated or semi-automated systems whose operators are closely and electronically monitored. Throughout the sector, high-trust relations within well-organised collective bargaining systems have been replaced by low-trust relations. Meanwhile, the unions' role has been reduced to attempting to maintain the terms and conditions for a rapidly shrinking workforce and negotiating severance and early retirement packages in exchange for the jobs of the rest.[33]

By contrast, the regulatory framework that governs Germany's telecommunications industry, involving a wider range of stakeholders, has resulted in a more even distribution of the benefits of technical change. In a country where consumer and worker interests are well represented in the regulatory framework and in collective bargaining, widespread displacement of workers, downsizing and cost minimisation are often ruled out as approaches to the restructuring of industry, technology and work organisation. By eliminating these options and by restricting their ability to segment the domestic product market, the regulatory framework has obliged firms to offer a universally high level of service and to adopt a revenue-enhancing, up-market, strategy to which the unions have lent their full support.[34]

If we compare the different systems, we see that, in the Anglo-American case, economic uncertainty triggered by regulatory changes and new technology has been exacerbated by the social uncertainty associated with the process of dismantling the traditional social relations of production. In the process, the short-term benefits to management from their largely unrestricted exercise of prerogative have been achieved at considerable expense to the workforce and a restriction of the benefits of new technology for the customers with least countervailing power.[35] And the longer-term costs include the detrimental effects on productivity and employee commitment that accompanies increased insecurity, low morale and the creation of antagonistic, non-cooperative and low-trust employment systems. This contrasts with the German case where the greater certainty generated by well-established and collective social relations of production has served to ameliorate the economic uncertainty of the information technology revolution and allowed its benefits to be more widely shared. The comparison reminds us that the regulation of technical change and the political and legal constitution of markets create the frameworks within which national competences evolve, and, as such, they play a central role in determining technological trajectories.

The failure to recognise this systemic effect is apparent when it is uncritically argued that the USA leads in radical new technology. Whilst there is no doubt that the USA has taken the lead in the 'newly emerging' phases of many recent new technologies, much of the lead in incorporating these generic changes into productive systems has come from Japan and Europe rather than the USA. The failure of US businesses, in this respect, cannot be simply attributed to the fact that exploration for and pioneering of new technologies has beneficially crowded out their exploitation. It is, more likely, a reflection of the aggressive individualism and antagonistic inter- and intra-firm relationships that prevents US industry from developing effective cooperative learning processes in its workplaces and supply chains. The absence of such processes, which marks the continued prevalence of Taylorist forms of work organisation (with their emphasis on managerialism) and the persistent belief that skilled work can be readily replaced by technology.

The contrasting experiences of Britain, Germany, the USA and Japan should make us reassess the claim that the need to negotiate technical change slows down the development process. This might be true from the perspective of the distributive interests of the large corporations, but only at great cost to a large proportion of the workforce and many customers. And what the overall costs and benefits are judged to be will depend upon the relative weights attached to the different interests and the extent to which the assessor subscribes to the view that what is good for the corporation is necessarily good for the system. In any case, in evaluating the longer-term effects, the risk of destroying cooperative and trusting inter- and intra-firm relations and those in the wider society would need to be added to the cost side of the balance sheet.

As for the claim that the globalisation of trade and production has robbed the nation-state of its regulatory powers, we remain sceptical. For, as Hirst and Thompson have argued, if government regulations and extended welfare states were such a threat to international competitiveness and economic performance then states such as Denmark and the Netherlands should not exist. With their small, highly internationalised, economies, these countries demonstrate that 'a high level of international exposure does not automatically require the responses of cut-throat competition between firms and the slashing of welfare provision'. On the contrary, it is precisely because their economies are so exposed to external shocks that they have developed the regulatory means by which to cushion their firms and workers against the vicissitudes of the global markets. And, in doing so, they have *strengthened*, rather than weakened, their international competitiveness. By restraining wages, by coordinating action between firms and by offering security to workers, these countries have demonstrated that 'a form of negotiated social governance can work and deliver the goods better than strong states enforcing free markets'.[36]

As we enter the twenty-first century, the policies pursued by our governments need to be adaptive to the challenges of the new technological, organisational and market forms spawned by the pressure of scientific discovery and intensified competition. Past experience suggests that the success of these policies, and their impact on the speed and direction of technical change, will depend on the extent to which our regulatory frameworks and codes of practice succeed in restricting the over-exploitation of bargaining advantage. And yet, in Britain today, as was true of the years which preceded the Great Depression, 'the freedom that regulation creates is denounced as unfreedom' and 'the justice, liberty and welfare it offers are decried as a camouflage of slavery'.[37] But to acknowledge the current hegemony of the neo-liberal philosophy is not to endorse it. On the contrary, the experience of other countries suggests that the institutions which regulate the markets for labour and capital can help to preserve, rather than undermine, the *real* freedoms enjoyed by workers and their families.

Appendix A

Organisations participating in the study

Case No.	Description
Case 1	is a large independent utilities company. Its shares are quoted on the stock market.
Case 2	is a medium-sized independent utilities company. Its shares are quoted on the stock market.
Case 3	is a medium-sized transport company which is part of a British-owned corporation. Its shares are quoted on the stock market.
Case 4	is a large government agency.
Case 5	is a medium-sized independent corporation providing educational services to the further education sector. It receives a substantial proportion of its finances from a government funding agency.
Case 6	is a medium-sized independent corporation providing educational services to the further education sector. It receives a substantial proportion of its funding from a government funding agency.
Case 7	is a public corporation supplying a wide range of communications and other services directly to the private and business sectors.
Case 8	is a large independent manufacturing company in the building materials sector, its shares are quoted on the stock market.
Case 9	is a large manufacturing company in the food and drinks sector which is owned by a British corporation. It is quoted on the stock market.
Case 10	is a large manufacturer of components for the telecommunications and IT markets which is owned by a British corporation. Its shares are quoted on the stock market.
Case 11	is a large independent food manufacturer. Its shares are traded on the stock market.
Case 12	is a small independent private construction company.
Case 13	is a large financial services company owned by a British corporation. Its shares are quoted on the stock market.
Case 14	is a large financial services company owned by a foreign corporation. Its shares are quoted on the stock market.
Case 15	is a large independent retailer of travel and related service. Its shares are quoted on the stock market.
Case 16	is a large independent retailer of mainly food and household products. Its shares are quoted on the stock market.
Case 17	is a small independent, privately owned employment agency.
Case 18	is a medium-sized, independent, privately owned employment agency.
Case 19	is a large, independent, privately owned employment agency.
Case 20	is a public provider of health services.

Appendix B

Changes in job content and related institutional arrangements over the last five years

Organisation (by case no.)	Practices which have helped reduce traditional job demarcations		
	'Multi-skilling' and related training	Team working/task participation	De-layering of management/ reduction of grades
8	Manual workers, management, support staff, emphasis on NVQs, Institute of Management	Move to team working; empowerment to place daily decisions in the hands of employees themselves, self-directed team working, move from shift managers to team leaders and area improvement managers	Reduction in number of managers
9	Multi-skilling and related training of manual workers	Shopfloor undertaking quality checks/problem solving, move towards self-managing work teams (SMWTs)	Reduction in number of managers
10	Manual workers	Move to team working, delegation of decisions to working team leaders to replace non-working supervisors	Taken out four layers of management
2	Multi-skilling occurred already	SMWTs in place already	Management team reduced from 7 to 5
1	Broadening of roles for all white-collar workers; up-skilling, multi-tasking for blue-collar workers	Programme of job redesign, empowerment, giving people the opportunity to do more in their own way, SMWTs	Reduction in number of job-titles
13	Training for multi-skilled multi-functioning workforce, plans for 'self-organising' training	Multi-functioning team-based operations, more delegation, empowerment, self-controlling teams replacing management	Substantial de-layering of managerial levels (190 management roles eliminated); elimination of lower-value jobs

Organisation (by case no.)	Practices which have helped reduce traditional job demarcations		
	'Multi-skilling' and related training	*Team working/task participation*	*De-layering of management/ reduction of grades*
14	Job content of clerical workers shifted from admin towards providing customer care and wider range of services, on-going training because of higher skills requirements	Team working introduced in large branches (has SMWTs)	Fewer job titles; reduced managerial population through closure of area offices (giving responsibilities to branch offices)
11	Manual workers	Semi-autonomous team working for cleaning crew	Fewer grades
16	Shelf-fillers working on check-out, move to multi-functioning managers; behavioural skill training on-going, e.g. motivation and adaptability	Empowerment of managers	Flattening of managerial hierarchies
15	Multi-roles for customer facing staff with less demarcation		Slimming down of occupational grades; no. of job titles fallen.
3	Training staff now doing cleaning (broadening roles of managers in head office, same responsibilities, but more of them)		Fewer managers
5	Broadening role of lecturers (more management *and* teaching responsibilities)		No. of middle managers reduced from thirty-four to two
6		Move to SMWTs	
4	(Same responsibilities for managers, but more of them)	Empowerment	De-layering of management grades
7		Quality control becomes the responsibility of all; move to SMWTs	De-layering of management grades

Appendix C

Sample sizes in the World Values Surveys

Full details of the World Values Surveys can be obtained from:

The Inter-University Consortium for Political and Social Research (ICPSR)
P.O. Box 1248
Ann Arbor
Michigan 48106

The ICPSR web address is: http://www.icpsr.umich.edu

The sample sizes for the five countries which appear in both the first (1981–4) and third (1995–97) waves of the WVS are tabled below.

Country	Year	Fieldwork organisation	N
Norway	1982	Central Bureau of Statistics	1,246
Norway	1996	Central Bureau of Statistics	1,127
Spain	1981	DATA SA	2,303
Spain	1995	ASEP (Madrid)	1,211
Sweden	1982	Gallup-Sweden	954
Sweden	1996	TEMO (Solna)	1,009
USA	1982	The Gallup Organization	2,325
USA	1995	The Gallup Organization	1,542
West Germany	1981	Institut für Demoskopie	1,305
West Germany	1997	FORSA (Berlin)	1,017

Notes

Introduction

1 OECD (1998b).
2 For criticisms of our 1999 report, see Guest and Conway (1999) and Furedi (1999).
3 For a more detailed examination of moderators – and, in particular, those which moderate the stress of job insecurity – see Wichert *et al.* (2000) and Nolan *et al.* (1999).

1 More pressure, less protection

1 For example, of the twenty organisations that took part in the JIWIS survey, eighteen described their product market as increasingly competitive. In addition to the pressure exerted by their competitors, most of the senior managers we spoke to claimed they were coming under greater price pressure from their customers (in the public sector they spoke of increased 'budget pressure') and 35 per cent claimed that they had also been forced to extend better credit terms to their customers. As for scheduling the production of their goods and services, most of the senior managers we spoke to suggested that they were under pressure to meet the immediate requirements of their customers; putting the customer 'on hold' – via waiting lists or variations in delivery times – was not an option.
2 Quoted by Bannister and Barrie (1999).
3 See Dicken (1992, pp. 115–19).
4 Castells (1996, p. 248); Dicken (1992, p. 379).
5 Both firms had introduced Expert Information Systems (EIS) which make suggestions and reach conclusions in a similar way to a human 'expert'. These systems relied on a computerised knowledge base and an inference engine which is a method of processing a large number of rules. Besides their use in financial services, expert systems are also used in process control to optimise the utilisation of large and expensive plant and equipment. In the public sector, expert systems are being introduced in the health service to enable non-specialist clinical staff to diagnose problems beyond their normal knowledge and expertise.
6 Achieved through a variety of devices ranging from computerised tills where operators enter the data to various forms of scanning machines.
7 Crooks (2000).
8 Crooks (2000).
9 Castells (1996, p. 437).
10 Standing (1999, p. 62).

11 See Dicken (1992, p. 18) and the World Bank (1999, Table 4.5).
12 Dicken (1992, p. 18). The speed at which commercial services globalised during the 1980s is well illustrated in the three case examples described by Hood and Peters (2000, pp. 91–5) representing the areas of information technology (Electronic Data Systems), express transport (FedEx) and management and technology consulting (Andersen Consulting).
13 Castells (1996, p. 235) and UNCTAD (1999, p. 1).
14 By the end of 1993, the number of people employed in transnational corporations was estimated at less than 3 per cent (approximately 73 million) of the global workforce (Kolodner 1994, p. 6).
15 Kolodner (1994).
16 See Castells (1996, Figure 4.3).
17 Dicken (1992, p. 51) notes that during the 1960s the foreign output of TNCs was growing at twice the rate of growth of world gross national product and 40 per cent faster than world exports.
18 Burbach and Robinson (1999).
19 UNCTAD (1999).
20 Dicken (1992, p. 48).
21 Sauvan (1999).
22 Burbach and Robinson (1999).
23 Toonen and Raadschelders (1997). See also Wright (1994, pp. 10–13).
24 See Farnham and Horton (1996, p. 18).
25 Descriptions of these programmes can be found in Chapter 2 and Appendix B.
26 Walsh (1995, p. 121).
27 Walsh (1995, p. 120).
28 Walsh (1995, p. 139).
29 See Walsh (1995, p. 133); Toonen and Raadschelders (1997); OECD (1998a).
30 Walsh (1995, p. 111). A comprehensive summary of the public sector reforms introduced in Europe, the US, Australia and New Zealand can also be found in the 'country files' contained in Pollitt and Bouckaert (2000, pp. 192–287).
31 Price *et al.* (1999).
32 Quoted in Price *et al.* (1999).
33 Quoted in Price *et al.* (1999, p. 1890).
34 Hutton (1995), Akyüz and Cornford (1995).
35 Hutton (1995, p. 133).
36 By 1998, 14 per cent of all equity trades in the US were on-line, a 50 per cent increase on 1997 (see Castells 2000, p. 58).
37 Collinson (2000).
38 Schmidt *et al.* (2000).
39 Castells (2000, p. 54).
40 Launched by OM Group of Sweden and Morgan Stanley Dean Witter.
41 According to a press release issued by Sir David Walker, Chairman of Morgan Stanley, on 8 February 2000.
42 UNCTAD (1999, p. 20).
43 UNCTAD (1999, p. 21).
44 The federal regulators who repealed the Glass Steagall Act may (or may not) have forgotten that the Act was introduced in the wake of a string of bank failures due to unwise investments in securities and mutual funds. The Act was designed 'to force banks, especially at state level, to become less market-based and so develop longterm relationships with their customers' (Hutton 1995, p. 260).
45 Dickson (2000, p. 13).
46 Dickson (2000, p. 13).

47 Wilks (1999, pp. 194–242). It is no surprise, therefore, that of the 6,220 mergers which qualified for scrutiny by the MMC only 211 were referred to the Commission and, of these, only 81 were found to be against the public interest and only 48 were eventually blocked. In other words, less than 1 per cent of mergers were prevented during this period (Wilks, p. 194).

48 Price *et al.* (1999, p. 1891).

49 See Standing (1999, p. 136).

50 Standing (1999, pp. 138–45).

51 To be included in the ILO unemployment category the jobless are: people without a job who were available to start work in the two weeks following their LFS interview and who had either looked for work in the four weeks prior to the interview or were waiting to start a job they had already obtained.

52 TUC (1999).

53 During 1989, 568,000 employees were made redundant – 25.6 per 1,000 employees. In 1997, the number of redundancies was 799,000 – 36.3 per 1,000 employees (Turnbull and Wass 2000, p. 60).

54 Turnbull and Wass (2000, p. 64).

55 In the BLS statistics, displaced workers consist of those who lost their job because a plant or company closed or moved, because their position or shift was abolished, or because they had insufficient work.

56 ILO (1998).

57 Unions have found it much more difficult to organise 'flexiworkers' (e.g. temporary and casual workers, freelancers and contract workers) because of 'the organisational difficulty of reaching and retaining such workers, the tendency for them not to identify with unions, the difficulty of integrating flexiworkers into union structures, and the legal ambiguity over the position of contingent workers' (Standing 1999, p. 199).

58 Standing (1999, p. 202).

59 Functioning consultative committees consist of those which meet at least once every three months. The declining incidence of these committees affected all sizes of workplace. For the smallest workplaces (25–49 employees) it fell from 21 to 14 per cent. For the largest workplaces (500 or more employees) it fell from 70 to 58 per cent (Millward *et al.* 2000, p. 109).

60 In contrast to the decline in representative consultation (via trade unions) direct forms of communication (e.g. workplace-wide meetings, team meetings and ad hoc problem-solving groups) had proliferated.

61 Millward *et al.* (2000, p. 113).

62 Looking at the results from the 1998 Workplace Industrial Relations Survey, Millward *et al.* arrive at a similar conclusion when they note that: 'Non-union or direct voice mechanisms may be more effective than union-related or representative forms of voice in enhancing the responsiveness (or apparent responsiveness) of management to specific employee issues. Yet, they appear to be less effective at promoting fair treatment for the workforce. Instead, it is the influence of the trade union that appears to be decisive in this regard' (2000, p. 135).

63 Burchell *et al.* (1999, p. 35).

64 Burchell *et al.* (1999, p. 34).

65 W. Brown *et al.* (1998) argue that 'implicit' de-recognition has occurred in organisations that provide apparently substantial recognition rights, but which have, in practice, narrowed the scope of bargaining so substantially that there has been a measure of 'implicit' or partial de-recognition.

66 Bertola *et al.* (1999), Brandão (1998), OECD (1997), Raines (1998).

67 Brandão (1998, p. 20).

68 The Redundancy Payments Act requires the provision of statutory redundancy payments, advance notice of any impending redundancies and written information to recognised trade unions or employee representatives, specifying the reasons for any redundancies and the number of employees involved. But as summarised in the work of Turnbull and Wass:

> The need to declare redundancies, the scale of any job losses, and the selection of workers for redundancy are essentially determined by managerial prerogative . . . The only statutory requirement is that the employer must experience 'a reduction or cessation of work of a particular kind', but the legal test is simply whether, *in the employer's opinion,* fewer workers are required to perform the particular task in question. The most prevalent, and indeed most straightforward, form of redundancy is where the employer simply declares a particular job redundant, along with the job holder.
>
> (2000, p. 65)

69 It was not until 1999 that the Blair administration reduced the qualifying period – for all workers – from two years to one year.
70 Deakin (1990).
71 Because the wages gained by entering into paid employment are counterbalanced by the income lost through the diminution or termination of means-tested benefits.
72 Deakin and Wilkinson (1991).
73 Standing (1999, p. 234).
74 Calculated as the ratio of payments of unemployment insurance benefits to number of unemployed, with respect to the average gross pay of all production workers.
75 Standing (1999, p. 243) and Blondal and Pearson (1995).
76 Examples drawn from the late 1990s include Spain, where benefits for single people were reduced by 22 per cent between 1995 and 1998, and Sweden, whose gross replacement rate fell from 80 per cent to 75 per cent in 1997.
77 OECD (1999).
78 In addition, the maximum period for the receipt of Danish unemployment benefits has been reduced from seven to five years.
79 The TANF took effect as of 1 July 1997.
80 Furthermore, the deduction for shelter costs (rent) in counted income for determining food stamps has been abandoned since 1 January 1997, thereby reducing social assistance benefits still further.
81 Marshall (1950, p. 8).
82 In other words, although there was a good deal of *potential* demand, the markets for labour and products were stuck in a Catch 22, the resolution of which could only be achieved through the demand-boosting efforts of the government. During the Great Depression, employers would have been willing to increase their payrolls were it not for the lack of demand. But the only way to increase consumer demand was to increase the payrolls. Keynes' 'General Theory' provided one solution: the use of government loan expenditure to break the impasse and inject enough demand into the economy to create a virtuous circle whereby investment would feed employment, employment would feed consumer demand, and consumer demand would feed more investment. This very solution was adopted by the US government when it endorsed the New Deal put forward by Roosevelt's economic advisers.
83 Wilkinson (1988).
84 Meade (1995).

85 Standing (1999, p. 61).
86 Standing (1997, p. 61).
87 For a pungent description of this process see Galbraith (1993).
88 L. Brown *et al.* (1998).
89 Polanyi (1957, p. 73).

2 Flexibility and the reorganisation of work

1 Those which reported the most success in squeezing their suppliers were the large private sector corporations (the two utilities and the three manufacturing companies) and the large public sector provider of communication services. The manufacturer of IT components was as weak in the market for its supplies as it was in the market for its products. Otherwise, the organisations we interviewed reported little change in the relationship with their suppliers.
2 See Atkinson (1984, 1987); Atkinson and Gregory (1986).
3 See, for example, Harrison's prediction that the spread of flexible production and related practices of lean production across the manufacturing and service sectors would involve the 'explicit reinforcement or creation of *de novo* sectors of low-wage "contingent" workers, frequently housed within small business suppliers and subcontractors linked to a growing, and international, problem of working poverty' (Harrison 1994, p. 12).
4 See Pollert (1988, 1991).
5 Robinson (2000, p. 33).
6 Purcell *et al.* (1999, p. 5).
7 Cully *et al.* (1999, pp. 35–8).
8 See Robinson (2000, p. 36).
9 Or, less frequently, by 'upsizing' the workforce through new recruitment.
10 Of course, the demand for locational flexibility was often linked to other factors besides the need to adjust the demand and supply of labour. For example, in the retailing and financial services industries, we found mobility clauses that were specifically designed to ensure that employees could move between branches to attain 'the correct skill level'.
11 Workers sent to the company by another, often related, company or by a recruiting agent.
12 Castells (1996, p. 269).
13 As described by Peter Dicken:

> Conditions in the myriad of small subcontracting firms are very different from those in the major firms. The subcontracting segment has none of the much lauded qualities of lifetime employment and corporate paternalism which exist in the major corporations. Competitiveness within the subcontracting segment is fierce; the small firms are very heavily subservient to the stringent demands of the principal companies.
>
> (1992, p. 217)

See also Kyotani (1999, pp. 191–2) and Shire (2000).
14 Castells (1996, p. 272).
15 See Gronning (1998, p. 298).
16 See Kyotani (1999, pp. 183–4 and pp. 189–90). Drawing on Kamata's study of the Japanese shipbuilding industry, Berggren and Nomura (1997, p. 73) note that when managers announce 'voluntary' retirement schemes, they often identify which categories of employees should volunteer – on the basis of their past performance (as measured by their sickness record, their willingness to change and their morale). Some of the costs of this increased drive to flexibility are

described by Hampson (1999, pp. 379–80) who illustrates the growing incidence of *karoshi* (i.e. deaths attributed to overwork) the causes of which range from long working hours, a sudden increase in workload and the added mental pressures of expanded responsibilities and production quotas.

17 Among the more (in)famous advocates of this model were the three members of the International Motor Vehicles Project Team (IMVP) whose publications, such as *The Machine that Changed the World*, exhorted organisations to adopt the lean production methods used in Japanese auto assembly (Womack *et al.* 1990). For an extensive review of the literature on lean production see Hampson *et al.* (1999).

18 Of course, functional flexibility is more prevalent in some industries and occupational sectors than in others. For example, the 1998 Workplace Employee Relations Survey found that:

> The lowest levels of functional flexibility are found among workplaces where technical and scientific workers make up the core workforce – in over 80% of these cases either no or very few workers have been trained to be functionally flexible, and in only 7% of cases were most so trained. By way of contrast, in workplaces where sales workers constituted the core workforce, 45% had trained most of these workers to be functionally flexible while 36% had none or few so trained.
>
> (Cully *et al.* 1999, p. 40)

19 For example, training initiatives, some of which led to formal qualifications such as NVQs.

20 Although this was particularly true of the service sector, when we asked senior managers what things were important when it came to maintaining the performance of their organisations, customer service and the quality of the workforce were stressed by all the organisations participating in the JIWIS. And pre-existing or new quality frameworks spanned the manufacturing, public and private service sectors.

21 See Elger (1991) for an analysis of developments in manufacturing, the sector which received the most research attention during the 1980s.

22 Rinehart (1995) and MacDuffie (1996).

23 Cameron *et al.* (1993, p. 34). For another account of the way in which restructuring aims at transforming people's attitudes, see Halford *et al.* (1997).

24 Womack *et al.* (1990, p. 12).

25 Rinehart (1995).

26 A phrase originally used by Parker and Slaughter (1988).

27 Quinn (1999, p. 28).

28 Sennett (1998).

29 The extract from Muetzelft is cited in Sewell and Wilkinson (1992, p. 102). There is considerable agreement to be found on Muetzelft's stance. Like Quinn, and at least in part Sennett, Durand also feels that the possibility for better, more autonomous, jobs is limited by the obsession with just-in-time production methods (Durand 1998). And, whereas Sandberg (1998) claims that 'team work' can open up the possibility for a more humane and creative organisation of work, Durand worries that team-based working will lead, in practice, to a more intense form of exploitation.

30 For further detail on this point see Ake Sandberg's editorial introduction to *Economic and Industrial Democracy* (1998).

31 The distinction between consultative and delegative participation is described at greater length in Geary (1994).

32 Cully *et al.* (1999, p. 67).

33 See Rosenblatt and Ruvio (1996).
34 Hutton (1995, p. 83).
35 See Davies and Freedland (1993) for a detailed exposition of the measures taken to reduce trade union industrial (and political) power.
36 See Deakin (1998, esp. pp. 24–31). In their review of the Workplace Employee Relations Survey, Millward and his colleagues predict that collective bargaining is likely to decline still further, in extent and effectiveness (2000, p. 235).
37 As noted in the work of Applebaum and Batt, the real challenge for British and American unions lies in the need 'to define a new role for themselves in representing the interests of workers in production systems in which workers' skills and participation in decision-making are the basis of competitive advantage. Unions must expand their role from one of safeguarding workers' interests to participating in the critical business decisions that ultimately determine the working conditions, employment security, and economic welfare of workers' (Applebaum and Batt 1994, pp. 24–5).
38 European Commission (1997). The notion that flexibility is best achieved through partnership was echoed in subsequent EC employment guidelines and in the government's own Fairness at Work White Paper (DTI, Cm 3963, May 1998, HMSO). In similar vein, Hampson argues that a system of 'balanced production' (which takes account of the waste involved in overburdening workers as well as machines) requires, in turn, a cooperative relationship between the actors who participate in the 'political institutional' framework which shapes industrial adjustment (Hampson 1999, p. 379).
39 Wilkinson (1998) and Biracree *et al.* (1997).
40 Knell (1999).
41 For a review see Buchanan and Preston (1994).

3 The prevalence and redistribution of job insecurity and work intensification

1 Burgess and Rees (1996); Gregg and Wadsworth (1999).
2 See Aaronson and Sullivan (1998).
3 Robinson (2000).
4 Standing (1999).
5 Further details of these two surveys can be found in Felstead *et al.* (1998).
6 We are grateful to Phil Wyatt of the GMB for supplying us with these figures.
7 OECD (1998c).
8 Thanks to Nick Buck of the BHPS team at the University of Essex for providing us with some of this information.
9 For more information, see Felstead *et al.* (1998).
10 The correlation = −0.54 (p<0.05). Without the UK the correlation improves to −0.63.
11 The discrepancy between the two figures makes it all the more likely that the ISR's figures exaggerate the increase in job insecurity which took place in the UK during the 1980s and 1990s.
12 Unfortunately, because their data only goes back to 1977, Aaronson and Sullivan (1998) are unable to chart what may have been a big hike in job insecurity in the early 1970s.
13 Greenhalgh and Rosenblatt (1984).
14 Green (1999, 2000).
15 Wheatley (2000) and Glynn and Holbeche (2000).
16 Thanks to the European Foundation for the Improvement of Living and Working Conditions for making this data available.
17 Green (1999, 2000).
18 Not that he saw any reason to 'risk it'.

4 Disappearing pathways and the struggle for a fair day's pay

1 Jenkins and Sherman wrote of a jobs holocaust. They argued that the growth of knowledge based work put at risk: 'the unskilled, semi-skilled and skilled manual jobs, clerical, administrative and managerial posts and the whole information industry workforce' (1979, p. 105).

2 By the late 1980s Scase and Goffee (1989, pp. 9–10) were describing how a reduction in the size and extent of management hierarchies in Britain had resulted from the adoption of flatter, relatively decentralised structures, linked to the introduction of computerised technologies. Organisations were increasing their trading activities without having to increase staff levels. Merger and takeover activities and ensuing rationalisations of production systems in manufacturing and retail outlets also reduced the need for managerial and supervisory staff.

3 For an especially egregious example of this philosophy see the section entitled 'We're All in This Together' in Bridges (1994).

4 Waterman *et al.* (1994).

5 See Applebaum and Batt (1994), Hecksher (1995). An insightful account focusing specifically on developments in managerial careers can also be found in a collection of papers edited by Paul Osterman (1996).

6 Quoted in Harrison 1994 (p. 199). The quotation is taken from Noyelle's book, *Beyond Industrial Dualism* (1987).

7 Gittleman and Howell (1993, p. 19).

8 Castells (1996, p. 225).

9 Gershuny (1993, p. 162). Or to use the colloquial language employed by the *Guardian*'s Richard Thomas: 'Gershuny's findings indicate that mobility is about what happens right at the beginning – with the one-chance saloon of education. Do well at school and college and you'll be OK; mess up, and that's pretty much it. The labour market no longer gives you a second chance' (Thomas 1996).

10 Gershuny (1983, p. 163).

11 Lovering (1990). See especially his discussion of the restructuring of the map of labour market places (1990, pp. 12–16; already touched on in Chapter 2).

12 As emphasised in the work of Savage *et al.*, in Britain, the decline of internal labour markets poses 'a particularly acute crisis for managerial workers' for whom 'self-directed career paths' are becoming almost as common as 'conventional career patterns' (1995, pp. 58–66).

13 Papers by Scott *et al.*, Batt and MacDuffie are all chapters in Osterman (1996).

14 Cf. Zabusky and Barley (1996), Scarborough (1998).

15 The independent food manufacturer was the exception; and even here it was reported that there were fewer grades across the workforce.

16 Levy and Murnane (1992, pp. 1340–6).

17 Someone whose earnings exceeded those of 90 per cent of all workers.

18 As measured by Gini coefficients (see note 21).

19 Freeman and Katz (1994, p. 32).

20 Bernstein and Mishel (1997).

21 The Gini coefficient is an index of inequality which would take the value of zero if all incomes were identical and would approach 100 per cent if all income were received by one person.

22 The growth in *wage* inequality was mirrored by the growth in *income* inequality. The Joseph Rowntree Inquiry into Income and Wealth Distribution in Britain found that average incomes grew by approximately 40 per cent between 1979 and 1994/5. For the richest tenth the rate of growth was 60–68 per cent. For the poorest tenth it was only 10 per cent before housing costs and actually fell by 8 per cent after housing costs (JRF 1998).

23 Kohn (1986, p. 2).
24 Kohn also draws on the fields of psychoanalysis, leisure studies, cultural anthropology, evolutionary biology and education.
25 Quoting from Wachtel's *The Poverty of Affluence*, Kohn notes that: 'Our obsession with growth is the expression of neither inexorable laws of human nature nor inexorable laws of economics . . . It is a cultural and psychological phenomenon, reflecting our present way of organising and giving meaning to our lives . . . [that] is now maladaptive' (1986, p. 73). Robert Bellah and his colleagues make a similar argument, although from a different disciplinary base. In their *Habits of the Heart: Individualism and Commitment in American Life*, they argue that: 'We have been called a people of plenty, and though our per capita GNP has been surpassed by several other nations, we are still enormously affluent. Yet the truth of our condition is our poverty' (1996, p. 295).
26 Kohn (1986, p. 71).
27 Wilkinson (1996, p. 1). See also Kaplan (1999) and Bishop and Smith (1991).
28 Wilkinson (1996, p. 3). Oliver James makes the same observation when he notes that: 'It is almost a tenet of modern life that as a nation becomes wealthier, the satisfaction and well-being levels of its citizens will rise accordingly – affluence should breed happiness and this is the ultimate justification offered by politicians for placing increased prosperity at the heart of their politics. Yet this principle only seems to apply up to a basic level and not beyond' (1998, p. 44).
29 Wilkinson (1999, p. 258).
30 Wilkinson (1994, p. 42).
31 Wilkinson (1996, p. 115).
32 Sen (1999, p. 49).
33 Klerman (1992), 'The changing rate of major depression', *Journal of the American Medical Association*, 268: 21, 3098–3105 (cited in James 1998, pp. 344–5).
34 The term 'major depression' refers to feelings of worthlessness or excessive guilt; recurrent suicidal tendencies, having a depressed mood for most of the day nearly every day for at least two weeks for no good reason.
35 James (1998, p. 326).
36 A good illustration of James' argument can be found in the comparison of social class differences in mortality rates between Sweden and England and Wales. In Sweden, which has one of the advanced world's most egalitarian distributions of income, the poorest social classes have lower mortality rates than the highest social classes in England and Wales (Wilkinson 1996, p. 86).
37 See, for example, Brown and Sisson (1975); Brown and Walsh (1994); W. Brown *et al.* (1995, 1998).
38 Brown *et al.* (1995, p. 133).
39 Kohn (1986, pp. 121–2) writes that 'a structured imperative to beat others invites the use of any means available. Whilst employers have not been wholly indifferent to the impact of workplace innovations on employees, 'structural imperatives' appear paramount. In this sense, Sennett's conclusion that a regime of indifference dominates the corporate landscape under the new capitalism seems rather apt (2000, p. 190).

5 Job insecurity and work intensification: the effects on health and well-being

1 Van Vuuren *et al.* (1991).
2 Warr (1987).
3 Lazarus and Folkman (1984, p. 21).
4 Cox (1993).
5 Kuhnert *et al.* (1989).

6 Lim (1996), Van Vuuren *et al.* (1991), Barling and Kelloway (1996), Mattiasson *et al.* (1990).
7 Burchell (1997).
8 Burchell (1994).
9 Amick *et al.* (1998).
10 See Goldberg (1972).
11 Warr (1990).
12 Instead of analysing each item separately, a summary score was produced for each construct (i.e. GHQ, work-related well-being, work intensification and job insecurity) by adding up the scores of the individual items. All items were answered on a 5-point Likert-type scale.
13 Ferrie *et al.* (1995).
14 Lazarus and Folkman (1984).
15 Heaney *et al.* (1994).
16 Burchell (1997). See also Dekker and Schaufeli (1995).
17 The experience of unemployment has been widely shown to be detrimental for psychological health and well-being. See, for example, the studies by Warr (1983) and Dooley and Catalano (1988).
18 Ferrie *et al.* (1995, p. 1269).
19 Winnubst *et al.* (1996).
20 French *et al.* (1982).
21 See Cox (1993).
22 Warr (1987).
23 Hardy *et al.* (1997).
24 Within this sample, an increase in work demands was associated with a linear increase in job-related depression. But there was a non-linear relationship between work demands and anxiety: very high and very low levels of work demands were *both* associated with the highest anxiety scores (De Jonge and Schaufeli 1998).
25 Miller *et al.* (1999).
26 Barnett and Brennan (1995).
27 Janssen *et al.* (1999).
28 Bromet *et al.* (1992).
29 Warr (1987).
30 Wheatley (2000).
31 Warr (1987).
32 Rystedt and Johansson (1998).
33 Stansfeld *et al.* (1997).
34 Büssing and Jochum (1986), Depolo and Sarchielli (1986, re job insecurity) and Caplan *et al.* (1975, re work intensification).
35 James (1998, p. 326).
36 See Barling and Kelloway (1996), Heaney *et al.* (1994), Joelson and Wahlquist (1987), Jacobson (1987), Roskies and Louis-Guerin (1990).
37 Lazarus and Folkman (1984).
38 Warr (1987).
39 Dekker and Schaufeli (1995).
40 Burchell (1994).
41 Joelson and Wahlquist (1987, p. 179).
42 Dekker and Schaufeli (1995).
43 See Roskies *et al.* (1993).
44 Jacobson (1987).
45 Joelson and Wahlquist (1987).
46 Sutherland and Cooper (1988).
47 Winnubst *et al.* (1996).

48 Matteson and Ivancevich (1988) also point to research findings suggesting that chronic overload may cause biochemical changes, specifically, elevations of blood cholesterol levels.
49 Lazarus and Folkman (1984).
50 For a more detailed examination of moderators – and, in particular, those which moderate the stress of job insecurity – see Wichert *et al.* (2000) and Nolan *et al.* (1999).
51 Stansfeld *et al.* (1999).
52 Roskies and Louis-Guerin (1990), Hallier and Lyon (1996).
53 Burchell *et al.* (1999).
54 Burchell (1994) and Ferrie *et al.* (1995).
55 Wheatley (2000), Stansfeld *et al.* (1999).
56 Kuhnert and Palmer (1991), Rystedt and Johansson (1998), Barnett and Brennan (1995), Narayanan *et al.* (1999).
57 Kuhnert and Vance (1992), Mattiasson *et al.* (1990).
58 Schabracq and Winnubst (1996).
59 Janssen *et al.* (1999).
60 Miller *et al.* (1999).
61 Winnubst *et al.* (1996).
62 Roskies *et al.* (1993).
63 Armstrong-Stassen (1994) and Barling and Kelloway (1996) both examine the link between job insecurity and perceptions of control. Van der Doef and Maes (1999) provides an extensive review of the large literature on work intensification and control.
64 Greenhalgh and Rosenblatt (1984) for job insecurity and Winnubst and Schabracq (1996) for work intensification.
65 Kuhnert *et al.* (1989).
66 House (1981, p. 26).
67 Thoits (1995, p. 64).
68 Berkman (1985), Kessler and McLeod (1985).
69 House (1981).
70 Dekker and Schaufeli (1995).
71 Armstrong-Stassen (1993, 1994).
72 Kaufmann and Beehr (1986).
73 Lim (1996).
74 Bromet *et al.* (1992).
75 Winnubst *et al.* (1988).
76 Wells (1982).
77 See Buunk (1990) and House (1981).
78 Cohen and Cohen (1983).
79 See Buunk (1990) for a review of this literature.
80 Burchell *et al.* (1999).
81 As suggested by the experience of Ganster *et al.* (1986; see also House 1981; Buunk 1990), the difference between the two sets of findings might be explained by the use of different stressor measures and different statistical methods.
82 Our results are in line with other studies which have reported either none or very few buffering effects (e.g. Dekker and Schaufeli 1995; Seers *et al.* 1983).
83 Cutrona (1996).

6 The intensification of everyday life

1 Beck (1992, p. 184).
2 Putnam (2000, p. 184).
3 Cf. Giddens (1992).

4 Giddens (2000, p. 27).
5 Popenoe (1987, p. 528).
6 Cf. Hakim (1996), Humphries and Rubery (1992), McRae (1991), Siltanen (1994).
7 Although there are colourful debates over the degree to which this outcome is the result of women's personal 'choices' (see Hakim 1996; Crompton and Harris 1998).
8 Cf. Lewis (1999).
9 The fact that in Northern Europe and the USA, high female labour force participation coexists with high divorce rates whereas in Southern Europe women's low involvement in paid labour coexists with (relatively) low rates of divorce.
10 That is, the extent to which our emotional experiences at work influence the dynamics of our family life.
11 Putnam (2000, pp. 187 and 258).
12 Putnam (2000, p. 283). It should be emphasised that Putnam's observations are made with specific reference to America's declining participation in voluntary associations. His book does not contain any estimates of the extent to which 'pressures of time and money' were responsible for the growth in divorce rates and lone-parent families.
13 Sennett (1998, p. 21).
14 Sennett (1998, p. 24).
15 Sennett (1998, p. 26).
16 Beck (1992, p. 135).
17 On the same page, Beck also claims that:

> If thought through to its conclusion, the basic figure of fully developed modernity is the single person. In the requirements of the market, the requirements of family, marriage, parenthood, or partnership are ignored. Those who demand mobility in the labour market in this sense without regard to private interests are pursuing the dissolution of the family – precisely in their capacity as apostles of the market.
>
> (Beck 1992, p. 123)

18 As portrayed in his description of Rico, whose 'fear of losing his control went much deeper than worry about losing his job . . . he feared that the actions he needed to take and the way he has to live in order to survive in the modern economy have set his emotional, inner life adrift' (Sennett 1998, p. 20).
19 What Beck refers to as the 'self-reflexive' obsession with an individual 'career' or 'performance' (Beck 1992, pp. 131–7).
20 $U = 11782$, non-significant .135.
21 Davies and Joshi (1998), Meadows (1996).
22 Although the association between insecurity and household tension appears quite modest on the basis of the measurements taken from the JIWIS survey, the longitudinal research conducted by Elder *et al.* (1984, 1986) suggests that the spillover effects of job insecurity can leave a lasting impression upon the individuals affected. Their studies show how fathers who were in insecure employment during the 1930s exhibited inconsistent parental discipline, which in turn, was associated with difficult behaviour and temper tantrums in their children. Moreover, insecure fathers were also more likely to 'reject' their children and their daughters in particular. And the daughters of rejecting fathers were subsequently found to have lower employment ambitions than other girls.
23 Wheatley (1992).

24 Ryan (1999).
25 Office for National Statistics (1998).
26 Rones *et al.* (1997).
27 Green (1999).
28 Cf. Guest and Conway (1996).
29 Beatson 1995.
30 Cooper and Williams (1994).
31 Wheatley (1992).
32 $F = 14.08$, $p = 0.001$
33 Ferri and Smith (1996).
34 Hochschild (1997).
35 Burgoyne and Clark (1985), Khare and Rao (1986), DeVault (1991).
36 Kotalova (1996).
37 Greenhaus and Beutell (1985).
38 See Lewis (1997) for a review.
39 This is largely because research in this area has tended to fall into two ideological camps. On the one hand, there are feminist researchers who emphasise the cultural and social constraints 'imposed' on women in a patriarchal society (e.g. Coontz *et al.* 1999; Stacey 1990; Walby 1990) . On the other hand, is a group of commentators who see working mothers as the source of most social evils (Dench 1997; James 1998; Popenoe 1987).
40 Cutrona (1996).
41 Cowan and Cowan (1992).
42 As can be seen from Figure 6.7, being a mother is, in itself, associated with greater job-related tension at home (see Chapter 5 for a discussion of the distinction between 'main' and 'buffering' effects).
43 Galambos and Walters (1992), Hughes and Galinsky (1994).
44 In a very broad sense, 'kinship' refers to the ways in which human reproduction is socially organised. It also relates to the societal values and attitudes which regulate relationships.
45 Simpson (1999, p. 119).
46 Simpson (1998).
47 Cooper and Lewis (1993).
48 Hass and Hwang (1995).
49 Charlesworth (1996).
50 Galinsky and Bond (1996).
51 Cf. Business in the Community (1993), Fletcher and Rapoport (1996).
52 Lewis (1997).
53 Purcell (2000).
54 Cockburn (1991), Cunnison and Stageman (1993), Creese (1999).
55 Creese (1999).

7 The organisational costs of job insecurity and work intensification

1 Hecksher (1995).
2 Hallier's work also points to the resentment generated by managers who continue to use redundancy as a 'cost control measure' even when their companies are recording profits (Hallier 2000, p. 2).
3 The bitterness experienced by workers in the financial services industry has also been noted in Makin *et al.* (1996, p. 137).
4 Ridderstråle and Nordström (1999, p. 143). The short-termism implicit in the perspective of companies which initiate redundancies at a time of rising profitability is reflected in the recent survey of British managers conducted by Les Worrall and Cary Cooper. The survey revealed that the companies which were

most aggressive when it came to implementing large-scale redundancies (and de-layering and outsourcing their workforce) were also the *least* likely to seek to expand into new markets. In other words, they tend to concentrate on holding on to what they have rather than seeking to stretch themselves (Worrall and Cooper 1999, p. 18).

5 Greenhalgh and Rosenblatt (1984, p. 433).

6 Needless to say, insecurity does not always lead to lowered job performance. For some individuals, insecurity can serve as a challenge or an 'activator'. But, as noted in the work of D.J. Abramis, such individuals are in the minority. Having set out to evaluate the potential *positive* effects of role ambiguity, role conflict and job security – he discovered that, for the majority of his respondents, all three of these 'stressors' were negatively correlated with job performance and positively correlated with job dissatisfaction, anxiety and depression (Abramis 1994).

7 Hecksher (1995, p. 45).

8 The Health and Safety Commission describe stress as 'the reaction people have to excessive pressures or other types of demand placed on them' (HSC 1999, p. 2).

9 Although the British Institute of Directors prefers to understate the health costs derived from stress at work, its report on 'managing stress at work' acknowledges the link between stress and coronary heart disease (and other illnesses caused by high blood pressure, including strokes). But, as with the Health and Safety Commission, it also emphasises that stress at work is caused by a variety of factors including, but not restricted to, long working hours. Indeed, it suggests that although illnesses resulting from long working hours are undesirable, they are 'unlikely to be one of the major causes of public ill-health' (Day 1998, p. 2). And it emphasises that 'there are likely to be other work-related factors that may well have larger influences'. Nonetheless, whether or not long hours or other work-related factors have the greater influence on health, there is a growing recognition (not just in Britain but across the industrialised world) that the absences and poor performance caused by work-related illnesses represent a considerable cost to the employer, in lost production, replacement staff, sick-pay and/or sick-leave, and disruption of operations.

10 HSC (1999, p. 3).

11 It is a point which has also been strongly emphasised by Cary Cooper and Stephen Worrall. In their recent *Quality of Working Life* survey, they note that job pressures – especially when these translate into longer working hours – frequently exert a deleterious effect on people's social life and, in particular, in their relationships with their families (Worrall and Cooper 1999, pp. 59–63).

12 L. Harris (1985), Poll conducted for the Metropolitan Life Foundation and A. J. Elkin and P. J. Rosch (1990), 'Promoting mental health at the workplace: the prevention side of stress management', *Occupational Medicine: State of the Art Review*, 5(4), 739–54. Both cited in Cooper *et al.* (1996, p. 2).

13 Of which, 88 per cent is attributed not to absenteeism but to 'lost productivity whilst at work' (Greenberg *et al.* 1999).

14 The figures are quoted by Felix (1998) who also cites other estimates putting the cost of workplace stress in the USA at more than $65 billion per annum.

15 Cooper *et al.* (1996, p. 3).

16 According to the UK Health and Safety Commission at least half of these days can be attributed to workplace stress.

17 CBI (1999).

18 Complementing the issue of work overload, our respondents found the lack of adequate staffing critical as a cause of stress in the workplace. An employee in the financial services industry made a typical comment:

Stress in general I think could be sorted out a lot by having the right number of people to do the work. That's the main thing – we've had meetings of the employee groups in the last three or four months and that's the one thing that always comes out, the fact that if we had enough bodies in the right places, then a lot of stress would disappear.

19 'Work-related stress cases hit all-time high' (*The Independent*, 7 December 1999).
20 'Pioneers who broke new legal ground' (*Guardian*, 22 January 2000).
21 Indeed, this is one of the few areas where the trade union movement has been able to demonstrate its continuing relevance following the sharp decline in membership numbers since the early 1980s. The trade unions have long warned industry of the dangers inherent in ignoring work-related health problems and they have been at the forefront of the campaign – through the courts and industrial tribunals – to gain recognition of the employers' responsibilities, and to win compensation where employers have been negligent. By contrast, the British government has long appeared reluctant to strengthen employment protection legislation, preferring to leave employers a relatively free hand in order not to increase their costs and competitiveness. However, EU directives on working conditions are increasingly being introduced and enforced, with consequences which will inevitably be reflected in penalties and compensation claims if regulations are ignored.
22 'Work-related stress claims soar' (*Guardian*, 6 December 1999).
23 'Payouts predicted for stressed teachers' (*Guardian*, 5 October 1999).
24 'Stress at work', *Unison Health and Safety Information Sheet* (Unison, 1999, p. 2).
25 Unison (1999, pp. 3–4).
26 Mack *et al.* (1998: 230)
27 Altogether, 46 per cent of the employees who identified a motivation policy mentioned their organisation's financial incentives, 32 per cent talked about their employer's training and development programmes, 19 per cent talked about 'team-building' initiatives, 15 per cent talked about 'performance appraisal' and 14 per cent talked about their organisation's communication policies.
28 The 'certainty' with which their respondents intended to leave their organisation for another job within the next twelve months.
29 Guerts *et al.* (1999, p. 261).
30 Worrall and Cooper (1999, p. 76).
31 Makin *et al.* (1996, pp. 234, 240).

8 Stress intervention: what can managers do?

1 Shumaker and Brownell (1984).
2 Shumaker and Brownell (1984).
3 Shumaker and Brownell (1984).
4 Cohen and Syme (1985), House (1981).
5 Shumaker and Brownell (1984).
6 The importance of talking can also be seen in the responses to our self-completion questionnaire. In response to the quetion 'Do you believe that it should be part of a supervisor's job to provide support to employees when they face difficulties and problems at work', 98 per cent of the respondents who answered this question (88 per cent of the whole sample) answered 'yes'. When respondents were then asked the open-ended question of what kinds of support they thought a supervisor should be providing, the majority of respondents had a very clear idea of what kinds of support they wanted. The most frequently mentioned form of support was 'being listened to' with 31 per cent of respondents mentioning this form of support. Another 16 per

cent of respondents mentioned wanting 'talking', 'discussions and regular meetings' with their supervisors. In connection with being listened to by a supervisor and being able to talk to him or her about problems, 'having time', 'being approachable' and 'having an open-door policy' were also mentioned by 15 per cent of the respondents. In other words, various aspects of communication were mentioned by more than half the respondents.

7 Barling and Kelloway (1996); Greenhalgh and Rosenblatt (1984).
8 Warr (1987). Research by Burchell (1994) has also pointed to the link between stress and the inability to plan.
9 Shumaker and Brownell (1984).
10 Greenberg and Baron (1995), Alderfer (1972), Maslow (1970).
11 Greenberg and Baron (1995, pp. 422–3).
12 Wheatley (2000).
13 Kiesler (1985).
14 Wheatley (2000).
15 Greenberg and Baron (1995).
16 Wheatley (2000).
17 Austin (1991).
18 Seyper *et al.* (1989).
19 Brownell (1990).
20 Weissenberg and Kavanagh (1972).
21 Bass (1990).
22 Greenberg and Baron (1995).
23 Blake and Mouton (1969).
24 Cox (1993).
25 HSC (1999).
26 Lazarus and Folkman (1984, p. 350).

9 What can governments do?

1 Smith (1976, Vol. 2, p. 49).

2   People of the same trade seldom meet together, even for merriment and diversion, but the conversation ends in a conspiracy against the public, or in some contrivance to raise prices . . . [and] though the law cannot hinder people of the same trade from sometimes assembling together, it ought to do nothing to facilitate such assemblies; much less to render them necessary.

                                          (Smith 1976, Vol. 1, p. 144)

3 Kirzner (1997).
4 Schumpeter (1994, p. 84).
5 Stakeholders in an organisation consist of any individual or group who can affect or is affected by the activities of the organisation.
6 The essence of this philosophy has been stated as follows:

    Corporate liberalism conceived property and economic development prior to the will of collective or democratic choice. *The laws of trade,* its adherents were fond of saying, *are stronger than the laws of men.* Thus, the modern corporation, like the liberal person, owed its existence first and foremost to private purpose. If the result of economic development rooted in such pre-social entitlement was to concentrate market power in huge monopolistic firms, this was deemed inevitable. The only economic role left to the democratic state was to redress the concentration of excessive wealth in the modern corporation through regulated monopoly. The goal of regulation, in other words, was to balance the interests of consumers in redistribution with those of the corporation in accumulation.

(Berk 1994, pp. 13–14)

7 Deakin and Slinger (1997).

8 The current Labour administration has proved less hostile to stakeholder legislation than its Conservative predecessors, as demonstrated by the reintroduction of minimum wage laws and the strengthening of the right to unfair dismissal (for part-time workers).

9 In the late seventeenth and early eighteenth centuries, William Temple and Bernard Mandeville were convinced that 'those that get their living by their daily labour . . . have nothing to stir them up to be serviceable but their wants, which it is prudent to relieve, but folly to cure'. Three centuries later, many of the arguments marshalled in support of welfare-to-work are predicated on the same conviction, viz. that too much money renders the poor 'insolent and lazy' (see Kaye's introduction to Mandeville 1988 and Peck and Theodore 2000a, 2000b).

10 Roethlisberger and Dickson (1939).

11 Baritz (1964).

12 Slinger (2000).

13 Trist and Murray (1993).

14 Blyton and Turnbull (1992); Towers (1996); and Applebaum and Batt (1994) provide surveys of the HRM literature and debates about its deployment. Cully *et al.* (1999) report on the use of HRM practices in Britain as do Wood and de Menezes (1998).

15 Guest (1987).

16 Applebaum and Batt (1994, p. 22).

17 For example, a fall in product demand or an unanticipated technical change.

18 Deakin and Wilkinson (1998).

19 Polanyi (1957, p. 73).

20 Deakin (2000, p. 13).

21 For a review see Buechtemann (1993).

22 EC Directive/93/104.

23 Purcell *et al.* (1999).

24 Witness the growing number of cases in which individual employees have successfully sought compensation from their employers on the grounds of work-induced stress (as described in Chapter 7).

25 For a further discussion of these issues, see Ewing (1996, pp. 96–101).

26 Hutton (1995, p. 159).

27 Sawyer (1992, p. 331).

28 Dei Ottati (2000).

29 Best (1990).

30 Gallie (2000).

31 Persson (1997).

32 Batt and Darbyshire (1997).

33 Wilkinson (1998, p. 30).

34 Batt and Darbyshire (1997).

35 In a similar way, the rivalry created by the use made by Microsoft of its market power and the outcome of the current anti-trust suit against Microsoft can be expected to have important consequences for innovation in information technology and for the structuring of the market for Internet services.

36 Hirst and Thompson (1999).

37 Polanyi (1957, pp. 256–7).

References

Aaronson, D. and Sullivan, D. G. (1998) 'Recent trends in job displacement', Federal Reserve Bank of Chicago, *Chicago FG Letter* 136 (December).

Abramis, D. J. (1994) 'The relationship of job stressors to job performance', *Psychological Reports* 75(1): 547–58.

Akyüz, Y. and Cornford, A. (1995) 'International capital movements: some proposals for reform', in J. Michie and J. Grieve Smith (eds) *Managing the Global Economy*. Oxford: Oxford University Press.

Alderfer, C. P. (1972) *Existence, Relatedness and Growth*. New York: Free Press.

Amick, B., Kawachi, I., Coakley, E., Lerner, D., Levine, S. and Colditz, G. (1998) 'Relationship of job strain and iso-strain to health status in a cohort of women in the United States', *Scandinavian Journal of Work Environment and Health* 24(1): 54–61.

Applebaum, E. and Batt, R. (1994) *The New American Workplace: Transforming Work Systems in the United States*. New York: ILR Press.

Armstrong-Stassen, M. (1993) 'Production workers' reaction to a plant closing: the role of transfer, stress, and support', *Anxiety, Stress and Coping* 6: 201–14.

Armstrong-Stassen, M. (1994) 'Coping with transition: a study of layoff survivors', *Journal of Organizational Behavior* 15: 597–621.

Atkinson, J. (1984) 'Manpower strategies for flexible organisations', *Personnel Management August*: 28–31.

Atkinson, J. (1987) 'Flexibility or fragmentation: the United Kingdom labour market in the eighties', *Labour and Society* 12, January: 87–105.

Atkinson, J. and Gregory, D. (1986) 'Flexible future: Britain's dual labour force', *Marxism Today* April: 12–17.

Austin, N. K. (1991) 'Why listening's not as easy as it sounds', *Working Woman*: 46–48.

Bannister, Nicholas and Barrie, Chris (1999) 'Murdoch's spin on the Web', *Guardian* 2 July.

Baritz, L. (1964) *Servants of Power*. Middletown, CT: Wesleyan University Press.

Barling, J. and Kelloway, E. K. (1996) 'Job insecurity and health: the moderating role of workplace control', *Stress Medicine* 12: 253–9.

Barnett, R. C. and Brennan, R. T. (1995) 'The relationship between job experiences and psychological distress: a structural equation approach', *Journal of Organizational Behavior* 16: 259–76.

Bass, B. M. (1990) *Bass and Stogdill's Handbook of Leadership*. New York: Free Press.

Batt, R. (1996) 'From bureaucracy to enterprise? The changing jobs and careers of managers in telecommunications service', pp. 55–80 in P. Osterman (ed.) *Broken Ladders: Managerial Careers in the New Economy.* New York: Oxford University Press.

Batt, R. and Darbyshire, O. (1997) 'Institutional determination of deregulation and restructuring in telecommunications: Britain, Germany and the United States compared', *International Contributions to Labour Studies* 7(3): 57–79. Special Issue on Co-operative and Antagonistic Work Organisation.

Beatson, M. (1995) *Labour Market Flexibility,* Employment Department Research Series No. 48. Sheffield: UK Employment Department.

Beck, U. (1992) *Risk Society: Towards a New Modernity.* London: SAGE.

Bellah, R. (1996) *Habits of the Heart: Individualism and Commitment in American Life,* 2nd edn, California: University of California Press.

Berggren, C. and Nomura, M. (1997) *The Resilience of Corporate Japan.* London: Paul Chapman.

Berk, G. (1994) *Alternative Tracks: The Constitution of American Industrial Order, 1865–1917.* Baltimore, MD: The Johns Hopkins University Press.

Berkman, L. F. (1985) 'The relationship of social networks and social support to morbidity and mortality', in S. Cohen and S. L. Syme (eds) *Social Support and Health.* London: Academic Press.

Bernstein, Jared and Mishel, Lawrence (1997) 'Has wage inequality stopped Growing?' *Monthly Labor Review* 120(12): 3–16.

Bertola, Giuseppe, Boeri, Tito and Cazes, Sandrine (1999) 'Employment protection and labour market adjustment in OECD countries: evolving institutions and variable enforcement', Geneva: ILO.

Best, M. (1990) *The New Competition: Institutions of Industrial Restructuring.* Cambridge, MA: Harvard University Press.

Biracree, A., Konzelmann Smith, S. and Wilkinson, F. (1997) 'Productive systems, competitive pressures, strategic choices and work organisation: an introduction', *International Contributions to Labour Studies* 7(3): 3–17. Special Issue on Co-operative and Antagonistic Work Organisation.

Bishop, J. and Smith, W. J. (1991) '26 international comparisons of income inequality: tests for Lorenz dominance across nine countries', *Economica* 58(232): 461.

Blake, R. R. and Mouton, J. S. (1969) *Building a Dynamic Corporation through Grid Organizational Development.* Reading, MA: Addison-Wesley.

Blondal, Sveinbjorn and Pearson, Mark (1995) 'Unemployment and other non-employment benefits', *Oxford Review of Economic Policy* 11(2): 136–69.

BLS (Bureau of Labor Statistics) (1999) *Comparative Civilian Labor Force Statistics, Ten Countries, 1959–1998.* Washington, DC: US Department of Labor.

BLS (Bureau of Labor Statistics) (2000) *Labor Force Statistics from the Current Population Survey.* Washington, DC: US Department of Labor.

Blyton, P. and Turnbull, P. (1992) 'Debates, dilemmas and contradictions', in P. Blyton and P. Turnbull (eds) *Reassessing Human Resource Management.* London: Sage Publications.

Brandão, Sandra (1998) *Regulation and Labor Market Performance: The Experience of Five Developed Countries.* Washington, DC: Institute of Brazilian Issues, The George Washington University.

Bridges, William (1994) *Job Shift: How to Prosper in a Workplace without Jobs.* New York: Addison Wesley.

Bromet, E. J., Dew, M. A., Parkinson, D. K., Cohen, S. and Schwartz, J. E. (1992) 'Effects of occupational stress on the physical and psychological health of women in a microelectronics plant', *Social Science and Medicine* 34: 1377–83.

Brown, Lester, Flavin, Christopher and French, Hilary (1998) *State of the World.* London: Earthscan Publications.

Brown, W. and Sisson, K. F. (1975) 'The use of comparisons in workplace wage determination', *British Journal of Industrial Relations* 13(1): 23–53.

Brown, W. and Walsh, J. (1994) 'Managing pay in Britain', in K. Sisson (ed.) *Personnel Management in Britain,* 2nd edn. Oxford: Blackwell.

Brown, W., Marginson, P. and Walsh, J. (1995) 'Management: pay determination and collective bargaining', in P. Edwards (ed.) *Industrial Relations: Theory and Practice in Britain.* Oxford: Blackwell.

Brown, W., Deakin, S., Hudson, M., Pratten, C. and Ryan, P. (1998) *The Individualisation of Employment Contracts in Britain.* Employment Relations Series, Department of Trade and Industry. London: HMSO.

Brownell, J. (1990) 'Perceptions of effective listeners: a mangement study', *Journal of Business Communication* 27: 401–15.

Buchanan, D. and Preston, D. (1994) 'Cellular manufacture and the role of teams', in J. Storey (ed.) *New Wave Manufacturing Strategies: Organizational and Human Resource Management Dimensions.* London: Paul Chapman.

Buechtemann, C. F. (1993) 'Introduction: employment security and labor markets', in C. F. Buechtemann (ed.) *Employment Security and Labour Market Behavior: Inter-disciplinary approaches and International Evidence.* New York: ILR Press.

Burbach, Roger and Robinson, William (1999) 'The fin de siècle debate: globalization as epochal shift', *Science and Society* 63(1): 10–39.

Burchell, B. (1994) 'The effects of labour market position, job insecurity, and unemployment on psychological health', in D. Gallie, C. Marsh and C. Vogler (eds) *Social Change and the Experience of Unemployment.* Oxford: Oxford University Press.

Burchell, B. (1997) 'Job security and psychological well-being: preliminary analyses of the British Household Panel Survey', paper for the JRF Work and Opportunity Workshop, 16–17 October.

Burchell, B. (1999) 'The unequal distribution of job insecurity, 1966–86', *International Review of Applied Economics* 13(3): 437–58.

Burchell, B., Day, D., Hudson, M., Ladipo, D., Mankelow, R., Nolan, J., Reed, H., Wichert, I. and Wilkinson, F. (1999) *Job Insecurity and Work Intensification.* York: Joseph Rowntree Foundation.

Burgess, S. and Rees, H. (1996) 'Job tenure in Britain 1975–92', *Economic Journal* 106(435): 334–44.

Burgoyne, J. and Clark, D. (1985) 'You are what you eat: food and family reconstitution', in A. Murcott (ed.) *The Sociology of Food and Eating.* Aldershot: Gower.

Business in the Community (1993) *Corporate Culture and Caring.* London: Business in the Community/IPM.

Büssing, A. and Jochum, I. (1986) 'Arbeitsplatzunsicherheit, Belastungserleben und Kontrollwahrnehmung: Ergebnisse einer Quasi-Experimentellen Untersuchung in der Stahlindustrie', *Psychologie und Praxis* 30: 180–91.

Buunk, B. P. (1990) 'Affiliation and helping interactions within organizations: a critical analysis of the role of social support with regard to occupational stress', in W. Stroebe and M. Hewstone (eds) *European Review of Social Psychology 1.* Chichester: John Wiley and Sons.

Cameron, K., Freeman, S. J. and Mishra, A. K. (1993) 'Downsizing and redesign-
ing organisations', pp. 19–65 in G. P. Huber and W. Glick (eds) *Organisational
Change and Redesign*. New York: Oxford University Press.

Caplan, R. D., Cobb, S., French, J. R. P., van Harrison, R. and Pinneau, S. R.
(1975) *Job Demands and Worker Health*, US Department of Health, Education and
Welfare Publication No. NIOSH 75–160. US Government Printing Office, Washington, DC.

Castells, Manuel (1996) *The Rise of the Network Society (Volume 1 of the The Information
Age: Economy, Society and Culture)*. Oxford: Blackwell.

Castells, Manuel (2000) 'Information Technology and Global Capitalism', in Will
Hutton and Anthony Giddens (eds) *On the Edge: Living with Global Capitalism*.
London: Jonathan Cape.

CBI (Confederation of British Industry) (1999) *Focus on Absence*. London: Confederation of British Industry.

Chang, Clara and Sorrentino, Constance (1991) 'Union membership statistics in
12 countries', *Monthly Labor Review* December: 46–53.

Charlesworth, K. (1996) *Are Managers under Stress? A Survey of Management Morale*.
London: Institute of Management.

Cockburn, C. (1991) *In the Way of Women: Men's Resistance to Sex Equality in Organisations*. London: Macmillan.

Cohen, S. and Cohen, P. (1983) *Applied Multiple Regression for the Behavioral Sciences*.
Hillsdale, NJ: Erlbaum.

Cohen, S. and Syme, S. L. (1985) 'Issues in the study and application of social
support', in S. Cohen and S. L. Syme (eds) *Social Support and Health*. London:
Academic Press.

Collinson, Patrick (2000) 'Call dealing has them hanging on', *Guardian* 26 February.

Coontz, S., Parson, M. and Raley, G. (eds) (1999) *American Families: A Multicultural
Reader*. London: Routledge.

Cooper, C. and Lewis, S. (1993) *The Workplace Revolution: Managing Today's Dual-
Career Families*. London: Kogan Page.

Cooper, C. L. and Williams, S. (1994) *Creating Healthy Work Organizations*. Chichester:
John Wiley and Sons.

Cooper, Cary, Liukkonen, Paula and Cartwright, Susan (1996) *Stress Prevention in
the Workplace: Assessing the Costs and Benefits to Organisations*. European Foundation
for the Improvement of Living and Working Conditions. London: Kogan Page.

Cowan, C. and Cowan, P. (1992) *When Partners Become Parents: The Big Life Change
for Couples*. New York: Basic Books.

Cox, T. (1993) *Stress Research and Stress Management – Putting Theory to Work*. Contract Research Report No. 61/1993. London: Health and Safety Executive.

Creese, G. (1999) *Contracting Masculinity*. Oxford: Oxford University Press.

Crompton, R. and Harris, F. (1998) 'Explaining women's employment patterns:
"orientations to work" revisited', *British Journal of Sociology* 49(1): 118–35.

Crooks, Ed (2000) 'Arguments start over net effect of e-commerce', *Financial Times*
21 February.

Cully, Mark, Woodland, Stephen, O'Reilly, Andrew and Dix, Gill (1999) *Britain at
Work: As Depicted by the 1998 Workplace Employee Relations Survey*. London: Routledge.

Cunnison, S. and Stageman, J. (1993) *Feminising the Unions*. Aldershot: Avebury.

Cutrona, C. (1996) *Social Support in Couples: Marriage as a Resource in Times of Stress*.
London: SAGE.

Davies, H. and Joshi, H. (1998) 'Gender and income inequality in the UK 1968–1990: the feminization of earnings or poverty?', *Journal of the Royal Statistical Society* 161(1): 33–61.

Davies, P. and Freedland, M. (1993) *Labour Legislation and Public Policy*. Oxford: Clarendon Press.

Day, Geraint (1998) *Health Matters in Business – Health at Work*. London: Institute of Directors.

De Jonge, J. and Schaufeli, W. B. (1998) 'Job characteristics and employee well-being: a test of Warr's Vitamin Model in health care workers using structural equation modelling', *Journal of Organizational Behavior* 19: 387–407.

Deakin, S. (1990) 'Equality under a market order: the Employment Act 1989', *Industrial Law Journal* 19: 1–19.

Deakin, S. (1998) *Organisational Change, Labour Flexibility and the Contract of Employment*. ESRC Centre for Business Research, University of Cambridge, Working Paper No. 106.

Deakin, S. (2000) 'Social Rights and the Market: An Evolutionary Perspective', paper presented to the 22nd International Working Party on Labour Market Segmentation, Manchester, 12–15 July.

Deakin, S. and Slinger, G. (1997) *Hostile Takeovers, Corporate Law and the Theory of the Firm*, University of Cambridge, ESRC Centre for Business Research, Working Paper No. 56.

Deakin, S. and Wilkinson, F. (1991) 'Labour law, social security and economic inequality', *Cambridge Journal of Economics* 15: 125–48.

Deakin, S. and Wilkinson, F. (1998) 'Cooperation, contract law and economic performance', in I. Jones and M. Pollitt (eds) *The Role of Business Ethics in Economic Performance*. Basingstoke: Macmillan.

Dei Ottati, G. (2000) *Exit, Voice and Loyalty in Industrial Districts: The Case of Prato*, University of Cambridge, ESRC Centre for Business Research, Working Paper No. 175.

Dekker, S. W. A. and Schaufeli, W. B. (1995) 'The effects of job insecurity on psychological health and withdrawal: a longitudinal study', *Australian Psychologist* 30: 57–63.

Dench, G. (1998) *Rewriting the Sexual Contract*. London: Institute of Community Studies.

Denman, James and McDonald, Paul (1996) 'Unemployment statistics from 1881 to the present day', *Labour Market Trends* January: 5–17.

Depolo, M. and Sarchielli, G. (1986) 'A socio-cognitive approach to the psychology of unemployment', in G. Debus and H.-W. Schroiff (eds) *The Psychology of Work and Organization*. North Holland: Elsevier Science.

DeVault, M. (1991) *Feeding the Family: The Social Organisation of Caring as Gendered Work*. Chicago: University of Chicago Press.

Dicken, Peter (1992) *Global Shift: The Internationalization of Economic Activity*. London: Paul Chapman Publishing.

Dickson, Martin (2000) 'We are all venture capitalists in the brave new world', *Financial Times* 11 March.

Dooley, D. and Catalano, R. (1988) 'Recent research on the psychological effects of unemployment', *Journal of Social Issues* 44: 1–12.

Durand, J. (1998) 'Is the "Better job" still possible today?', *Economic and Industrial Democracy* 19(1): 185–98 (Special Issue on Productivity and Good Work).

Elder, G. H., Caspi, A. and Van Nguyen, T. (1986) 'Resourceful and vulnerable children: family influences in stressful times', in R. K. Silbereisen, K. Eyforth and G. Rudinger (eds) *Development as Action in Context.* New York: Springer-Verlag.

Elder, G. H., Liker, J. and Cross, C. (1984) 'Parent–child behavior in the Great Depression: life course and intergenerational influences', in P. B. Baltes and O. G. Brim (eds) *Life-span, Development and Behavior* 6. New York: Academic Press.

Elger, T. (1991) 'Flexibility and intensification in manufacturing', pp. 46–66 in A. Pollert (ed.) *Farewell to Flexibility.* Oxford: Basil Blackwell.

European Commission (1997) 'Partnership for a New Organisation of Work, Green Paper', Bulletin of the European Union Supplement 4/97. Luxembourg: Office for Official Publications of the European Community.

European Working Conditions Survey, Dublin: European Foundation for the Improvement of Living and Working Conditions.

Eurostat, New Cronos Database, Durham: University of Durham.

Ewing, K. (ed.) (1996) *Working Life: A New Perspective on Labour Law.* London: Lawrence and Wishart.

Farnham, David and Horton, Sylvia (1996) *Managing the New Public Services.* Basingstoke: Macmillan.

Felix, Sonya (1998) 'Taking the sting out of stress', *Benefits Canada* November.

Felstead, A., Burchell, B. and Green, F. (1998) 'Insecurity at work', *New Economy* 5: 180–4.

Ferri, E. and Smith, K. (1996) *Parenting in the 1990s.* London: Family Policy Studies Centre, in association with the Joseph Rowntree Foundation.

Ferrie, J., Shipley, M., Marmot, M. G., Stansfeld, S. and Smith, G. (1995) 'Health effects of anticipation of job change and non-employment: longitudinal data from the Whitehall II study', *British Medical Journal* 311: 1264–9.

Fletcher, J. and Rapoport, R. (1996) 'Work–family issues as a catalyst for organizational change', in S. Lewis and J. Lewis (eds) *The Work–Family Challenge: Rethinking Employment.* London: Sage.

Freeman, Richard B. and Katz, Lawrence F. (1994) 'Rising wage inequality: the United States vs. other advanced countries', pp. 29–62 in Richard B. Freeman (ed.) *Working Under Different Rules (NBER Project Report).* New York: Russell Sage.

French, J. R. P., Caplan, R. D. and Van Harrison, R. (1982) *The Mechanisms of Job Stress and Strain.* New York: Wiley.

Furedi, F. (1999) 'Diseasing the workplace', *Occupational Health Review* November/ December: 2–4.

Galambos, N. L. and Walters, B. J. (1992) 'Work hours, schedule inflexibility, and stress in dual-earner spouses', *Canadian Journal of Behavioural Science* 24: 290–302.

Galbraith, John Kenneth (1993) *The Culture of Contentment.* Harmondsworth: Penguin.

Galinsky, E. J. and Bond, J. T. (1996) 'The role of employers in addressing the needs of employed parents', *Journal of Social Issues* 52: 111–36.

Gallie, D. (2000) 'The quality of working life: is Scandinavia really different?', paper presented to the 22nd meeting of the International Working Party on Labour Market Segmentation, Manchester, 12–15 July.

Ganster, D. C., Fusilier, M. R. and Mayes, B. T. (1986) 'Role of social support in the experience of stress at work', *Journal of Applied Psychology* 71: 102–10.

Geary, J. F. (1994) 'Task participation: employees' participation enabled or constrained?', in K. Sisson (ed.) *Personnel Management: A Comprehensive Guide to Theory and Practice in Britain*. Oxford: Basil Blackwell.

Gershuny, J. (1993) 'Post-industrial career structures in Britain', in Gosta Esping-Andersen (ed.) *Changing Classes: Stratification and Mobility in Post-Industrial Societies*. London: SAGE.

Giddens, A. (1992) *The Transformation of Intimacy: Sexuality, Love and Eroticism in Modern Societies*. Stanford, CA: Stanford University Press.

Giddens, A. (2000) 'Anthony Giddens and Will Hutton in conversation', in W. Hutton and A. Giddens (eds) *On the Edge: Living with Global Capitalism*. London: Jonathan Cape.

Gittleman, Maury B. and Howell, David R. (1993) *Job Quality and Labor Market Segmentation in the 1980s: A New Perspective on the Effects of Employment Restructuring by Race and Gender*, Jerome Levy Economics Institute Working Paper No. 82. New York: Jerome Levy Economics Institute.

Glynn, C. and Holbeche, L. (2000) *The Roffey Park Management Agenda*. West Sussex: Roffey Park Management Institute.

Goldberg, D. P. (1972) *The Detection of Psychiatric Illness by Questionnaire*. Oxford: Oxford University Press.

Green, F. (1999) *It's Been a Hard Day's Night: The Concentration and Intensification of Work in Late 20th Century Britain*. Studies in Economics, 99/13, Canterbury, University of Kent.

Green, F. (2000) 'Why has work become more intensive? Conjectures and evidence about effort-based technical change, and other stories', paper presented to the 22nd meeting of the International Working Party on Labour Market Segmentation, Manchester, 12–15 July.

Greenberg, J. and Baron, R. A. (1995) *Behavior in Organizations: Understanding and Managing the Human Side of Work*. London: Prentice-Hall International.

Greenberg, O. E., Sisitsky, T. and Kessler, R. C. (1999) 'The economic burden of anxiety disorders in the 1990s', *Journal of Clinical Psychiatry* 60(7): 427–35.

Greenhalgh, L. and Rosenblatt, Z. (1984) 'Job insecurity: towards conceptual clarity', *Academy of Management Review* 9: 438–48.

Greenhaus, J. H. and Beutell, N. J. (1985) 'Sources of conflict between work and family roles', *Academy of Management Review* 10: 76–88.

Gregg, P. and Wadsworth, J. (1999) 'Job tenure, 1975–98', in P. Gregg and J. Wadsworth (eds) *The State of Working Britain*. Manchester: Manchester University Press.

Gronning, Terje (1998) 'Whither the Japanese employment system? The position of the Japan Employers' Federation', *Industrial Relations Journal* 29(4): 295–303.

Guerts, Sabine A., Schaufeli, Wilmar B. and Rutte, Christel G. (1999) 'Absenteeism, turnover intention and inequity in the employment relationship', *Work & Stress* 13(3): 253–67.

Guest, D. (1987) 'Human Resource management and industrial relations', *Journal of Management Studies* 24(5): 503–21.

Guest, D. E. and Conway, N. (1997) *Employee Motivation and the Psychological Contract*. Plymouth: Plymouth Distributors.

Guest, D. and Conway, N. (1999) 'How dissatisfied and insecure are British workers? A survey of surveys', London: Institute of Personnel and Development.

Hakim, C. (1996) *Key Issues in Women's Work.* London: Athlone.

Halford, S., Savage, M. and Witz, A. (1997) *Gender, Careers and Organisations: Recent Developments in Banking, Local Authorities and Nursing.* London: Macmillan.

Hallier, J. (2000) 'Security abeyance: coping with the erosion of job conditions and treatment', *British Journal of Management* 11: 107–23.

Hallier, J. and Lyon, P. (1996) 'Job insecurity and employee commitment: managers' reactions to the threat and outcomes of redundancy selection', *British Journal of Management* 7: 107–23.

Hampson, I. (1999) 'Lean production and the Toyota production system – or, the case of the forgotten production concepts', *Economic and Industrial Democracy* 20(3): 369–91.

Hardy, G. E., Shapiro, D. A. and Borrill, C. S. (1997) 'Fatigue in the workforce of National Health Service Trusts: levels of symptomatology and links with minor psychiatric disorder, demographics, occupational and work role factors', *Journal of Psychosomatic Research* 43: 83–92.

Harrison, B. (1994) *Lean and Mean: The Changing Landscape of Corporate Power in the Age of Flexibility.* New York: Basic Books.

Hass, L. and Hwang, P. (1995) 'Company culture and men's use of family leave in Sweden', *Family Relations* 44: 28–36.

Heaney, C. A., Israel, B. A. and House, J. S. (1994) 'Chronic job insecurity among automobile workers: effects on job satisfaction and health', *Social Science and Medicine* 38: 1431–7.

Hecksher, Charles (1995) *White-Collar Blues: Management Loyalties in an Age of Corporate Restructuring.* New York: Basic Books.

Hill, Ian (1999) *Share Ownership: A Report on the Ownership of Shares at 31st December 1997.* London: Office for National Statistics.

Hipple, Steven (1999) 'Worker displacement in the mid-1990s', *Monthly Labor Review* 122(7): 15–32.

Hirst, P. and Thompson, G. (1999) *Globalization in Question.* Cambridge: Polity Press.

HMSO (1998) Fairness at Work White Paper: Employment Relations Bill, Cm 3968, May. London: HMSO.

Hochschild, A. (1997) *The Time Bind: When Work Becomes Home and Home Becomes Work.* New York: Metropolitan Books.

Hood, Neil and Peters, Ewen (2000) 'Globalisation, corporate strategies and business services', in Neil Hood and Stephen Young (eds) *The Globalisation of Multinational Enterprise Activity and Economic Development.* London: Macmillan.

House, J. S. (1981) *Work Stress and Social Support.* London: Addison-Wesley.

HSC (Health and Safety Commission) (1999) *Managing Stress at Work.* London: Health and Safety Commission.

Hughes, D. and Galinsky, E. (1994) 'Work experiences and marital interactions: elaborating the complexity of work', *Journal of Organizational Behavior* 15: 423–38.

Humphries, J. and Rubery, J. (1992) 'Women's employment in the 1980s: integration, differentiation and polarisation', in J. Michie (ed.) *The Economic Legacy: 1979–1991.* London: Academic Press.

Hutton, W. (1995) *The State We're In.* London: Jonathan Cape.

ILO (International Labour Organization) (1998) *World Labour Report 1997–8: Industrial Relations, Democracy and Social Stability.* Geneva: ILO.

IMF (International Monetary Fund) (1999) *World Economic Outlook Database, September 1999.* Paris: IMF.

Jacobson, D. (1987) 'A personological study of the job insecurity experience', *Social Behaviour* 2: 143–55.

James, Oliver (1998) *Britain on the Couch: Why We're Unhappier than We Were in the 1950s – Despite Being Richer.* London: Arrow.

Janssen, P. P. M., Schaufeli, W. B. and Houkes, I. (1999) 'Work-related and individual determinants of the three burnout dimensions', *Work & Stress* 13: 74–86.

Jenkins, C. and Sherman, B. (1979) *The Collapse of Work.* London: Eyre Methuen.

Joelson, L. and Wahlquist, L. (1987) 'The psychological meaning of job insecurity and job loss: results of a longitudinal study', *Social Science and Medicine* 25: 179–82.

JRF (Joseph Rowntree Foundation) (1998) 'Income and wealth: the latest evidence', *Findings*, March, York: Joseph Rowntree Foundation.

Kaplan, G. (1999) 'Inequality in income and mortality in the United States: analysis of mortality and potential pathways', in I. Kawachi *et al.* (eds) *The Society and Population Health Reader: Income Inequality and Health.* New York: The New Press.

Kaufmann, G. M. and Beehr, T. A. (1986) 'Interactions between job stressors and social support: some counterintuitive findings', *Journal of Applied Psychology* 71: 522–6.

Kessler, R. C. and McLeod, J. D. (1985) 'Social support and mental health in community samples', in S. Cohen and S. L. Syme (eds) *Social Support and Health.* London: Academic Press.

Khare, R. S. and Rao, M. S. (ed.) (1986) *Food, Society and Culture.* Durham, NC: Carolina Academic Press.

Kiesler, C. A. (1985) 'Policy implications of research on social support and health', in S. Cohen and S. L. Syme (eds) *Social Support and Health.* London: Academic Press.

Kirzner, I. (1997) *How Markets Work: Disequilibrium, Entrepreneurship and Discovery,* IEA Paper No. 133, London: Institute of Economic Affairs.

Kitson, Michael and Michie, Jonathan (1995) 'Trade and growth: a historical perspective', in Jonathan Michie, and John Grieve Smith (eds) *Managing the Global Economy.* Oxford: Oxford University Press.

Knell, J. (1999) *Partnership at work*, Employment Relations Research Series, Department of Trade and Industry. London: HMSO.

Kohn, A. (1986) *No Contest: The Case Against Competition.* Boston, MA: Houghton Mifflin Company.

Kolodner, Eric (1994) 'Transnational corporations: impediments or catalysts of social development?', Occasional Paper No. 5, World Summit for Social Development. Geneva: United Nations Research Institute for Social Development.

Kotalova, J. (1996) *Belonging to Others: Cultural Construction of Womanhood in a Village in Bangladesh.* Dhaka: University Press Limited.

Kuhnert, K. W. and Palmer, D. R. (1991) 'Job security, health and the intrinsic and extrinsic characteristics of work', *Group and Organization Studies* 16: 178–92.

Kuhnert, K. W. and Vance, R. J. (1992) 'Job insecurity and moderators of the relation between job insecurity and employee adjustment', in J. C. Quick, L. R. Murphy and J. J. Hurrell (eds) *Stress and Well-being at Work.* Washington: American Psychological Association.

Kuhnert, K. W., Sims, R. R. and Lahey, M. A. (1989) 'The relationship between job security and employee health', *Groups and Organization Studies* 14: 399–410.

Kyotani, E. (1999) 'New managerial strategies of Japanese corporations', in A. Felstead and N. Jewson (eds) *Global Trends in Flexible Labour*. London: Macmillan.

Lazarus, R. S. and Folkman, S. (1984) *Stress, Appraisal and Coping*. New York: Springer.

Levy, Frank and Murnane, Richard J. (1992) 'US earnings levels and earnings inequality: a review of recent trends and proposed explanations', *Journal of Economic Literature* 30: 1333–81.

Lewis, J. (1999) *Individualism and Commitment in Marriage and Cohabitation*, Research Papers 8, 99. London: Lord Chancellor's Department.

Lewis, S. (1997) ' "Family friendly" employment policies: a route to changing organizational culture or playing about at the margins?', *Gender, Work and Organization* 4(1): 13–23.

Lim, V. K. G. (1996) 'Job insecurity and its outcomes: moderating effects of work-based and nonwork-based social support', *Human Relations* 49: 171–93.

Lovering, J. (1990) 'A perfunctory sort of post-Fordism: economic restructuring and labour market segmentation in Britain in the 1980s', *Work, Employment and Society* May: 9–28 (Special Issue).

LRA (Labor Research Association) (1999) *Unions Trends and Data*. New York: LRA.

MacDuffie, J. P. (1996) 'Automotive White-Collar: The Changing Status and Roles of Salaried Employees in the North American Auto Industry', pp. 81–125 in P. Osterman (ed.) *Broken Ladders: Managerial Careers in the New Economy*. New York: Oxford University Press.

Machin, Stephen (1999) 'Wage Inequality in the 1970s, 1980s and 1990s', in Paul Gregg and Jonathan Wadsworth (eds) *The State of Working Britain*. Manchester: Manchester University Press.

Machin, Stephen (2000) 'Union decline in Britain', Discussion Paper 455, London: Centre for Economic Performance.

Mack, David A., Nelson, Debra L. and Quick, James C. (1998) 'The stress of organisational change: a dynamic process model', *Applied Pyschology: An International Review* 47(2): 219–32.

Makin, Peter, Cooper, Cary and Cox, Charles (1996) *Organizations and the Psychological Contract: Managing People at Work*. Leicester: The British Psychological Society.

Mandeville, B. (1988) *The Fable of the Bees, or Publick Benefits, with a Commentary, Critical, Historical and Explanatory by F. B. Kaye*. Indianapolis: Liberty Classic.

Marshall, T. H. (1950) *Citizenship and Social Class*. Cambridge: Cambridge University Press.

Maslow, A. H. (1970) *Motivation and Personality*. New York: Harper and Row.

Matteson, M. T. and Ivancevich, J. M. (1988) 'Health promotion at work', in C. L. Cooper and I. Robertson (eds) *International Review of Industrial and Organizational Psychology 1988*. Chichester: John Wiley and Sons.

Mattiasson, I., Lindgärde, F., Nilsson, J. A. and Theorell, T. (1990) 'Threat of unemployment and cardiovascular risk factors: longitudinal study of quality of sleep and serum cholesterol concentrations in men threatened with redundancy', *British Medical Journal* 301: 461–6.

McRae, S. (1991) 'Occupational change over childbirth: evidence from a national survey', *Sociology* 25(4): 589–604.

Meade, J. E. (1995) 'Full employment regained? An Agathotopian dream', University of Cambridge, Department of Applied Economics.

Meadows, P. (1996) *Work Out – or Work In? Contributions to the Debate on the Future of Work.* York: Joseph Rowntree Foundation.

Miller, R. L., Griffin, M. A. and Hart, P. M. (1999) 'Personality and organizational health: the role of conscientiousness', *Work & Stress* 13: 7–19.

Millward, N., Bryson, A. and Forth, John (2000) *All Change at Work? British Employment Relations 1980–1998, as Portrayed in the Workplace Industrial Relations Survey Series.* London: Routledge.

Miyake, Maiko and Thomsen, Stephen (1999) 'Recent trends in Foreign Direct Investment', *Financial Market Trends (OECD)* 73(July): 109–26.

Narayanan, L., Menon, S. and Spector, P. E. (1999) 'Stress in the workplace: a comparison of gender and occupations', *Journal of Organizational Behavior* 20: 63–73.

Nolan, J. P., Wichert, I. C., Burchell, B. J. (1999) 'Job insecurity, psychological well-being and family life', in E. Heery and J. Salmon (eds) *The Insecure Workforce.* London: Routledge.

Noyelle, Thierry (1987) *Beyond Industrial Dualism.* Boulder, CO: Westview Press.

OECD (Organisation for Economic Co-operation and Development) (1997) *Implementing the OECD Jobs Strategy: Lessons from Member Countries' Experience.* Paris: OECD.

OECD (Organisation for Economic Co-operation and Development) (1998a) *Public Management Developments in the United States, Update 1998.* Paris: OECD.

OECD (Organisation for Economic Co-operation and Development) (1998b) *The OECD Jobs Study.* Paris: OECD.

OECD (Organisation for Economic Co-operation and Development) (1998c) *Economic Outlook.* Paris: OECD.

OECD (Organisation for Economic Co-operation and Development) (1999) *Benefit Systems and Work Incentives.* Paris: OECD.

Office for National Statistics (1998) *Social Trends 1998.* London: HMSO.

Osterman, P. (ed.) (1996) *Broken Ladders: Managerial Careers in the New Economy.* New York: Oxford University Press.

Parker, M. and Slaughter, J. (1988) *Choosing Sides: Unions and the Team Concept.* Boston, MA: South End Press.

Parker, M. and Slaughter, J. (1995) 'Unions and management by stress', pp. 41–53 in S. Babson (ed.) *Lean Work: Empowerment and Exploitation in the Global Auto Industry.* Detroit: Wayne State University Press.

Peck, J. and Theodore, N. (2000a) 'Work first: Workfare and the regulation of contingent labour markets', *Cambridge Journal of Economics* 24(1): 119–38.

Peck, J. and Theodore, N. (2000b) 'Beyond employability', *Cambridge Journal of Economics* 24(6): 119–38.

Persson, B. (1997) 'Unions, management and the government: the Swedish model', *International Contributions to Labour Studies* 7: 119–33. Special Issue on Co-operative and Antagonistic Work Organisation.

Polanyi, Karl (1957) *The Great Transformation: The Political and Economic Origins of Our Time.* Boston, MA: Beacon Press.

Pollert, A. (1988) 'The flexible firm: fixation or fact?' *Work, Employment and Society* 2: 281–316.

Pollert, A. (ed.) (1991) 'The orthodoxy of flexibility', pp. 3–31 in A. Pollert (ed.) *Farewell to Flexibility.* Oxford: Basil Blackwell.

Pollitt, Christopher and Bouckaert, Geert (2000) *Public Management Reform: A Comparative Analysis.* Oxford: Oxford University Press.

Popenoe, D. (1987) 'Beyond the nuclear family – a statistical portrait of the changing family in Sweden', *Journal of Marriage and the Family* 49: 173–83.

Price, David, Pollock, Allyson M. and Shaoul, Jean (1999) 'How the World Trade Organisation is shaping domestic policies in health care', *Lancet* 354(9193): 1889–92.

Purcell, K. (2000) 'Gendered employment insecurity?', in E. Heery and J. Salmon (eds) *The Insecure Workforce*. London: Routledge.

Purcell, K., Hogarth, T. and Simm, C. (1999) *Whose Flexibility? The Costs and Benefits of Non-Standard Working Arrangements and Contractual Relations*. York: JRF.

Putnam, R. (2000) *Bowling Alone: The Collapse and Revival of American Community*, New York: Simon and Schuster.

Quinn, J. (1999) 'Is empowerment ethical? Why ask the question?', in John Quinn and Peter Davies (eds) *Ethics and Empowerment*. London: Macmillan.

Raines, Philip (1998) *Labour Standards and Industrial Restructuring in Western Europe*. Geneva: ILO.

Ridderstråle, J. and Nordström, K. (1999) *Funky Business: Talent Makes Capital Dance*. Stockholm: BookHouse Publishing AB.

Rinehart, J. (1995) 'The ideology of competitiveness', *Monthly Review*. October: 14–23.

Robinson, P. (2000) 'Insecurity and the flexible workforce: measuring the ill-defined', in A. Heery and J. Salmon (eds) *The Insecure Workforce*. London: Routledge.

Roethlisberger, F. J. and Dickson, W. J. (1939) *Management and the Worker*. Cambridge, MA: Harvard University Press.

Rones, P., Ilg, R. and Gardner, J. (1997) 'Trends in hours of work since the mid-1970s', *Monthly Labor Review* 4: 3–12 (US Bureau of Labor Statistics).

Rosenblatt, Z. and Ruvio, Z. (1996) 'A test of a multi-dimensional model of job insecurity: the case of Israeli teachers', *Journal of Organizational Behavior* 17: 587–605.

Roskies, E. and Louis-Guerin, C. (1990) 'Job insecurity in managers: antecedents and consequences', *Journal of Organizational Behavior* 11: 345–59.

Roskies, E., Louis-Guerin, C. and Fournier, C. (1993) 'Coping with job insecurity – how does personality make a difference?' *Journal of Organizational Behavior* 14: 617–30.

Ryan, S. (1999) 'Work–family issues', in S. Coontz, M. Parson and G. Raley (eds) *American Families: A Multicultural Reader*. London: Routledge.

Rystedt, L. W. and Johansson, G. (1998) 'A longitudinal study of workload, health and well-being among male and female urban bus drivers', *Journal of Occupational and Organizational Psychology* 71: 35–45.

Sandberg, A. (1998) 'Editorial introduction', *Economic and Industrial Democracy* 19(1): 5–16 (Special Issue on Productivity and Good Work).

Sauvan, Karl P. (1999) 'Global and Regional FDI Trends', Report presented to the Troisième Séminaire sur L'Investissement, Le Commerce et Le Développement Economique held in Evian, France, 21–22 April. UNCTAD.

Savage, Mike, Barlow, James, Dickens, Peter and Fielding, Tony (1995) *Property, Bureaucracy and Culture: Middle Class Formation in Contemporary Britain*. London: Routledge.

Sawyer, M. (1992) 'The industrial policy legacy', in J. Michie (ed.) *The Economic Legacy 1979–1992*. London: Academic Press.

Scarborough, Harry (1998) 'The unmaking of management? Change and continuity in British management in the 1990s', *Human Relations* 51: 691–716.

Scase, R. and Goffee, R. (1989) *Reluctant Managers: Their Work and Life Styles.* London: Unwin Hyman.

SCELI (Social Change and Economic Life Initiative Surveys) (1986) Study Number 2798, UK Data Archive, University of Essex.

Schabracq, M. J. and Winnubst, J. A. M. (1996) 'Senior employees', in M. Schabracq, J. A. M. Winnubst and C. L. Cooper (eds) *Handbook of Work and Health Psychology.* Chichester: John Wiley and Sons.

Schmidt, Carsten, Condon, Cliff and Lee, Sandi (2000) *Online Trading Skyrockets in Europe.* Cambridge, MA: Forrester Research Inc.

Schor, Juliet B. (1992) *The Overworked American: The Unexpected Decline of Leisure.* New York: Basic Books.

Schumpeter, J. (1994) *Capitalism, Socialism and Democracy.* London: Routledge.

Scott, E. D., O'Shaughnessy, K. C. and Cappelli, P. (1996) 'Management Jobs in the Insurance Industry: Organisational De-skilling and Rising Pay Inequity', pp. 126–54 in P. Osterman (ed.) *Broken Ladders: Managerial Careers in the New Economy.* New York: Oxford University Press.

Seers, A., McGee, G. W., Serey, T. T. and Graen, G. B. (1983) 'The interaction of job stress and social support: a strong inference investigation', *Academy of Management Journal,* 26: 273–84.

Sen, Amartya (1999) *Development as Freedom.* Oxford: Oxford University Press.

Sennett, R. (1998) *The Corrosion of Character: The Personal Consequences of Work in the New Capitalism.* London: W. W. Norton.

Sennett, R. (2000) 'Street and office: two sources of identity', in W. Hutton and A. Giddens (eds) *On the Edge: Living with Global Capitalism.* London: Jonathan Cape.

Sewell, G. and Wilkinson, B. (1992) 'Empowerment or emasculation? Shopfloor surveillance in a total quality organisation', in P. Blyton and P. Turnbull (eds) *Reassessing Human Resource Management.* London: SAGE.

Seyper, B. D., Bostrom, R. N. and Seibert, J. H. (1989) 'Listening, communication abilities and success at work', *Journal of Business Communication* 26: 293–303.

Shire, K. (2000) 'Women's employment: between equal opportunities and deregulation – the absence of a social model in Japan', Paper presented at the International Working Party on Labour Market Segmentation, UMIST, Manchester, July.

Shumaker, S. A. and Brownell, A. (1984) 'Toward a theory of social support: closing conceptual gaps', *Journal of Social Issues* 40: 11–36.

Siltanen, J. (1994) *Locating Gender.* London: UCL Press.

Simpson, B. (1999) 'Nuclear fallout: divorce, kinship and the insecurities of contemporary family life', in J. Vail, J. Wheelock and M. Hill (eds) *Insecure Times: Living with Insecurity in Contemporary Society.* London: Routledge.

Simpson, R. (1998) 'Organizational restructuring and presenteeism: the impact of long hours on the working lives of managers in the UK', *Management Research News* 21: 19–20.

Slinger, G. (2000) 'Essays on Stakeholders and Takeovers', University of Cambridge PhD (unpublished).

Smith, A. (1976) *The Wealth of Nations.* Chicago: University of Chicago Press.

Stacey, J. (1990) *Brave New Families: Stories of Domestic Upheaval in Late Twentieth-century America.* New York: Basic Books.

Standing, G. (1993) 'Labor regulation in an era of fragmented flexibility', pp. 425–41 in C. Buechtemann (ed.) *Employment Security and Labour Market Behavior: Interdisciplinary Approaches and International Evidence.* ILR Report No. 23. Ithaca, NY: ILR Press.

Standing, G. (1999) *Global Labour Flexibility: Seeking Distributive Justice.* London: Macmillan.

Stansfeld, S. A., Fuhrer, R., Head, J., Ferrie, J. and Shipley, M. (1997) 'Work and psychiatric disorder in the Whitehall II study', *Journal of Psychosomatic Research* 43: 73–81.

Stansfeld, S. A., Fuhrer, R., Head, J., Ferrie, J. and Shipley, M. (1999) 'Work characteristics predict psychiatric disorder: prospective results from the Whitehall II study', *Occupational and Environmental Medicine* 56: 302–7.

StatBase (2000) *Claimant Count 1950–2000.* London: Office for National Statistics.

Sutherland and Cooper, C. G. (1988) 'Sources of work stress', in J. J. Hurrell Jr, L. R. Murphey, S. L. Sauter and C. L. Cooper (eds) *Occupational Stress: Issues and Developments in Research.* London: Taylor & Francis.

Thoits, P. A. (1995) 'Stress, coping, and social support processes: where are we? What next?', *Journal of Health and Social Behaviour 1995* (Extra Issue), pp. 53–79.

Thomas, Richard (1996) 'Get on down, move on up', *Guardian*, p. 318.

Thornton, Shelley (1998) *Reforming Public Enterprises – Case Studies: United Kingdom.* Paris: OECD Public Management Service.

Toonen, Theo and Raadschelders, Jos (1997) 'Public sector reform in Western Europe', Department of Public Administration, Leiden University

Towers, B. (ed.) (1996) *The Handbook of Human Resource Management,* 2nd edn. Oxford: Basil Blackwell.

Trist, E. and Murray, H. (1993) 'Historical overview', in E. Trist, F. Emery and H. Murray (eds) *The Social Engagement of Social Science: II, The Socio-Technical Perspective.* Philadelphia: University of Pennsylvania Press.

TUC (Trades Union Congress) (1999) *The Regional Policy Divide.* London: TUC Economic and Social Affairs Department.

Turnbull, P. and Wass, V. (2000) 'Redundancy and the paradox of job insecurity', in E. Heery and J. Salmon (eds) *The Insecure Workforce.* London: Routledge.

UNCTAD (United Nations Conference on Trade and Development) (1999) *World Investment Report: Foreign Direct Investment and the Challenge of Development.* Geneva: United Nations.

Unison (1999) 'Stress at work' (Unison Health and Safety Information Sheet). London: Unison.

Van der Doef, M. and Maes, S. (1999) 'The job demand-control (-support) model and psychological well-being: a review of 20 years of empirical research', *Work and Stress* 13: 87–114.

Van Vuuren, T., Klandermans, B., Jacobson, D. and Hartley, J. (1991) 'Employees' reactions to job insecurity', in J. Hartley, D. Jacobson, B. Klandermans and T. van Vuuren (eds) *Job Insecurity – Coping with Jobs at Risk.* London: SAGE.

Wachtel, P. L. (1989) *The Poverty of Affluence: A Psychological Portrait of the American Way of Life,* Philadelphia, PA: New Society.

Walby, S. (1990) *Theorizing Patriarchy.* Oxford: Blackwell.

Walsh, Kieron (1995) *Public Services and Market Mechanisms: Competition, Contracting and the New Public Management.* London: Macmillan.

Warr, P. (1983) 'Work, jobs and unemployment', *Bulletin of the British Psychological Society* 36: 305–11.

Warr, P. (1987) *Work, Unemployment and Mental Health.* Oxford: Oxford University Press.

Warr, P. (1990) 'The measurement of well-being and other aspects of mental health', *Journal of Occupational Psychology* 63: 193–210.

Waterman, R. H., Waterman, J. A. and Collard, B. A. (1994) 'Toward a career resilient workforce', *Harvard Business Review* July–August: 87–95.

Weissenberg, P. and Kavanagh, M. H. (1972) 'The independence of initiating structure and consideration: a review of the evidence', *Personnel Psychology* 25: 119–30.

Wells, J. A. (1982) 'Objective job conditions, social support and perceived stress among blue collar workers', *Journal of Occupational Behaviour* 3: 79–94.

Wheatley, M. (1992) *The Future of Middle Management.* Corby: Institute of Management.

Wheatley, R. (2000) *Taking the Strain: A Survey of Managers and Workplace Stress.* London: Institute of Management Reseach.

Wichert, I. C., Nolan, J. P. and Burchell, B. J. (2000) *Workers on the Edge: Job Insecurity, Psychological Well-being, and Family Life.* Washington, DC: Economic Policy Institute.

Wilkinson, F. (1988) 'Real wages, effective demand and economic development', *Cambridge Journal of Economics* 12: 179–91.

Wilkinson, F. (1998) *Co-operation, the Organisation of Work and Competitiveness,* University of Cambridge, ESRC Centre for Business Research, Working Paper No. 85.

Wilkinson, Richard (1994) 'Health, redistribution and growth', in Andrew Glyn and David Miliband (eds) *Paying for Inequality: The Economic Cost of Social Injustice.* London: IPPR/Rivers Oram Press.

Wilkinson, Richard (1996) *Unhealthy Societies: The Afflictions of Inequality.* London: Routledge.

Wilkinson, Richard (1999) 'Putting the picture together: prosperity, redistribution, health and welfare', in Michael Marmot and Richard Wilkinson (eds) *Social Determinants of Health.* Oxford: Oxford University Press.

Wilks, Stephen (1999) *In the Public Interest: Competition Policy and the Monopolies and Mergers Commission.* Manchester: Manchester University Press.

Winnubst, J. A. M. and Schabracq, M. K. (1996) 'Social support, stress and organization: toward optimal matching', in M. Schabracq, J. A. M. Winnubst and C. L. Cooper (eds) *Handbook of Work and Health Psychology.* New York: Wiley.

Winnubst, J. A. M., Buunk, B. P. and Marcelissen, F. H. G. (1988) 'Social support and stress: perspectives and processes', in S. Fisher and J. Reason (eds) *Handbook of Life Stress, Cognition and Health.* Chichester: John Wiley and Sons.

Winnubst, J. A. M., de Jong, R. D. and Schabracq, M. J. (1996) 'The diagnosis of role strains at work: the Dutch version of the Organizational Stress Questionnaire', in M. Schabracq, J. A. M. Winnubst and C. L. Cooper (eds) *Handbook of Work and Health Psychology.* Chichester: John Wiley and Sons.

Winnubst, J. A. M., Marcelissen, R. H. G., Bastelaer, A. M. L., De Wolff, Ch. J. and Leuftink, A. E. (1984) 'Type A behaviour pattern as a moderator in the stressor–strain relationship', in A. M. Koopman-Iwema and R. A. Roe (eds) *Advances in the Psychology of Work and Organizations: European Perspectives.* Lisse: Swets and Zeitlinger.

Womack, J., Jones, D. and Roos, D. (1990) *The Machine that Changed the World.* New York: Rawson Associates.

Wood, S. and de Menezes, L. (1998) 'High commitment management in the UK: evidence from the Workplace Industrial Relations Survey and Employers' Manpower and Skill Practice Survey', *Human Relations* 51(4): 485–515.

World Bank (1999) *World Development Report: World Development Indicators.* Washington, DC: World Bank.

World Trade Organization (WTO) (2000) *International Trade Statistics 2000.* Geneva: World Trade Organization.

Worrall, Les and Cooper, Cary L. (1999) *The Quality of Working Life.* London: Institute of Management.

Wright, Vincent (1994) *Privatization in Western Europe: Pressures, Problems and Paradoxes.* London: Pinter.

Zabusky, S. E. and Barley, S. R. (1996) 'Redefining Success: Ethnographic Observations on the Careers of Technicians', pp. 185–214 in P. Osterman (ed.) *Broken Ladders: Managerial Careers in the New Economy.* New York: Oxford University Press.

Index